THE LOST YEARS

THE LOST YEARS

RADICAL ISLAM, INTIFADA, AND WARS
IN THE MIDDLE EAST 2001-2006

CHARLES ENDERLIN
translated by SUZANNE VERDERBER

OTHER PRESS · NEW YORK

Permission to reprint Nathan Alterman's "The Besieged" and "For This" is gratefully acknowledged. Copyright © by Hakibbutz-Hameuchad.

Copyright © 2006 Librairie Arthème Fayard
First published in 2006 as *Les Années Perdues: Intifada et guerres au Proche-Orient 2001-2006* by Librairie Arthème Fayard, France.

Translation copyright © 2007 Suzanne Verderber

Production Editor: Robert D. Hack

Text designer: Jeremy Diamond
This book was set in Minion by Alpha Graphics of Pittsfield, New Hampshire.

10 9 8 7 6 5 4 3 2 1

Library of Congress Cataloging-in-Publication Data

Enderlin, Charles.
  [Années perdues. English]
  The lost years : radical Islam, intifada, and wars in the Middle East, 2001-2006 / Charles Enderlin ; translated from the French by Suzanne Verderber.
    p. cm.
  "First published in 2006 as Les années perdues: intifada et guerres au Proche-Orient 2001-2006 by Librairie Arthème Fayard, France."
  Includes bibliographical references and index.
  ISBN-13: 978-1-59051-171-8 (hardcover : alk.paper) 1. Al-Aqsa Intifada, 2000- 2. Arab-Israeli conflict–1993–Peace. 3. Israel–Politics and government–21st century. 4. Palestinian Arabs–Politics and government–21st century. I. Title
  DS119.765.E6313 2007
  956.05'4–dc22
                          2007014195

To Amit and Niv, my grandchildren

The great tragedies of history often spellbind men with their terrible faces. They are transfixed by them, incapable of making any decision other than to wait.

—ALBERT CAMUS

CONTENTS

INTRODUCTION

The connection is unmistakable. While the Israeli Defense Forces (IDF) were conducting major operations in the West Bank and Gaza with the intention of "burning into the [Palestinian] conscience" the idea that they would gain nothing through violence, the U.S. army invaded Iraq "to disarm this country of weapons of mass destruction, to end Saddam Hussein's support for terrorism, and to free the Iraqi people."[1] Ariel Sharon believed that he would change the fundamentals of the Israeli-Palestinian conflict and put an end to terror by removing Yasser Arafat. The Bush administration believed that democracy would be born across the Middle East by freeing Iraq from Saddam Hussein's bloody dictatorship. In both cases, flawed intelligence and baseless analysis were used to justify the exercise of military muscle with identical devastating results. The IDF easily reconquered the autonomous Palestinian territories in the West Bank and won battles against terrorism, but in doing so it weakened the moderates of Fatah and the Palestine Liberation Organization (PLO) and contributed to the rise of Hamas. The United States, meanwhile, swiftly destroyed Saddam Hussein's regime, but transformed Iraq into a major training ground for radical Islam. Each demonstrated the inherent weakness of military force when applied without the support of legitimate policies. In today's world, bayonets are not magic wands—generals cannot transform Middle Eastern societies into modern Western societies.

The same school of thought, an ideology of action based on the principle of unilateralism, is at the center of this catastrophic failure. Within the span of six years, American and Israeli leaders brought the Middle East to the brink of a major victory for radical Islam.

During that time, Israeli leaders had succeeded in persuading their public, the American administration, and a portion of international opinion that Arafat fomented the intifada. This accusation, incessantly repeated by the military and by politicians, served as a pretext for a rejection of the Oslo Accords and the systematic destruction of the Palestinian Authority.

At last, in June 2004, heads of military intelligence and analysts of Shin Bet publicly unveiled the truth for the first time, poking holes in the propaganda and revealing the decision-making process that led to the present situation. The Israeli press, patriotic for the most part during the first two years of the intifada, finally entered the debate as well. Akiva Eldar from *Haaretz*, the Israeli moderate newspaper, was the first to break the dam of silence. On the Palestinian side, talk began to flow more openly after the death of Yasser Arafat in November 2004.

In *The Lost Years*, I recount those six years lost for peace. This book is the sequel to *Paix ou guerres*, the story of the secret negotiations that were conducted by the Palestinians and Israelis for decades before culminating in the handshake between Yitzhak Rabin and Yasser Arafat on September 13, 1993, and *Shattered Dreams*, which examines the string of events leading up to the collapse of the Oslo negotiations.

My thanks to all those who, by providing information and advice, made the existence of this book possible. The Israelis: Lieutenant General Moshe Yaalon, General Amos Malka, Brigadier General Zvi Fogel, Brigadier General Dov Sedaka, Brigadier General Ilan Paz, Colonel Ephraim Lavi, Matti Steinberg, Israel Hasson, Ami Ayalon, and Dan Meridor.

The Palestinians: Saeb Erekat, Yasser Abed Rabbo, Ahmed Qureia, Mohammed Dahlan, Jibril Rajoub, and Marwan Barghouti (before his arrest).

In the United States: Larry Wilkerson, Dan Kurtzer, Mike Scheuer, and Clayton Swisher.

Several Israelis and Palestinians have taken me into their confidence under the seal of anonymity. Their contribution to my research was significant.

The research conducted for this book led to the production of a televised documentary broadcast by France 2, *Les Années de sang*, which I coauthored with director Dan Setton. I thank him for allowing me to quote his filmed interviews of Salah Taamri, Avi Dichter, Giora Eiland, and Uzi Dayan. The documentary was also shown on the Discovery Channel under the title *Years of Blood*.

My thanks also go to Abigail Yohanan, my excellent assistant, and to Talal Abou Rahmeh, the correspondent for France 2 in Gaza.

This book was made possible thanks to the encouragement of my French publisher Olivier Bétourné. All my thanks also go to Suzanne Verderber, who produced this excellent translation, to Judith Gurewich and her team from Other Press, especially Corinna Barsan, the indefatigable editor.

Danièle Kriegel-Enderlin, my wife, accompanies and supports me throughout the often arduous trials involved in covering the Middle East conflict. Without her, this book would never have seen the light of day.

Charles Enderlin
Jerusalem, May 2007

CHAPTER 1

LIES AND TRUTHS

February 6, 2001. The Middle East entered the Sharon era. Triumphantly elected with 62.39 percent of the vote, at the age of 71 the old general became the master of Israel's destiny. A mere six months earlier, no Israeli political correspondent would have bet money on him. He owed his rise to power not only to shifting public opinion that no longer had faith in the possibility of peace, but also to a monumental error committed by his predecessor. On December 9, 2000, Ehud Barak had in effect resigned, calling for a special election within sixty days for the post of prime minister, despite anticipated general elections planned for April. By doing this, Barak, who would stand as a candidate for his own seat, hoped to create an obstacle for Benjamin Netanyahu, for whom all the polls predicted victory, and to face instead the opponent he thought he could beat more easily: Ariel Sharon. A delay of eight weeks would have permitted progress to be made in negotiations, and perhaps even allowed for the conclusion of an agreement with the Palestinians. But on December 26, during a late-night conversation, Ehud Barak secretly informed Bill Clinton that he would not sign any agreement before the election, and could not accept the parameters for an agreement that the American president had presented to the parties three days earlier. The Israeli prime minister allowed the Taba negotiations to proceed in January 2001 knowing perfectly well they would lead nowhere.[1] During an interruption in talks one week before the election, Shlomo Ben Ami, the Israeli minister of foreign affairs, declared: "The parties confirm that they have never been so close to an agreement, and believe that the differences that remain can be surmounted when the negotiations are taken up again. . . . We leave Taba conscious of having established the foundations of an agreement concerning all problems." For his part, Saeb Erekat, the Palestinian negotiator, predicted that a few more weeks of discussion would be sufficient to bring the negotiations to a conclusion.

More importantly, by proclaiming before the election that Arafat was not a "partner" for peace and that at Camp David he had unveiled the "true face" of the leader of the PLO, Ehud Barak convinced a majority of Israelis that the Oslo Accords had failed. In the absence of any possible agreement, he argued that the only remaining option was to repress the intifada. As leader of the Labor Party, Barak presented himself to voters after proclaiming that peace was impossible without a Palestinian partner—a veritable political suicide, according to Shimon Peres.[2]

THE CAMP DAVID SPIN

In reality, the slogan "no partner," now engraved in the collective Israeli conscience, was the brainchild of public relations specialists. Even before the Camp David summit, Moshe Gaon and Tal Zylberstein, communications advisors to Barak, had concluded, after having examined the consequences of a potential failure of the negotiations: "It is necessary to shift the responsibility to Arafat: it has been demonstrated that Arafat does not want to reach an agreement. Barak went further than any other Israeli leader to determine whether or not it was possible to put an end to the conflict, and it is clear that Arafat refuses."[3]

This theme—taken up successfully by Likud during the electoral campaign and later by the Bush administration—was subsequently debunked by most of the leaders of the Israeli intelligence services, both civil and military. In early July 2000, before going to Camp David, Ehud Barak had consulted with all of his specialists. General Amos Malka, chief of military intelligence, had told him that Arafat was ready to sign an agreement according to the following conditions: an independent Palestinian state with its capital in East Jerusalem; sovereignty over the Temple Mount, which is also the Haram al-Sharif, the third most holy site of Islam; and 97 percent of the West Bank, on the condition of an exchange of territory for the remaining 3 percent. The PLO leader would save face by accepting a compromise: he would renounce the right of return of Palestinian refugees in exchange for a declaration from Israel accepting responsibility for the tragedy of the refugees and permitting the return of 20,000 to 30,000 among them to Israeli territory. But Malka warned his prime minister: "I told him that that there was no way that Arafat would accept a compromise on 90 percent of the territory, or even 93 percent. He isn't a real estate agent, and he will not stop halfway. Barak answered: 'You're telling me that if I offer him 90 percent he won't accept? I don't accept your analysis.' . . . Barak felt he was capable of doing his own analysis without the facts provided by military intelligence. He believed that he was more intelligent."[4]

Malka's opinion was also supported by Matti Steinberg, the principal analyst of Shin Bet, the internal security agency, experts from Mossad, as well Colonel (res.) Shaul Arieli, who directed the department of negotiations at the prime minister's office at the time. They railed against the propaganda according to which, at Camp David, "Yasser Arafat rejected a generous Israeli proposal in order to instigate a war against the Jewish state."[5] Even Shlomo Ben Ami, the minister of foreign affairs and principal Israeli negotiator—overall a critic of Arafat—finally admitted in 2006: "If I were a Palestinian, I would have rejected Camp David as well."[6]

Years after the summit, some American and Israeli politicians claim that Arafat rejected a proposal that would have given him almost a hundred percent of the West Bank. In fact, the figure never went over 91 percent and the Palestinians, taking into account the security zones the Israelis intended to keep, believed they would get 82 percent.[7]

THE NON-PARTNER

In January 2001, three months after the beginning of the intifada, a simple message was broadcast by the majority of Israel's media outlets: "The leader of the PLO has unleashed the Palestinian uprising and directs it himself." General Amos Gilaad, the head of the evaluation department of military intelligence, presented his personal interpretation of Arafat's aims to the government: "Arafat intends to use the Oslo process within the framework of his strategy for the destruction of Israel. His aim is the creation of a 'great Palestine.' During the course of negotiations, he demanded the right of return of Palestinian refugees in order to liquidate Israel using the weapon of demography."[8]

However, the official report drawn up by his own department and submitted to the government as is required, affirmed the contrary. The report was based on information collected from diverse sources by all Israeli services. Its author, Colonel Ephraim Lavi, who was in charge of the Palestinian desk, was unequivocal: "No document issued from our department contained facts that could have served as the basis for such a theory. . . . The postulate that Arafat had no other interest than the destruction of Israel by means of the right of return became dogma."[9] The notes taken in real time by Camp David participants, Israelis and Palestinians, confirm that at no point did Arafat's negotiators demand the return of millions of refugees to Israel. The numbers discussed during the talks ranged from a few hundred to a few thousand Palestinians.[10] But Shlomo Ben Ami, the foreign minister, would only permit discussion of "a limited number of reunifications of families."[11] Gilead Sher, head of Ehud Barak's cabinet and one of the principal negotiators, thinks today that, in this instance, his Palestinian interlocutors were mainly concerned with saving face, and that it would have been possible to arrive at a satisfactory solution for Israel.[12] Even Amos Gilaad had spoken differently of Arafat only two months earlier in December 2000. During a conference at Herzliya, he had in effect declared that the leader of the PLO "wanted to create a Palestinian state within the 1967 borders [West Bank, Gaza, East Jerusalem] and was seeking a just solution to the refugee problem." Not a word was said about Arafat's strategy to destroy Israel.

MUTINY

Meanwhile, in November 2000, Yuval Diskin, the number two at Shin Bet, had submitted a report to Barak entitled "The Myth of Arafat's Control." Based on intelligence in his possession, he confirmed that the latest Palestinian uprising had been spontaneous and that Arafat did not control it. This conclusion was shared by experts from the other services —notably those from Mossad. But the truth would emerge far too late to have an impact on public opinion, not only in Israel but also in the United States, where the Bush administration was to adopt an identical position.

The slogan "Arafat the terrorist" suited the Israeli military leadership. It fit their strategy perfectly. Since he became chief of staff in 1998, Lieutenant General Shaul Mofaz had sped up preparations of the army for a full-fledged confrontation with the Palestinians. He reiterated—to both his subordinates and to politicians—that Israel had to reconstitute its capacity for deterrence toward the Arab world in general, and toward the Palestinians in particular. Dennis Ross, the American mediator, wrote: "the chief of staff of the Israeli army worried that the Israelis had largely lost their ability to deter Palestinian violence after more than a week back in May—when Fatah activists and Palestinian forces had fired on the IDF but had been met with a relatively weak response.[13] He vowed the IDF would be much stronger in response next time. If they were not, the Palestinians would lose all respect for the IDF and act accordingly. Mofaz told me that only an immediate, strong, and preemptory response would reestablish the Israeli deterrent."[14]

Close to Likud, the nationalist Right, Mofaz was fifty-two years old at the time. He began his military career in the paratroopers brigade and the elite special forces known as the Sayeret Matkal, the commando unit of the general staff. He belonged to a group of superior officers who felt that the Israeli military reaction during the first Palestinian uprising, in December 1987, had been notoriously insufficient, thereby ensuring PLO political gains. He also criticized politicians for having ordered the unilateral retreat of the IDF from south Lebanon on May 25, 2000. The operation had fallen into disarray and made it possible for Hezbollah to proclaim that its heroic fighters triumphed over the Zionist enemy on the battlefield. The Israeli army subsequently believed it had to restore its honor. Brigadier General Zvi Fogel, at the time chief of staff of the Southern Command, which included Gaza, described the situation thus: "As we saw it, the retreat from south Lebanon had been an enormous trauma. We had the feeling that we were fleeing with our tails between our legs. And what's the best way to get over feelings like that? To prepare for another confrontation!"[15]

Mofaz did not appreciate the efforts of the Barak government to achieve a cease-fire agreement and to pursue negotiations with the Palestinians. The confrontation between the military and the prime minister had come to a head on December 27, 2000, when the Israeli cabinet had to agree on its response to President Clinton's proposal for compromise. The chief of staff was sharply critical of all elements of the American plan, and elicited an equally sharp response from Barak: "Shaul! It is not possible that you really think that Israel cannot exist without dominating the Palestinian people! That's what your comments suggest!"[16] A few hours later, the press was informed of Mofaz's criticisms. On December 29, after the government's approval of Clinton's plan, the general was quoted in the daily *Yedihot Aharonot*: "Clinton's plan works against Israel's security interests. If it is implemented, it will put the security of the state in danger!" That same day, in *Haaretz*, the army directly attacked the government, which it criticized for "what appear to be exaggerated concessions to the Palestinians while large-scale combat is being pursued in the territories."[17] A military commentator defined the situation this way: "Tsahal [the IDF] intends to win the conflict and will not allow the politicians, through their contradictory instructions, to dampen its victory. . . . No one will tell the army how to fight!"[18]

Artfully manipulating euphemism, Gilead Sher, the head of Ehud Barak's cabinet, expressed regret that during the first four months of the intifada the military had not collaborated "in efforts to restore calm. . . . Eyewitness accounts from the ground indicated that there had been, on numerous occasions, deviations with respect to instructions issued on the political level. A number of decisions and engagements [toward the Palestinians] drawn up by the prime minister and transferred to the army 'evaporated': tanks had not been redeployed, officers being content with leaving the tanks in place and merely turning the cannons away. The fishing zone off Gaza had not been reopened. Against the directives [of the government], only a small number of Palestinians had been authorized to work in Israel. Checkpoints had not been removed."[19] Published a year later, in October 2001, these accusations would pass unnoticed.

It wasn't until 2004 that Shlomo Ben Ami, formerly Barak's minister of foreign affairs, revealed that he also knew the Israeli military command was following its own plan[20] . . .

which led to the widening of the infernal circle of violence rather than narrowing it. The minister Amnon Lipkin-Shahak,[21] also a former chief of staff, who, in the name of the prime minister, did what he could to achieve a cease-fire, told me on numerous occasions of his anger and his frustration at the fact that the army was executing an entirely different war on the ground from what had been decided upon at the [Israeli] political level. Colonels and officers were conducting independent operations. Merchandise that had to be delivered to the Palestinian population [according to political decisions] was blocked by checkpoints on the order of local commanders. Bulldozers destroyed greenhouses and plantations allegedly for security reasons, which exacerbated Palestinian rage to unprecedented levels. These policies of 'collective reprisals,' including economic ones, did not correspond to the intentions of the government, whose objective was to restore calm. It was a plan executed by the military leadership, which willfully ignored the instructions and intentions of political directives. It is clear that at this moment Tsahal [the IDF] determined the chain of events. The government was incapable of imposing its will on the army or of assuming control of it—even when certain ministers remarked upon it to Barak, the leader of the government and the defense minister.

A MILLION CARTRIDGES

Beginning in the first days of the intifada, Mofaz himself set in motion "Field of Thorns," a plan he had been preparing for years to repress a Palestinian uprising.[22] The IDF's response was massive. Amos Malka would recount—four years later!—how, a month into the intifada, he had asked the intelligence officer of the Central Command, Brigadier General Yossi Kuperwasser, to verify the quantity of ammunition fired by his units against the Palestinians: "He asked me: 'Why is that important?' I answered: 'You'll see!' When he returned with the number— 800,000 cartridges, 200,000 for the south region [Gaza]—I said to him: 'Now you understand why it's important.' He realized that the numbers were significant."[23] The death toll spoke eloquently: in September and October 2000, 115 Palestinians were killed, as opposed to only twelve Israelis. Shin Bet analysts and military intelligence drew the same conclusion: the IDF was changing the reality on the ground.

Individual soldiers allowed themselves to react more spontaneously. They no longer feared being the target of an inquiry by the military police each time a Palestinian civilian was killed. Beginning in November 2000, the IDF officially designated the intifada an "armed conflict: combat against terrorist groups." New procedures were put in place. The military police no longer immediately investigated the circumstances of a civilian death. As a result, the commander of the unit concerned would hold a so-called "debriefing," the conclusions of which were sent to a military prosecutor who, himself, decided whether proceedings were justified.[24] As a result, between September 29, 2000 and June 22, 2005, the Israeli military police only investigated 131 cases in which soldiers shot at Palestinians, and only eighteen proceedings resulted in indictments. And yet, during this period, 3,185 Palestinians died, among whom were hundreds of bystanders.[25]

In the West Bank and Gaza, with some exceptions, officers and soldiers had few qualms about proceeding against the Palestinians. The military staff vigilantly spread its version of the intifada: the Palestinian uprising had been planned and organized by Arafat. Today, Brigadier General Zvi Fogel sees things differently: "After Camp David, everyone was saying that there was no one to negotiate with and that confrontation was inevitable. From the point of view of intelligence, there was an incompatibility between the level of Palestinian preparations on the ground and the analysis that we were receiving from military intelligence. [On the Palestinian side] there was no sign of new fortified positions or of any specific deployment of equipment or arms, while the intelligence was telling us all the time about instructions from Arafat. A posteriori [it seemed to me that] they were overestimating the [Palestinians]. It's the typical process in which, based on partial intelligence, I assume the worst even if there is nothing to confirm it on the ground. . . . We understood later that the Palestinian preparations were defensive, concentrated in sectors [where there was a risk] of friction based on the preparations they observed on our side. . . . I think that our operations accelerated their own massive use of firearms and, at the same time, wrecked Palestinian services. We didn't create Hamas, but we helped it."[26]

As head of the department of negotiations at the prime minister's office and Ehud Barak's aide-de-camp during an interim period, Colonel Shaul Arieli was able to observe the behavior of the military leaders from the front row. He stated: "The army had a quasi-autonomous policy, under the direction of Mofaz, for whom force was the only solution against the intifada. In his view, he had responsibility for the security of the Israeli people, which he would assume in his own way, whatever the decisions of the government. The prime minister had decided that the responses should be proportional to Palestinian [attacks]. . . . Mofaz's policy was completely opposed to this principle and was founded exclusively upon the use of force. For example, Ephraim Sneh, the deputy defense minister at the time, decided one day to authorize the opening of the military checkpoint at the entrance to Gaza to allow for the transport of some merchandise. . . . And so the army, without informing anyone at all, did not execute this order issued from the political level. Later, the army apologized. But this kind of incident happened almost every day."[27]

This kind of blunder was often the work of local commanders, colonels commanding brigades deployed in the West Bank and Gaza. From the beginning of the intifada, they had obtained, for operational reasons and with Ehud Barak's consent, a kind of autonomy to act forcefully in the Palestinian territories. Known in certain command posts as the "Tanzim of Mofaz" (from the name of the Fatah armed militants), they willingly conducted operations in their own sectors that went against the government's instructions, but with the blessing of the chief of staff.[28]

Brigadier General Dov Sedaka, who led the department of civil affairs in the West Bank, perfectly described the prevailing atmosphere at the time: "At the beginning [of the intifada], I experienced a profound feeling of frustration and a veritable anger towards the Palestinians, especially after certain events like the death of a soldier in Joseph's Tomb in Nablus, in October 2000. [The Palestinians had prevented his evacuation.] I was saying: 'If that's what you want . . . that's what you'll get!' With me, at the time, anger triumphed over understanding of the situation. . . . And if I, a superior officer, the head of civil affairs, reacted this way after days of discussions with the other side, then the officers of inferior grades, the battalion chiefs, the lieutenants, could also only react very aggressively, and, in effect, it was guaranteed that this would be the case. [The message] was transmitted by the visits of generals to ground units and by declarations at the level of commanders of the region, of the senior staff."[29] Dov Sedaka ultimately found himself to be out of step with his superiors.

DOCTRINES

The IDF had its own conception of the Palestinian problem. In previous years, military strategists had studied low-intensity conflict. The Operational Theory Research Institute (OTRI), directed by Brigadier General (res.) Shimon Naveh and Brigadier General (res.) Dov Tamari, was installed near Tel Aviv in what was known as the Poum, the training academy for superior officers. With a think tank headed by Haim Assa, a mathematician and military analyst, and General (res.) Yedidia Yaari, a former commander of the navy, they introduced new strategic concepts that ultimately transformed the reality of the conflict.[30] The most important consisted of "burning into the conscience"[31] of the Palestinians the idea that they would gain nothing through violence. That entailed direct pressure on the populations of the West Bank and Gaza, where prolonged curfews and military checkpoints provoked an unprecedented economic crisis. In February 2001, according to Terje Larsen, the emissary of the United Nations, 32 percent of Palestinians lived below the poverty line, fixed at two dollars per day per person. In Gaza, the unemployment rate reached 50 percent, in the West Bank, 30 percent.[32]

This strategy to "burn the conscience" of the Palestinians was sharply criticized by analysts from military intelligence and by Shin Bet. One among them sent the following warning to Avi Dichter, head of the interior security service: "If the only option we give the Palestinians is surrender or confrontation, they will have nothing left to lose and will opt for suicide attacks. It's necessary to offer them a third way."

Lieutenant General Moshe "Boogie" Yaalon adopted and propagated the think tank's theories since he assumed control of the Central Command in 1998 (including the West Bank), and continued to do so when he became chief of staff in September 2000, two weeks before the start of the intifada. He also spent a significant portion of his military career in the Sayeret. He rejected the idea—essential in the eyes of the Israeli peace camp—that there was no military solution to the confrontation with the Palestinians. "There exists," he said, "a confrontation of interests, of wills, between our two peoples or between our two political entities. And I believe that we can reach a decision that allows us to achieve our objectives. We are not talking about a knockout victory but rather a win on points. Neither a final sprint nor a war that would only last two or three weeks, but a long-term effort. . . . The Palestinians have no other way of making us leave [the West Bank] than by beating us in a war of perception: I believe that we retreated from Lebanon because Israeli society was imbued with the idea that its army had been vanquished. . . ."[33] For Yaalon, the perception that each party drew from the conflict was fundamental, and he repeated to his subordinates that what was at play in "this war is the very existence of the Jewish state, which Arafat wants to destroy. In my opinion, it is of the utmost importance that the war conclude on the affirmation of a principle, which is that the Palestinians realize that violence does not pay."[34] According to this view, the intifada was only the continuation of the 1948 war of independence, when the Arab armies were tempted to destroy the young Jewish state.

THE SHARON PLAN

IDF leaders applauded the election of Ariel Sharon as prime minister. The new head of the government had always been opposed to the Oslo Accords, accusing Arafat of being a bloody terrorist. The Israeli voters overlooked his visit to the Jerusalem mosque complex forty-eight hours before the start of the intifada. They also did not want to remember his forced resignation as defense minister after the Sabra and Shatila massacres in Beirut, in September 1982.[35] Sharon, however, did not forget. During his eighteen years in the political wilderness, he had reflected, observed, and extracted lessons from his past mistakes. Moving forward, he would pay attention to opinion polls and heed the advice of communications experts. When Reuven Adler, one of the public relations experts who orchestrated his electoral campaign, proposed that he adopt the slogan "Only Sharon will bring peace!" he burst out laughing before making a correction: "No talks under fire!"[36] In the end, Sharon accepted the slogan "Peace with Security." But the Israelis still wanted to hear hopeful words from the mouths of their leaders. Through the years, Sharon had become aware of the futility of fighting tooth and nail against the negotiation process with the Palestinians. It is enough to play the game of diplomacy if one is in a position to impose the rules. It is easier to let talks stagnate than to oppose them. In 1998, Sharon had gone so far as to discreetly receive Mahmoud Abbas, at the time Arafat's top deputy in the PLO, at his home in the Negev, Sycamore Ranch. One year later, during the Wye River summit in Maryland, as the foreign minister under Benjamin Netanyahu, he had made his first forays into diplomatic engagement with the PLO, without going so far as to shake the hand of the man whom he had always considered to be a murderer: Yasser Arafat.

At the end of January 2001, two weeks before the rescheduled election, General (res.) Meir Dagan, one of his principal advisors, presented Sharon with a "Plan for Struggle Against Violence in the Territories." It was a plan intended to destroy the Palestinian Authority and to neutralize Arafat and the Palestinian leadership. The plan consisted of "the prohibition of the transfer of funds to the Palestinian Authority, and to infringe upon the wealth and personal fortune of its leaders. The members of the Autonomous Authority implicated in terrorism would be the objects of progressive 'individual treatment' extending, depending upon the case, from arrest . . . to expulsion from the region, all the way to the point of physical attack." In other words, assassination. In addition, Dagan proposed to execute "military and 'other' operations in [autonomous] zone A in order to send the message that these territories are not out of play!"[37] He also envisioned "psychological operations in order to encourage the creation of an alternative to the Autonomous Authority, due to deception experienced by the Palestinian public resulting from the dysfunction of the Authority and the fact that it is not possible to achieve a political solution."[38] These operations would be carried out within the framework of carrot and stick policies: the sectors in which the violence disappeared would be rewarded with the removal of military checkpoints.

VISIONS

Ariel Sharon was on the same wavelength as Mofaz and Yaalon. He knew that he could also count on Avi Dichter, the head of Shin Bet, who had an identical black-and-white vision of the conflict. At the age of forty-eight, Dichter had been named head of the internal security service in 2000, after the departure of Ami Ayalon. Ehud Barak preferred him to Israel Hasson, a moderate considered to be close to the Palestinian security services. Like the military leaders Mofaz and Yaalon, Dichter came from the Sayeret, where he had performed his compulsory military service before joining Shin Bet. In his view, there was no difference between the political direction and the military/terrorist level of Palestinian organizations. From this point to the end of the year, he would succeed in removing Matti Steinberg, the analyst whose critical reports he could not tolerate.

But in May 2006, Avi Dichter reexamined the vision he had espoused of the PLO leader at the time: "Arafat did not control the extent of the uprising, contrary to what we said at the time. Arafat did not foment the intifada. The intifada began like a snowball. . . . But he did not assume his historic role before the Palestinian people. . . . He was a political leader who did not assume his functions as we understood them. . . . Men whom he appointed and financed were transformed into terrorists. Arafat chose to do and say nothing [against terrorism]. In opposition to the image of an all-powerful Arafat thinking strategically, to my sorrow, I saw a weak Arafat, afraid of entering into Palestinian history by attacking an organization like Hamas."[39]

Ami Ayalon had a different vision of the conflict: "None among us could have comprehended the degree of energy that fed the uprising. It was like a wild horse that no one could manage to control, and by chance Arafat found himself in the saddle. But . . . if Arafat was in the saddle, we had to take care of him because he was the rider. That's what we had on our minds, but the reality was completely different."[40]

AMERICAN IDEOLOGIES

The question of the American government's responsibility remains to be discussed. Ariel Sharon had bad memories of the interventions of the Reagan administration during the war he waged in Lebanon in 1982. He believed that the State Department had insisted on creating obstacles, preventing him from achieving his objectives. Henceforth, the situation was to be different. The Israeli ambassador in Washington and other sources informed Sharon that Colin Powell, the new secretary of state, intended to negotiate a cease-fire, or even a political agreement. During the course of certain private conversations, the content of which was reported to Jerusalem, Powell declared himself to be in favor of the rapid creation of a Palestinian state and the immediate halting of Israeli settlement construction in the West Bank and Gaza. But, at the same time, Likud allies in the United States told Sharon that he did not have any reason to worry: they were well positioned within the corridors of power where they could influence George W. Bush, a novice in matters of foreign affairs.

These men, the "neoconservatives," in many cases originally emerging from the Democratic Party and even, for some, from the extreme Trotskyist Left, were the driving ideological force of the new administration. Several among them were signatories to a text entitled "A Clean Break: A New Strategy for Securing the Realm," sent in 1996 to Benjamin Netanyahu, the Israeli prime minister, several days before his visit to Washington. They proposed a renunciation of the principle of "territory for peace," which was the very foundation of the Israeli policy in negotiations with the Arab states and the Palestinians. They advised Israel to "work closely with Turkey and Jordan in order to contain, destabilize, and roll back some of its most dangerous threats. This implies a clean break from the slogan 'comprehensive peace' [which is replaced with] a traditional concept of strategy based on balance of power." They also advised Israel to "change the nature of its relations with the Palestinians, including the right of hot pursuit [of terrorists] for self defense into all Palestinian areas and nurturing alternatives to Arafat's exclusive grip on Palestinian society." Seven years before the Iraq war, the neoconservatives proposed the removal of Saddam Hussein in order to reestablish a Hashemite dynasty, the family of King Hussein of Jordan, in Baghdad! "The predominantly Shia population of southern Lebanon has been tied for centuries to the Shia leadership in Najf, Iraq rather than Iran. Were the Hashemites to control Iraq, they could use their influence over Najf to help Israel wean the south Lebanese Shia away from Hizballah, Iran, and Syria. Shia retain strong ties to the Hashemites: the Shia venerate foremost the Prophet's family, the direct descendents of which—and in whose veins the blood of the Prophet flows—is King Hussein."[41]

The principal author of this document was Richard Perle. Sixty years old, he was nicknamed the "prince of darkness," a reference to the period when, as advisor to Senate Democrat Henry Jackson from 1969 to 1980, he opposed arms control agreements with the USSR, believing that the United States would gain nothing in exchange. A virulent critic of the United Nations, this neoconservative was close to Benjamin Netanyahu. He believed that, at the very least, "the United States would be able to use its influence to negotiate the creation of a mini Palestinian state, neutralized and disarmed, in the West Bank and in Gaza with a part of Jerusalem for capital, under the leadership of a chairman who would not be suspected of extremism. Israel would remain powerful and rich. 'Palestine' would be weak and poor."[42] In July 2001, George Bush named Perle chairman of the Defense Policy Board.

Among the other signatories to the text, the name Douglas Feith also stands out, the new undersecretary of defense in charge of political strategy. He was from a family whose father escaped the Shoah and who, taking refuge in the United States, was a member of Betar, the Likud youth movement. He began his political career in 1981 at the National Security Council of Ronald Reagan's White House before serving as advisor to . . . Richard Perle. In 1986, Feith returned to the private sector by forming a law firm with Marc Zell, a fervent supporter of the Israeli settlements in Gaza and the West Bank, where he himself would settle with his family two years later, all the while developing his businesses in Israel.[43] Feith was hostile to the creation of a Palestinian state.[44]

David Wurmser and Meyrav, his wife of Israeli origin, also signed their names to the document. Wurmser is a former disciple of Perle. On November 1, 2000, in an editorial published in the *Washington Times*, he called upon the United States and Israel to "broaden" the conflict in the Middle East: "The conflict should be broadened to strike fatally, not only disarm, the centers of radicalism in the region to reestablish the certainty that fighting with either the United States or Israel is suicidal." Before the end of 2001, he would be recruited by Donald Rumsfeld, the head of the Pentagon, as a consultant to the department directed by Douglas Feith. Meyrav Wurmser, along with Colonel (res.) Yigal Carmon, a senior member of Israeli military intelligence and advisor to Prime Ministers Yitzhak Shamir and Yitzhak

Rabin, was the cofounder of the Middle East Media Research Institute (MEMRI). Officially independent, this institute had been, several times, accused of partiality and of emphasizing the most extremist elements of the Arab world.

Other neoconservatives were also named to important posts within the U.S. government. Elliott Abrams was appointed special assistant to the president and "Director of Democracy, Human Rights, and International Organization Affairs." He was born in New York in 1948 to a devout Jewish family. He was also one of the assistants to Senator Henry Jackson during the 1970s, which marked the beginning of a long career at the heart of the Reagan administration. As assistant to Secretary of State George Shultz, he fell into trouble with Congress following the Iran-Contra Affair, accused of giving false testimony, and ultimately pardoned by President Bush (Senior). In time, Abrams developed a communitarian, religious philosophy. In his view, atheism was a menace to society. In a book entitled *Faith or Fear: How Jews Can Survive in a Christian America*, he wrote: "Outside the land of Israel, there can be no doubt that Jews, faithful to the covenant between God and Abraham, are to stand apart from the nation in which they live. It is the very nature of being Jewish to be apart—except in Israel—from the rest of the population."[45] He thus condemned interfaith marriages, and, a faithful supporter of Likud, he rejected the Oslo Accords.

Paul Wolfowitz, perhaps the most influential figure in the group, was also very close to Israel, where he had stayed on several occasions and where his sister had emigrated. This talented academic became an aide to Donald Rumsfeld after a long political career that began in 1972 and led him to frequent both Democratic and Republican administrations. Even if he did not support the Israeli settlement policy in the occupied territories, he had nonetheless agitated for years in favor of the removal of Saddam Hussein. In January 1998, along with Richard Perle, Elliott Abrams, Donald Rumsfeld, and other neoconservatives, he signed a letter asking that President Clinton launch a military operation to oust Saddam Hussein.

These men, in just a few years, transformed the Middle East.

ARAFAT WAS MISTAKEN

Arafat, for his part, did not comprehend the scope of the changes taking place in Washington and Israel. During the preceding weeks, he insisted to his advisors that the Americans would not allow Ariel Sharon to be elected, and that Ehud Barak would stay in power. The surprise was bitter. The entourage of Hosni Mubarak vainly tried to assure him that the new Israeli prime minister "will be able to do more than his predecessor: remember, it's Sharon who caused the evacuation of Yamit [in the Sinai Peninsula]," but he believed that he had just received a veritable challenge, and his objective would henceforth be to prove that Sharon's policies would not bring peace to Israel.[46] "His iron fist," he told those closest to him, "will not break the Palestinian resistance, especially after his promise to end the intifada in a hundred days."[47] For months, Arafat would order the Palestinian security services to act against the violence only under pressure of events. Most of the time, such actions were in vain.

INTIFADA

On the ground, the situation was far from calm. On February 8, a car bomb exploded in Jerusalem, wounding two people. On the 11th, an Israeli from the Gush Etzion settlement was shot and killed. Two days later, in Gaza, in the Jebaliya refugee camp, the car of a colonel of Force 17, Yasser Arafat's Praetorian Guard, was targeted by a helicopter-launched missile, killing him on the spot. An Israeli spokesman confirmed that the officer was a suspected member of the Lebanese Hezbollah and was planning mortar attacks on Jewish settlers in Gaza. His son had been arrested by the Israeli army two weeks earlier. During the bombardment, six bystanders were wounded. According to the Palestinians, that same day a child had been killed during an exchange of gunfire near a checkpoint in southern Gaza. The next day, in a Tel Aviv suburb, bus driver Khalil Abu Elba of Gaza City, after having dropped off Palestinian workers, turned his vehicle on a group of soldiers and civilians. Eight were killed and twenty-six were wounded. The driver, who fled, was caught and seriously wounded by police. A thirty-five-year-old father, he had worked

for five years for an Israeli cooperative and he had, on that day, successfully passed through all of the security checks. Apparently, he did not
belong to any Palestinian organization. The West Bank and Gaza were
hermetically sealed off by the IDF.

Yasser Arafat reacted by declaring that it was a "response to the
Israeli military escalation, which has an influence over all Palestinians."
In Washington, Dore Gold, Sharon's emissary, declared during a meeting with Colin Powell: "Arafat has the means to put a stop to the violence. There are no spontaneous acts of violence. The latest attacks
against Israelis have their origin in the armed wing of Fatah and Force
17." George W. Bush condemned "the terrible act of violence in Israel
this morning. . . . I'm urging all parties to do their utmost to end the
violence." The president of the United States still had not taken a position on the conflict. He merely reiterated that his administration was
going to continue to work with all parties involved in order to restore
calm to the region. He decided to send Colin Powell to fulfill this task.

POWELL'S FIRST VISIT

The secretary of state arrived in Jerusalem on February 25. He was received by the prime minister, whom he knew personally. A few years
earlier, he had been a guest at Sharon's ranch. Powell explained that he
came first and foremost to listen. Sharon answered that, for his part, he
would only authorize the opening of checkpoints, the transport of merchandise, and the granting (under supervision) of permits to Palestinian workers if Arafat "publishes a declaration in Arabic calling for the
complete cessation of violence and brings about the restoration of the
coordination of law and order." It was not even a question, at this point,
of authorizing the transfer of funds collected by Israel as taxes and customs duties back to the Palestinian Authority. This money, Sharon explained, was used to pay the salaries of Palestinian police who fired on
the neighborhood of Gilo, in Jerusalem, and on Psagot, a settlement that
overlooks Ramallah. And he added: "As prime minister, I will conduct
negotiations with the Palestinian Authority following a cessation of hostilities." Powell reciprocated by inviting Sharon to visit Washington on

March 19 in order to meet George Bush, and, after holding a joint press conference, left for Ramallah.

Arafat was in a bad mood. His conversation with Powell was difficult. He told the American diplomat that the Israelis did not authorize him to use his helicopter to travel from Gaza to Ramallah. He had nevertheless been able to make the trip thanks to the king of Jordan, who had lent him his own helicopter. The Palestinian chairman demanded the opening of military checkpoints around Palestinian cities and the withdrawal of Israeli forces to the positions that they had held before the beginning of the intifada. He refused any new interim agreement with Israel.

But things appeared to be going badly for the leader of the PLO. During a stop in Kuwait, Colin Powell shared his impressions with the journalists accompanying him: "I found him [Sharon] very reflective, very thoughtful, very engaged on the issue—yes, Sharon—and realizing the enormity of the problem he has on his hands. And he also, I think, understands that people are remembering him from another day; and I think he now knows that he is prime minister of a country and he has a responsibility for all the lands under his stewardship at the moment and not just Israeli land. . . . [Arafat] held positions he has held all along. . . . But can he control all of [the violence]? I don't know anybody who can control all of it. The question is, is he exercising as much control as he can? That remains to be seen."

ARAFAT THE TERRORIST?

The political scene inside Israel was settling down. Shimon Peres, who assumed the leadership of the Labor Party after Ehud Barak's departure, negotiated a coalition agreement with Likud. In a highly emotional speech, the aging leader, who had received the Nobel Peace Prize for having negotiated the Oslo Accords, addressed the central committee of his own party, requesting that they cooperate without protesting: "We do not have a choice. The intifada and the dangers that haunt the country, like Iraq, which is developing a nuclear option, indicate that we cannot turn our backs on the challenges the country is facing. Do we have a replacement country? Do you want us to be forgotten in the opposition? What are we waiting for? Do you want to find your interviews on the inside pages of the newspapers?" Of the 1,600 delegates, 67 percent voted in favor of an alliance with Ariel Sharon. Henceforth, Israel would have a national unity government. Peres assumed the position of minister of foreign affairs. General (res.) Binyamin ("Fouad") Ben-Eliezer took charge of the Ministry of the Defense, where he was welcomed by Mofaz. The chief of staff believed he was still capable of asserting his authority, despite his new boss. Receiving a Jewish delegation from abroad, he accused Arafat by stating: "The Palestinian Authority is stocking light weapons, anti-tank and anti-air missiles, mortar shells . . . , it is using Fatah as its operational arm. That means that the Palestinian Authority is in the process of becoming a terrorist entity."[48] In other words, Mofaz wanted the Autonomous Authority to be declared an enemy of Israel, an enemy that it was necessary to destroy. Zeev Schiff, the military analyst for the daily *Haaretz*, grasped the significance of this declaration and suggested that such a far-reaching decision only be made, if it had to be, by the political leadership.[49] In Washington, two pro-Israeli senators, one a Republican and the other a Democrat, circulated a draft of a letter among their colleagues requesting that George Bush place the Tanzim, the armed branch of Fatah, and Force 17, Arafat's guard, on the list of terrorist organizations.

HAMAS

Eight days later, on March 4 after a weekend during which six Palestinians, including a nine-year-old child and a mother had been killed during clashes with the Israeli army, Hamas committed its first suicide attack since the beginning of the intifada. In Netanya, north of Tel Aviv, a few minutes before nine in the morning, Ahmed Alyan, the twenty-three-year-old muezzin of a mosque in Tulkarm, set off his explosive belt near a bus stop and killed three elderly Israelis. Sixty were wounded. Further away, at the marketplace, an angry crowd tried to lynch a Palestinian worker. The Israeli police managed to extricate him from his assailants;

he was only slightly hurt. In Israel, the incident caused a scandal. In Nablus and Gaza, as soon as the attack was announced, Palestinians took to the street, cheering and chanting: "We took revenge today in Netanya!"

In Jerusalem, Ariel Sharon announced: "We must remain united. That is the lesson we must take away from the latest attacks. We are facing a period that will not be easy and that demonstrates the importance of a national unity government." And the prime minister asked the Israelis to remain calm, and to not take justice into their own hands. For his part, Moshe Katsav, the head of state, criticized the leader of the PLO: "Arafat is leading a campaign to incite violence and is giving the green light to terrorist attacks." General Amos Malka, the head of military intelligence, got into line with the politicians in power and declared: "The intifada, in its present form, is no longer a popular uprising. The intifada is directed from on high. Arafat in person determines the level of violence." Nevertheless, responsibility for the Netanya attack had been claimed by Ezzedin al-Qassam, the armed branch of Hamas. In a statement published in Beirut, the organization recalled that it had warned Ariel Sharon of its intention to act: ten kamikazes, it had said, were ready to launch attacks on Israel to celebrate the arrival of Sharon to power. In Gaza, Mahmoud Zahar, a Hamas leader, warned: "We will continue to respond to Israel. While we are busy burying Palestinians, the Israelis, too, will have to collect the bodies of their dead."

GOD IS WITH US

The new government was presented to the Knesset on March 7. The army was on alert and had taken precautions. The principal Palestinian cities were sealed. A trench had been dug to isolate the village of Bir Zeit and its large university, north of Ramallah. Yasser Arafat, who, as a precaution, had sent a congratulatory telegram to Ariel Sharon, had the Israeli prime minister's inauguration speech translated in real time. "The supreme mission of the government is to reinforce the security of Israel, to guarantee the personal security of the citizens of the country while pursuing the struggle against violence," Sharon declared. . . . "We are extending a hand of peace towards the Palestinians. . . . We know that

peace entails painful compromises for both sides. Sadly, despite consid-
erable concessions that were made on the road to peace by all the governments of Israel in recent years, we still have not encountered, from
the other side, a will towards reconciliation and real peace. . . . We will
require that the Palestinians renounce violence, terrorism, and that the
Palestinian Authority fulfill its obligations and fight terrorism directed
against Israel, its citizens, and its soldiers." And the prime minister announced that he was ready to lead negotiations with the Palestinians in
order to reach a political agreement, "but not under the pressure of terrorism and violence." He added: "I understand the suffering of the Palestinian people and I believe that we can gradually advance towards
peace."

Gradually? Arafat clearly showed his reluctance. He would refuse any
new interim agreement. Two other statements uttered by Sharon caused
him to react. "The government will brandish the banner of Zionism in
education, in the integration of immigrants, and in the settlements,"[50] and
"Jerusalem is a great dream for which the Jews languished and prayed
from generation to generation. If we turn our backs on her, if we turn
our backs on her symbols and holy places, we risk mortgaging our future and our destiny." The Israeli prime minister, however, did confirm that he would not be involved in establishing new settlements. For
the head of the PLO, that was the sole positive point. On March 10,
for the first time since the beginning of the intifada, he brought together
the legislative council in Gaza and gave a radio broadcast. The Israelis
who hoped for a call to end the uprising (or at least a condemnation of
violence) were to be disappointed. Yasser Arafat reaffirmed his engagement in favor of a "way towards peace," and recognized the necessity
of according the Israelis the right to security. But, he added, Israelis
must understand that the Palestinians also have needs and rights.
Specifically, they had to be reminded of the Palestinian right to self-
determination and to an independent state, and of the right of return
of refugees as asserted by Resolution 194 of the United Nations General Assembly. He called upon Sharon's government to restart negotiations at the point where they had ended at Taba a month before, and

also called for the deployment of an international force "in Palestine, to protect the people." He knew that all of these proposals were perfectly unacceptable to the Israelis. Arafat violently criticized Ehud Barak's politics of repression, "the violent military aggression that caused the deaths of 500 martyrs, 20,000 wounded, and a loss of three million dollars to the Palestinian economy." And to the Palestinians who were asking whether the past five months of fighting and suffering could have been avoided, he answered: "Have we lost an opportunity for peace? I don't think so. You have witnessed a series of Israeli retreats that have followed the accords. I can say with all confidence that no opportunity was lost!. . . . Be patient! God is with you! Don't be sad!"

From September 30, 2000 to this point, according to the Palestinian Red Crescent, 381 Palestinians, sixty-one Israelis, and thirteen Arab Israelis were killed in clashes with Israeli police.

CHAPTER 2

LET'S ACT LIKE WE DIDN'T KNOW

Ariel Sharon's first visit to Washington, on March 19, 2001, could not have begun under more favorable auspices. As Thomas Friedman, editorialist for the *New York Times*, explained to an Israeli journalist: "Sharon was received here with open arms. He has not arrived in a city where the beautiful souls are the ones conducting politics. The Bush administration agrees with most of his analyses. Never have Arafat's actions been rated so low in the United States."[1] The Pentagon, the State Department, and the White House rolled out the red carpet. Sharon declared to Donald Rumsfeld: "One thing is certain. Like you, we will not sacrifice our lives for regional stability." With an approving air, the secretary of defense responded: "Israel is a small country and you cannot afford to make serious errors." George Tenet, however, did not react when Sharon explained to him that "Arafat is implicated personally in the attacks recently committed in Israel." The head of the CIA knew that his representatives on the ground had not obtained any concrete proof that Arafat was responsible.[2]

On March 20, George W. Bush invited the Israeli prime minister to lunch. At the end of their meeting, which lasted an hour and a half,

Sharon and his advisors were enchanted. Bush explained to his guests that he did not intend to get involved in the vigorous pursuit of an agreement in the Middle East. The new administration would offer its assistance in negotiations if the parties requested it, but its participation would be much more limited than that of Clinton's team. When Sharon advised him against inviting Arafat to the White House—an act "that would be saying that violence and terrorism pay off"—the following exchange took place:

> Bush: Do you really hate Arafat?
> Sharon: Yes!
> Bush: Do you intend to kill him?
> Sharon: No!
> Bush: Good![3]

Sharon would later admit that he regretted having made this promise to the president. Influenced by the American Israel Public Affairs Committee (AIPAC), the leading pro-Israeli lobby, eighty-seven senators and 209 members of the House of Representatives signed an appeal that called for the closure of the PLO office in Washington and the discontinuation of all American aid to the Palestinian Authority if violence continued in the Middle East. During a joint press conference with Sharon, Bush clarified his position on Jerusalem: "The final status of the city," he said, "will be ultimately determined by the interested parties."

As soon as he returned to Israel, Sharon was confronted with a situation he could have lived without. A commission, presided over by former Senator George Mitchell, was on the ground investigating the source of the violence. It had been created by Bill Clinton after the failure of the summit at Sharm el-Sheik in October 2000, and it was the summit's sole concrete result. In the presence of Hosni Mubarak, King Abdullah of Jordan, and the secretary-general of the United Nations, Clinton had, at the time, brought Ehud Barak and Yasser Arafat together to attempt to negotiate a cease-fire. Also serving on Mitchell's commission were Javier Solana, the European Union's senior representative for foreign politics; Souleyman Demirel, the former president of Turkey; and Thorbjoern Jagland, the Norwegian foreign minister. In an interview on Israeli radio, Ariel Sharon set the tone, warning the members of the commission: "[Ehud Barak] committed a grave historic error in giving his assent to the creation of such a commission, for no one has the right— no one!—to bring Israel before a world court!" When the commission tried to allay the fears of the Israeli prime minister by promising to deliver a "balanced" report, he retorted: "A balanced report will be a reward for the aggressor: Yasser Arafat, who made the decision to unleash the violence in order to gain political advantages. Any impartial examination of the facts will demonstrate the complete and total responsibility of Arafat."

HASSON NEGOTIATES

Israel Hasson, the former second-in-command at Shin Bet, had not yet left the prime minister's office, where he still worked in the department of negotiations with the Palestinians. The turn of events was causing him to become increasingly worried and on March 24, he traveled to Ramallah on his own to meet Jibril Rajoub, head of Palestinian preventive security in the West Bank. The three thousand agents in this service had not participated in any way in the intifada. Hasson and Rajoub, who had known each other for a long time, drew up a plan for an agreement, in stages, directed toward reestablishing calm. To demonstrate good faith, Palestinian security was required to initiate secret antiterrorist operations for the two weeks following a particularly odious attack. They cited as an example the murder, sharply criticized in the West Bank, of an Israeli adolescent lured near Ramallah by a young Palestinian woman who had contacted him through an internet chat room. The second phase would involve the opening of secret negotiations with the aim of concluding an interim agreement. Israel would make no territorial concessions but, on the ground, would redeploy its forces to the lines they had occupied before September 29, 2000.

Rajoub and Hasson next met with the Palestinian leaders who, after having familiarized themselves with the text, accepted it and proceeded to take all necessary measures to overcome Arafat's resistance if he refused it. Hasson then returned to Jerusalem and called Rafi Peled, the general manager of the prime minister's office, to request an urgent meeting with Sharon in the presence of the chief of staff of the prime minister, General Gadi Eizenkot. He received an answer ten minutes later: "The prime minister requests that you prepare a written report. He will read it tomorrow." Hasson got the underlying message that Sharon was putting him off and returned to his home in Galilee.

On the ground, the situation continued to deteriorate. Forty-eight hours later on March 26, in the Jewish settlement in Hebron, Shalhevet Pass, a ten-month-old Israeli girl, was killed in her father's arms by a Palestinian sniper. The settlers reacted by burning Palestinian cars and offices belonging to the Waqf, which administers Muslim property. The army imposed a curfew on the town. That day, General Gadi Eizenkot telephoned Israel Hasson to ask his opinion of the latest developments. Hasson discovered that his interlocutor was unaware of the plan for an agreement he had drawn up with Rajoub. "It is very important. I have to speak to the prime minister," Eizenkot insisted. Hasson sent the report to the prime minister's office, and fifteen minutes later, the general called back to say that "Ariel Sharon asks that you not concern yourself with that any longer. Only the head of Shin Bet is authorized to meet with the Palestinians." Hasson responded, "Under these conditions, I request that the prime minister accept my resignation," and in five minutes time, thereby renounced his Israeli public office.

MURDER ATTEMPTS AND REPRISALS

The next day, two explosions rocked Jerusalem six hours apart that wounded around thirty Israelis: a suicide bomber from Islamic Jihad and a car bomb. Colin Powell called Sharon, who told him that the situation was becoming intolerable. The government issued a statement: "The perpetrators of acts of terrorism will not escape without punishment and the Palestinian Authority will face the consequences." On that same day, the thirteenth Arab summit opened in Amman and Yasser Arafat gave a much-awaited speech: "The Palestinian people condemn terrorism in all its forms, including state-sponsored terrorism and aggression." He accused Israel of "stealing Palestinian land by expanding its settlements. . . . The Israeli army is pursuing a plan to assassinate our leaders, our citizens, and to destroy the peace process . . ." The leader of the PLO called for international protection for the Palestinians. But Bachar el-Assad, the son of the deceased Syrian president, stole the spotlight from Arafat by making declarations that immediately drew adamant condemnations from Europe and the United States: "We say that the [Israeli] prime minister is racist and that the army is racist but, when we speak of Israeli society, we do not have a voice . . . , it is more racist than the society of the Nazis . . ." The Arab summit ended the next day with a vote on a resolution to support the Palestinians and "their legitimate right to resist the occupation until they obtain their national rights." Arafat was promised a donation of around a million dollars, but he would discover quickly that the sum of money was a mirage. In the end, very little would be paid.

That same morning, Hamas committed yet another suicide attack in Neve Yamin, near the "Meeting Place of Peace," a gas station located near the border of the West Bank, close to Qalqilya. Two young students from a Talmudic school were killed and four others were wounded. The commando unit Ezzedin al-Qassam, the armed branch of the Islamic organization, issued a statement that promised future attacks. The Israeli government, which had pledged to the Bush administration that it would not pursue military operations during the Arab summit, could now respond. Helicopters and tanks attacked targets in Ramallah. And in Gaza, Force 17 bases were bombed, in addition to Arafat's house (he had not yet returned from Amman). Dozens were wounded and there was a death toll of two: a Palestinian soldier and a bystander. This was the first major military response since Ariel Sharon had assumed power. The Israeli tone grew harsher. The prime minister insisted that Arafat was a "terrorist leader." General Mofaz accused the Autonomous Authority of transforming itself into a "terrorist entity." In the Knesset, the leader of the peace camp, Yossi Sarid, a member of Meretz, a left-wing party, addressed the PLO leader: "It is time for you to stop your grotesque and pathetic participations in summits! Stay in Gaza and Ramallah and start to put things in order there! Because this anarchy is going to lead to a horrible disaster for your people and for ours! . . . Do not lead us to believe that you prefer the violence of armed struggle to the creation of a Palestinian state."

The Israeli peace camp was in a total state of collapse. Yoel Esteron, editor in chief of the moderate daily *Haaretz*, published an editorial in the *New York Times* on March 28, 2001, in which he addressed the question: "Where have all the peaceniks gone?" He wrote: ". . . 'two states for two peoples,' to quote the left-wing chant of the last 33 years. But for Yasser Arafat, and the majority of the Palestinians, this was not enough. In flagrant violation of their agreement at Oslo to resolve all matters of dispute by peaceful means, they launched into an armed struggle to pressure Israel. . . . Their chief demand: a return of all the refugees who fled or were evicted from their homes in a war that the Arabs forced on Israel in 1948. . . . What they seek, simply put, is the dissolution of the state of Israel."

The messages broadcast for months by politicians and military officials had been assimilated by practically the entirety of the Israeli public: Arafat was fully responsible for the situation. According to a poll conducted at the end of March 2001, 58 percent of those questioned affirmed that they would henceforth have a negative view of the Palestinian people. Sixty-three percent judged that it would no longer be possible to arrive at a peace agreement.[4] And 71 percent responded that they favored the sealing off of Palestinian cities and towns.[5] In the West Bank and Gaza, the mood in the street was no less belligerent: 62.3 percent of Palestinians supported the continuation of the intifada in two forms, namely, through popular demonstrations and armed struggle.[6]

March 30, Land Day. In the West Bank, Gaza, and in East Jerusalem, thousands of Palestinians demonstrated as a sign of their solidarity with Arab Israelis who were holding a general strike in memory of six among them killed in 1976 on the occasion of protests against the expropriation of land. In many places, the processions ended in front of Israeli military checkpoints. Rocks were thrown and shots fired. Six Palestinians were killed and dozens of others wounded. Arafat convened a government meeting, but close to a dozen Palestinian ministers were unable to attend because they did not receive authorization to pass through checkpoints. The news was not good for the Autonomous Authority. Meanwhile, at the Security Council in New York, the United States vetoed a resolution to deploy international observers in the Palestinian territories.

SHARON ESTABLISHES CONTACT

On April 2, heavy exchanges of gunfire exploded in the suburbs north of Bethlehem. An Israeli soldier was killed and several Palestinians were wounded, while in Ramallah, Israeli aviation destroyed prefabricated buildings belonging to Force 17. The next day, the Israeli army resumed a program of "targeted killings" of Palestinian militants, a program that had been suspended since February. In Gaza, a helicopter launched missiles on the car belonging to an Islamic Jihad leader, killing him. Later that evening Omri Sharon, the son of the prime minister, secretly arrived in Ramallah for a meeting with Arafat, a meeting organized by Yossi Ginosar, who was also in attendance. Ginosar, the former second-in-command at Shin Bet, had entered the private sector and was associated with Khaled Salam, the financial advisor to the leader of the PLO. The two men came bearing a firm message from the prime minister: "The violence must stop. When that happens, it will be possible to have a discussion." The subsequent discussion concerned the renewal of the coordination of security. A direct, secret line of communication would henceforth remain in place between Sharon and Arafat.

The first public meeting since Sharon's rise to power took place on April 4 in Athens. Shimon Peres, who knew nothing about Omri's mission, agreed to Javier Solana's proposal to meet with the Palestinians. Flanked by advisors, including Avi Gil, the head of his cabinet, they spoke at length with Saeb Erekat, the principal Palestinian negotiator, Nabil Shaath, the chief of foreign affairs, and Yasser Abed Rabbo, within the context of a conference on European-Mediterranean dialogue sponsored by the newsweekly the *Economist*. For three hours, the Palestinians, with the participation of Peres, described the situation in the West Bank and

Gaza—the sealed-off towns, the curfews, the difficulties of everyday life. And they warned that in the absence of a resumption of negotiations leading toward a definitive status of a Palestinian state, it would be impossible to restore calm if the Palestinians were left without hope. The two delegations departed after having discreetly promised to remain in contact.

Peres explained to his interlocutors that "Israel cannot negotiate in the midst of raging violence. The present government has neither a mandate to do that, nor the popular support to engage in serious negotiations while relations with Palestinians are closer to war than to the peace process."[7] Erekat and Shaath proposed at the time that Israel should at least send a positive message to the Palestinian population by freezing settlement activity. Peres responded by citing the government's agreement: no new settlements would be built, but construction would continue in existing settlements as part of their natural growth. The Palestinians refused to accept this argument and observed that numerous homes were uninhabited at these sites.

NEGOTIATIONS AND GUNFIRE

The American administration, for its part, had been informed of Omri Sharon's secret mission. Colin Powell had telephoned Yasser Arafat and Ariel Sharon; both agreed to the meeting of a "committee on the coordination of security." The session took place that very evening, in the home of the U.S. ambassador in Herzliya, north of Tel Aviv. The participants on the Palestinian side included the heads of preventive security for the Palestinians on the West Bank and Gaza, Jibril Rajoub and Mohammed Dahlan; the commander of the police force in Gaza, General Abdelrazik el-Majaida; and the head of Palestinian intelligence, Amin al-Hindi. Participants on the Israeli side included the director of Shin Bet, Avi Dichter, as well as the regional military commanders, Generals Doron Almog and Yitzhak Eytan, and Giora Eiland, of the military staff. The representative of the CIA in the region was also present, as well as American diplomats. The discussion was difficult. The Israelis demanded of their interlocutors that Hamas and Islamic Jihad activists, liberated at the beginning of the intifada, be imprisoned again and that a real effort be made to prevent future terrorist attacks. The Palestinians demanded the opening of sealed-off Palestinian towns, the withdrawal of Israeli forces to the positions they occupied before September 29, 2000, that is, their positions before the start of the intifada. They explained they would need several weeks to restore calm, and especially to give the population hope for a political solution. Bringing up accusations made against Yasser Arafat, Jibril Rajoub lashed out: "You describe him like a Pentium computer wearing a keffieh." Dahlan retorted: "You're wrong, Abu Amar [Yasser Arafat] is incapable of making the smallest decision. If we see real change on the ground, we will be able to try to appease the situation, but that will take time. . . . Several weeks at least."[8] The Israelis were not unhappy. Despite these reciprocal accusations, the Israelis nonetheless continued the dialogue with their Palestinian interlocutors, who appeared to be credible. The agenda for another meeting was discussed. It would take place the following week.

The Americans then gave the starting signal to depart. Dahlan, Hindi, and Majaida took their seats in the car belonging to the American embassy, which drove them to the Erez checkpoint, north of Gaza, where they were soon joined by the Palestinian convoy that was waiting for them. About a hundred meters away, shots were heard. Gunfire then broke out between an Israeli position and the security guards of the heads of Palestinian security. The American diplomat tried to stop the shooting. Dahlan, who was lying on the ground, protected by his wounded bodyguard, telephoned Arafat and against a background of gunfire, told him that they were stuck and in danger of being killed. The PLO leader immediately called King Abdullah of Jordan: "The Israelis want to kill Dahlan and the others!" The Hashemite sovereign relayed the information to Colin Powell, who personally woke up Ariel Sharon. The exchange of gunfire stopped. Three Palestinian security agents were wounded. Dahlan's 4x4 had been hit by seventy-two bullets. The Israelis claimed that the first shot came from the convoy of the Palestinian leaders, while the latter formally denied this and accused the IDF of wanting to assassinate them.

For months, Mohammed Dahlan would refuse to participate in any meeting with Israeli officials. He would now only move around Gaza in an unmarked car. Blunder or misunderstanding? The incident would, in any case, reinforce the Palestinians' feelings of suspicion toward the Israeli army.[9]

ASSASSINATION AND SETTLEMENTS

In the north of the West Bank on the morning of April 5 in Jenin, Iyad Hardan, the head of the military branch of Islamic Jihad, was killed in the explosion of a phone booth where he regularly made calls with the authorization of the guards of the prison (on the other side of the street!) where he was allegedly being held in detention "for his own security" according to the Autonomous Authority. The Israeli denial didn't fool anyone. Hardan had been accused of organizing several attacks. That same day, Binyamin Ben-Eliezer, the minister of defense, announced the lifting of the closure of the West Bank and Gaza. The Rafah border post located between Gaza and Egypt would be reopened and 3,200 Palestinian workers would be authorized to come back to work in Israel. However, this did not assuage the anger of the Palestinian leaders, who had learned that Nathan Shcharansky, Israeli minister of housing, had published a tender for the construction of 708 new flats in Maale Adumim, to the east of Jerusalem, and in Alfei Menashe, near Qalqilya. The announcement was accompanied by an explanation: "It is necessary to reinforce the Jewish enclaves of Judea-Samaria [the West Bank] due to the Palestinian attacks to which their inhabitants have been subjected. In addition, it is necessary to allow for the natural growth of these settlements . . ."

In Washington, the State Department's reaction to these events was immediate. Richard Boucher, the spokesman, revealed that Colin Powell was placing the responsibility for the incident that night at Erez on Israel. He stated: "The plan to extend the settlements is a provocation and risks to inflame an already complicated situation in the region even more." That evening, a mortar shell shot from Gaza exploded in Israeli territory without doing any damage. But this was not the first attack of this kind. On April 3 in the settlement at Netzarim, a fifteen-month-old Israeli child had been seriously wounded by a shell. In this instance as well, the Israeli army responded by bombarding Palestinian security buildings in the cities of Gaza and Beit Lahiya as well as in the refugee camp of Jebaliya, resulting in five wounded.

Several statements made by the grand rabbi, Ovadia Yosef, fanned the flames. An internet site revealed that the highly respected mentor of the Sephardic ultraorthodox Shas Party—the third most important political body in the country—declared during a sermon broadcast by satellite to his flock: "It is necessary to annihilate the Arabs. You must not be afraid of them. It is necessary to shoot super-missiles at them, wipe them out, these evil ones, these cursed ones!" There was a general outcry in Israel, with condemnations erupting from both the Left and the Right, as well as, evidently, from the Arab world. A Jordanian businessman put a price on the head of the rabbi: a million dollars! Several months earlier, Ovadia Yosef had already called the Arabs "snakes." Those close to him claimed that his statements had been taken out of context.

DESTROYING THE AUTONOMOUS AUTHORITY

On April 10, 2001, Ariel Sharon paid a visit to the troops in the south military region, accompanied by his minister of defense, Binyamin Ben-Eliezer, also a former general. This meeting between the IDF of 2001 and the two old military leaders who had not had the opportunity to familiarize themselves with modern military technology was a historical moment. The commander, General Doron Almog, launched straightaway into a power point presentation. He reviewed the situation in detail. Sharon and Ben-Eliezer, extremely bored, finally exclaimed: "But we know that! What are you doing to stop the mortar fire?" Almog tried to answer, but the prime minister immediately interrupted: "When I was an officer here, I focused on acts, not words." And he proceeded to recount how, when he was an officer, he succeeded in taking the enemy by surprise.[10] Right in the middle of this military discussion, three mortar shells fell on the settlement block of Gush Katif, in the south of the Gaza Strip. Authorization to respond was immediately granted. That night, missiles were fired at two Palestinian bases. The casualty toll: one dead (a Palestinian military doctor) and ten wounded. Sharon wanted results!

The army received new instructions. Colonel Gal Hirsch, chief of staff of the Central Command until 2002, was one of the men responsible for translating those instructions into operational terms in the West Bank. Close to General Moshe Yaalon, whose ideas concerning low-intensity warfare he shared, he commanded the Ramallah brigade during the first three months of the al-Aqsa intifada, and was a member of the group of colonels nicknamed "the Tanzim of Mofaz." To whoever was willing to listen, he claimed to possess evidence—which he did not reveal —that Yasser Arafat was controlling Palestinian violence himself.[11] Gal Hirsch, who later would be named commander of the officer's training school, thus claimed that the IDF had passed into a new phase. For him, it was no longer a question of "containing Palestinian violence," but rather of directly attacking the Autonomous Authority:

> The army assumed that on the other side there was a Palestinian system of control permitting and encouraging armed attacks. With increasing terrorist attacks, the strategic directives had changed, the command having shifted to the idea of 'leverage,' that is, the exertion of continued and permanent pressure on the Palestinian Authority to force it to continue to struggle against terrorism. . . . While that had not been officially announced, the Palestinian administration had become an objective and an adversary. The operations of the Israeli army aimed to demonstrate to the Palestinian Authority that it would pay the price for its support of terrorism.[12]

Numerous officers and reserve combat officers experienced a profound sense of unease in the face of the repression being conducted in the West Bank and Gaza. On January 25, 2001, several among them published a letter proclaiming their refusal to serve in the Palestinian territories:

> We, reserve combat officers and soldiers of the Israeli Defense Forces, who were raised upon the principles of Zionism, self-

sacrifice and giving to the people of Israel, . . . who have always served in the front lines, and who were the first to . . . protect the State of Israel and strengthen it. We . . . were issued commands and directives that had nothing to do with the security of our country, and that had the sole purpose of perpetuating our control over the Palestinian people. . . . We, who sensed how the commands issued to us in the Occupied Territories destroy all the values that we were raised upon, [w]e, who understand now that the price of Occupation is the loss of IDF's human character and the corruption of the entire Israeli society. . . . We shall not continue to fight beyond the 1967 borders in order to dominate, expel, starve and humiliate an entire people. . . .[13]

The two hundred signatories were for the most part expelled from their units. Some, not having responded to a mobilization order, were condemned in courts martial to imprisonment for several weeks.

FORTY-TWO PERCENT FOR THE PALESTINIANS

Ariel Sharon's entourage decided that it was time to dot the i's. Communications advisors chose Ari Shavit of the daily *Haaretz* for the task, a journalist who was not hostile to the prime minister. The interview was published on April 12:

Question: When quiet prevails, will you agree to recognize a Palestinian state on 40 to 50 percent of the territory [of the West Bank]?

Sharon: I did not say 50 percent. I said 42 percent. Maybe a bit more will be possible. But within the framework of a nonbelligerency agreement, for a lengthy and indefinite period, in an agreement that does not have a timetable but a table of expectations. Our expectations lie in three spheres: preventive action against terrorism and the infrastructures of terrorism; cessation of incitement and education for peace; economic cooperation. . . . As a Jew, I know that it is not easy to be a Palestinian. . . . There are things they definitely suffer from. They suffer from a lack of continuity of territory and we have to find a solution for that. They suffer from our roadblocks and that also needs a solution. They do not always behave properly at the roadblocks, but our soldiers also don't always behave as they should . . .

However, the evacuation of the settlements within the context of an agreement for nonbelligerency was out of the question. Netzarim, the settlement that cuts the Gaza Strip in half? Certainly not! This settlement has, he said, strategic importance. No concessions either on Jerusalem, on Hebron ("That is where King David was crowned!"), or on the Jordan Valley or the Golan Heights ("that would put Israel's security in danger"). The article was entitled, "Sharon Is Sharon."

Up north, after a Hezbollah mortar attack on Shebaa Farms, the Israeli position in Syrian-Lebanese territory, and the death of a soldier, the Israeli army responded by bombing a Syrian radar base near Beirut.[14] Three Syrian soldiers were killed. Binyamin Ben-Eliezer justified the raid, which he depicted as a "defensive reaction following the deaths of three soldiers and the kidnapping of three others by Hezbollah since the Israeli retreat in May 2000. Syria must understand that the rules of the game have changed. We have sent a clear message to the Syrians. They alone can stop Hezbollah."

On April 16, the IDF began a major operation in Gaza, the source of mortar shells launched against the Israeli town of Sderot. This Palestinian territory was split into three parts within forty-eight hours. Police stations and Force 17 offices were bombed or destroyed by bulldozer. The next day, Colin Powell released a statement in Washington criticizing "the excessive and disproportionate use of force by Israel." In reaction, the IDF withdrew its forces from the sectors it had just begun to occupy. In the West Bank and Gaza, these Israeli operations resulted in two deaths and several dozen wounded.

THE EGYPTIAN FAILURE

During this period, diplomats were getting more involved. The latest peace initiative was jointly proposed by Egypt and Jordan. It was presented in Jerusalem by the minister of foreign affairs of the Hashemite kingdom and consisted of three stages: the establishment of a cease-fire and the annulment of oppressive measures, both military and economic, on the part of the Israelis; the reestablishment of mutual confidence through the implementation of interim agreements; and finally, the resumption of negotiations on the definitive status of the Palestinian territories, which would necessarily terminate on a fixed date. Ariel Sharon did not look favorably upon this proposal. He would hear nothing of specific deadlines and favored a long-term interim agreement, but certainly not a definitive agreement that would restart negotiations concerning Israel's borders with Palestine. Shimon Peres, the minister of foreign affairs who was pursuing secret negotiations with Abu Ala, the president of the Palestinian parliament, and Mohammed Rashid, Arafat's financial advisor, was assigned the dossier and the mission of avoiding a crisis with Egypt and Jordan. He quickly made it known that the Israeli government accepted the framework of the Jordanian-Egyptian plan, but that it was necessary to add several clauses: "Israel will not accept a total freeze on the construction of settlements since Sharon's cabinet already promised to not build any new settlements, but only to accommodate the natural growth of existing settlements. Israel rejects the clause prohibiting the use of weapons banned by international law and demands that the Autonomous Authority stop the terrorists and seize illegal arms."[15]

Informed of these alterations, the Palestinians protested. They demanded a total halt to the settlement policy. On April 29, Shimon Peres went to Cairo after having met with King Abdullah in the Red Sea port of Aqaba in Jordan. The atmosphere of his meeting with Hosni Mubarak was pleasant. The Israeli foreign minister discussed his contacts with the Palestinian leaders. The Egyptian president was persuaded that an agreement was imminent, which he immediately announced on television and was picked up by the international media. Before leaving, Peres announced during a brief press conference: "Beginning this morning, we are going to take measures to make life easier, in all possible ways, for the populations in the territories." This declaration reinforced the feeling that a cease-fire was imminent. But, once he returned to Israel, he had to backtrack. Interviewed on Israeli television, Peres stated that no agreement had been reached with the Palestinians and that Hosni Mubarak was mistaken. The Egyptian president was furious. In a short speech broadcast by radio and television on May 1, he accused Peres of having led him astray: "The Israelis told us that they had come to an agreement with the Palestinians on the principles of a cease-fire. They asked me to make a statement concerning this, and I was surprised to hear from Arafat's mouth that it was not the case."

TEN CORPSES

On May 6 in Jerusalem, Shaul Mofaz held a meeting with the commanders deployed in the West Bank to boost their morale. He described the situation on the ground as he saw it, and then asked everyone to stop taking notes. The recording of his speech was stopped, and the chief of staff of the Israeli army declared to his officers: "You must seek out contact with the enemy!" "What is your definition of the enemy?" someone asked. Mofaz answered, "The armed [Palestinians]!" And then he added: "Each battle should result in ten corpses!" General Benny Gantz, who commanded the division, broke out into a cold sweat. Not only would that mean seventy Palestinian deaths each day, but, in addition, the order was totally illegal. After Mofaz's departure, the next day, Gantz again gathered together all those who might have interpreted Mofaz's words as an order: "It was only a way of speaking. Mofaz did not ask you to open fire indiscriminately!"

The next day, without warning, an Israeli unit shot at three Palestinian policemen posted at a checkpoint at the entry to Samua, a village close to Dahariya in the Hebron sector. One was killed and of the two wounded, one was disabled. Officially, the IDF announced that the incident concerned a "response to numerous Palestinian attacks," and then, forty-eight hours later, acknowledged that it was a "mistake" caused by faulty intelligence. The lieutenant colonel responsible for the operation later explained that he had only obeyed the order of the chief of staff. He would not be punished in any way. Shaul Mofaz would deny, for his part, that he had ever uttered these words, despite the fact that they were heard by several officers present.[16] "Fouad" Ben-Eliezer, the minister of defense, would only learn of this incident in the press.

MAHMOUD DARWISH: PEACE IS A MIRAGE

Another blunder took place on May 14 at two o'clock in the morning. According to intelligence received by the Israeli control post near Ramallah, a Force 17 unit was responsible for shots fired every night at the Ofer military base. An operation was mounted against the Palestinian checkpoint at the entrance to Beitunia, where the alleged attackers were stationed. Five perfectly innocent policemen were murdered, some in their sleep. The intelligence proved false.[17] Several hours later, thousands of Palestinians, among them numerous policemen, took part in the funeral for the victims, chanting "Vengeance!" and promising to continue the battle. The IDF acknowledged its error without offering apologies.

That day also marked the anniversary of the proclamation of Israel's independence and for the Palestinians, the *nakba*, or catastrophe, the 1948 defeat and the exile of hundreds of thousands of refugees. The previous year, in the more optimistic atmosphere that prevailed at the time, a text by the great poet Mahmoud Darwish had been solemnly read over Palestinian radio, evoking the conditions necessary for reconciliation between the two peoples and demanding that Israel acknowledge its responsibility for crimes committed against the Palestinians. But he also reminded Europe that it

> had to expiate the great crime committed against its Jewish citizens . . . and that it bears the responsibility for having created another problem: the Palestinian question. No tragedy justifies the creation of another tragedy. . . . We are not responsible for the great tragedy that Europe inflicted on the Jewish people. It is our moral responsibility to accept the Jewish history of the Holocaust as it is, without discussing

statistical aspects of the crime or amplifying our sympathy for the victims. We also have the right to demand that the children of the [Jewish] victims recognize the right of the Palestinians to life, to freedom, to independence . . .

An unprecedented gesture from the Palestinian national poet: he asked his people to recognize the Shoah at the very moment when negationism was gaining popularity in the Arab world.

Now, the following year, the tone had changed. At eleven o'clock, sirens wailed in the Palestinian territories. Imitating the commemoration of the Shoah in Israel, Palestinian drivers stopped their cars, passersby observed two minutes of silence, and a new text by Darwish was broadcast:

If the Israeli makers of this *nakba*, this catastrophe, are declaring this day of remembrance that the war of 1948 is not yet over, they are merely exposing the mirage of a peace which has loomed large over the past decade, in which they claimed to put an end to the conflict through the just apportionment of land. . . . When the moment of reckoning drew closer, the Israeli understanding of peace revealed its true colors: the resumption of the occupation under a different guise, under preconditions more favorable and less costly to the occupying power . . .

It amounted to saying, and it could not have been stated more clearly, that Palestinian society had returned to its prior status: peace with the Jewish state was now seen as impossible. Palestine was once again a mirror image of Israeli society, whose leaders compared the present conflict to the battle for independence, referring to the Shoah. The intifada and its repression now appeared in their true light: the result of the failure of the Oslo process to establish in both societies the basis for a lasting peace, which was ultimately impossible. Saeb Erekat would state with regret that the Israelis and Palestinians had returned to "the warm embrace of the conflict that all know only too well."[18]

ABU HANOUD ESCAPES

Early on the morning of May 18 in Tulkarm, Mahmoud Ahmed Marmash, a twenty-one-year-old carpenter, said good-bye to his mother after giving her a bag of sweets. She would only find his farewell letter later: "All those who believe that the religion of God will be victorious without engaging in holy war, without the shedding of blood, uniformed in human flesh, live in illusions!" He belonged to the Hamas commando unit Ezzedin al-Qassam, and late that morning activated his explosives in front of the entrance to a mall in Netanya, north of Tel Aviv. Five Israelis were killed and a hundred wounded. Hamas quickly released a statement announcing that it was in response to the killing of the five Palestinian policemen by the IDF in Beitunia earlier that week.

In Jerusalem, Ariel Sharon, after having consulted with Shimon Peres and the minister of defense, Binyamin Ben-Eliezer, authorized a series of aerial bombings against targets belonging to the Palestinian Authority. This time, F-16 warplanes were deployed for the first time in the West Bank since the 1967 Six-Day War. In Ramallah, an F-16 destroyed a Force 17 building, and in Nablus, several bombs were dropped on a prison. Eleven Palestinian policemen were killed, and around fifty more were wounded. To be precise, the IDF was aiming to kill—again—Mahmoud Abu Hanoud, one of the main leaders of the military branch of Hamas in the West Bank.[19] He had been incarcerated "for his own security," to use the expression of the Palestinian authorities. Israeli security officials accused the guards of letting him come and go as he pleased. Only slightly wounded, he was now free.

RAJOUB ESCAPES DEATH

On May 20 in Ramallah, after having hosted a group of Israeli journalists, Jibril Rajoub returned home. The moment he entered his bathroom, a tank shell exploded in his living room. Two other projectiles reached the house. The principal interlocutor to the Israelis had just escaped death. Five of his bodyguards were also wounded. According to an army spokesman, this operation was a reaction from the IDF position in Psagot, a settlement that overlooks Ramallah from the east, to Palestinian shots that had wounded an Israeli soldier while a checkpoint, situated several kilometers away, was being attacked. And he added: "The commander of the tank did not know that it was Rajoub's house." For his part, Ben-Eliezer, the minister of defense, stated: "Rajoub is obviously not a target. . . . I cannot imagine that officers in that sector would have wanted to kill Rajoub." The dozen journalists who rushed to the scene confirmed that no traces of ammunition were found and that a sole Israeli position, the headquarters of Beit El, a settlement to the northeast, was visible from the home of the Palestinian chief of preventive security. Above all, the surviving officers swore that they had not fired a single shot. This security service did not participate in the intifada, and the very notion that they would put their boss in danger was absurd. Ben-Eliezer published an apology, but did not talk to Rajoub directly: "The line was busy," he said.

Brigadier General Ilan Paz, the commander of the brigade deployed in this sector of Ramallah, made the following comment:

> The deputy commander of the battalion called to tell me that he had located armed men who were shooting on our forces from behind a wall. The identification was certain, he said, while demanding authorization to shoot mortar shells from a tank due to the distance. I told him to take the place of the commander in the tank to precisely show him where he had to shoot. I then authorized the launching of two shells. No one knew that it was Rajoub's house. Neither the commander of the battalion, Lieutenant-Colonel Erez Weiner, or his deputy were on site.[20]

So, the worst case scenario was that it was a targeting mistake. But Weiner could not manage to remain silent: the next day, he revealed on an Israeli radio program that he knew perfectly well that the targeted house was Rajoub's. An awkward situation for his superior officers, who told several military correspondents: "Weiner has committed an error that damages the honor of the IDF." Yet another press conference was called, this one involving Benny Gantz, the general commander of the division, and Weiner. According to the new version of the story, armed Palestinians had opened fire from the courtyard of Rajoub's home.

A former high official in Shin Bet pursued his own investigation and came to the conclusion that the incident stemmed from the initiative of a tank unit deployed in Psagot. The Israeli soldiers apparently wanted to seek revenge for one of their colleagues who had been wounded that morning. They allegedly lied to their superiors, who covered for them.[21] For an error of this kind to have occurred only a few weeks after the incident at the Erez checkpoint challenges the powers of the imagination. And for Palestinian security officials, it was not a coincidence.

THE MITCHELL REPORT

On May 21, the report of the investigative committee led by former senator George Mitchell was made public. Yasser Arafat and Ariel Sharon already had it in their possession for two weeks. The report treated both parties in an evenhanded fashion. In a chapter entitled "What Happened?" the members of the commission described the position of both camps at the time of the origin of the violence:

> The GOI [Government of Israel] asserts that the immediate catalyst for the violence was the breakdown of the Camp David negotiations on July 25, 2000 and the 'widespread appreciation in the international community of Palestinian responsibility for the impasse.' In this view, Palestinian violence was planned by the PA [Palestinian Authority] leadership, and was aimed at 'provoking and incurring Palestinian casualties as a means of regaining the diplomatic initiative.'
>
> The Palestinian Liberation Organization (PLO) denies the allegation that the intifada was planned. It claims, however, that 'Camp David represented nothing less than an at-

tempt by Israel to extend the force it exercises on the ground to negotiations,' and that 'the failure of the summit, and the attempts to allocate blame on the Palestinian side only added to the tension on the ground . . .'

From the perspective of the PLO, Israel responded to the disturbances with excessive and illegal use of deadly force against demonstrators; behavior which, in the PLO's view, reflected Israel's contempt for the lives and safety of Palestinians. For Palestinians, the widely seen images of the killing of 12-year-old Muhammed al Durra in Gaza on September 30, shot as he huddled behind his father, reinforced that perception.

From the perspective of the GOI, the demonstrations were organized and directed by the Palestinian leadership to create sympathy for their cause around the world by provoking Israeli security forces to fire upon demonstrators, especially young people. For Israelis, the lynching of two military reservists, First Sgt. Vadim Novesche and First Cpl. Yosef Avrahami, in Ramallah on October 12, reflected a deep-seated Palestinian hatred of Israel and Jews.

Accordingly, we have no basis on which to conclude that there was a deliberate plan by the PA to initiate a campaign of violence at the first opportunity; or to conclude that there was a deliberate plan by the GOI to respond with lethal force.

However, there is also no evidence on which to conclude that the PA made a consistent effort to contain the demonstrations and control the violence once it began; or that the GOI made a consistent effort to use nonlethal means to control demonstrations of unarmed Palestinians. Amid rising anger, fear, and mistrust, each side assumed the worst about the other and acted accordingly.

The Sharon visit [September 28, 2000, to the esplanade of the Haram al-Sharif/Temple Mount in Jerusalem] did not cause the 'al-Aqsa intifada.' But it was poorly timed and the

provocative effect should have been foreseen; . . . More significant were the events that followed: the decision of the
Israeli police on September 29 to use lethal means against the
Palestinian demonstrators; and the subsequent failure, as
noted above, of either party to exercise restraint.[22]

A footnote to the report indicated that the Israelis had communi-
cated to the commission a statement made by the Palestinian minister
of posts and telecommunications, in Lebanon in March 2001, confirming that the intifada had been planned by the Palestinian leadership
immediately following the Camp David summit in July 2000. The Palestinian Authority responded by transmitting the minister's denial to the
commission, which asserted that the statement had been misquoted and
taken out of context. An IDF intelligence officer subsequently told the
commission that this statement, while not constituting definitive evidence, was the "'open-source' version of what was known to the IDF
through 'other means'; knowledge and means not shared by the IDF with
the Committee." In this instance, the officer, whose name was not provided in the report, was not telling the truth: no Israeli intelligence service possessed a shred of evidence proving the existence of any Palestinian
planning of the intifada.

The commission analyzed the situation on the ground and noted the
striking absence of senior leadership on the Israeli side during confrontations with Palestinians throwing stones in Ramallah:

> Concerning such confrontations, the GOI takes the position
> that 'Israel is engaged in an armed conflict short of war. This
> is not a civilian disturbance or a demonstration or a riot. It is
> characterized by live-fire attacks on a significant scale. . . .
> [T]he attacks are carried out by a well-armed and organized
> militia.' Yet, the GOI acknowledges that of some 9,000 'attacks'
> by Palestinians against Israelis, 'some 2,700 [about 30 percent]
> involved the use of automatic weapons, rifles, hand guns,
> grenades, [and] explosives of other kinds.' Thus, for the first

three months of the current uprising, most incidents *did not* involve Palestinian use of firearms and explosives.

The commission also examined a crucial aspect of the policies of the IDF chief of staff, which explains why Israeli soldiers were less cautious about shooting: they had no reason to fear juridical investigations.

Moreover, by thus defining the conflict, the IDF has suspended its policy of mandating investigations by the Department of Military Police Investigations whenever a Palestinian in the territories dies at the hands of an IDF soldier in an incident not involving terrorism. In the words of the GOI, 'Where Israel considers that there is reason to investigate particular incidents, it does so, although, given the circumstances of armed conflict, it does not do so routinely.' We believe, however, that by abandoning the blanket 'armed conflict short of war' characterization and by re-instituting mandatory military police investigations, the GOI could help mitigate deadly violence and help rebuild mutual confidence. . . . [A]n effort should be made to differentiate between terrorism and protests.

When the widow of a murdered Israeli physician—a man of peace whose practice included the treatment of Arab patients —tells us that it seems that the Palestinians are interested in killing Jews for the sake of killing Jews, Palestinians should take notice. When the parents of a Palestinian child killed while in his bed by an errant .50 caliber bullet draw similar conclusions about the respect accorded by Israelis to Palestinian lives, Israelis need to listen. When we see the shattered bodies of children we know it is time for adults to stop the violence.

In their recommendations, Senator Mitchell and his colleagues refused to take sides. Israel and the Autonomous Authority were advised to work toward the establishment of measures to "restore calm" as a step toward rebuilding confidence, and to intensify their efforts to identify, condemn, and discourage the causes of violence in all its forms. The Autonomous Authority was advised, first, to clearly demonstrate to Palestinians and Israelis, through concrete actions, that terrorism is reprehensible and unacceptable, and second, to make a 100 percent effort to prevent terrorist operations and punish their perpetrators. For its part, Israel was advised to freeze all settlement activities, including those resulting from the "natural growth" theory of existing settlements.

THE BUSH ADMINISTRATION INTERVENES

From Washington, Colin Powell called Ariel Sharon to let him know that the Bush administration had adopted the Mitchell report. The secretary of state quickly rushed William Burns, the former ambassador to Jordan, and his assistant secretary of state for the Middle East, to the scene. His mission was not to set a new peace initiative in motion, but rather "to help the parties involved to create the conditions for a cease-fire." Sharon explained that, from his point of view, the Mitchell report was positive except for the passage concerning the freezing of construction in the settlements and the critical advice directed to the army. UN Secretary-General Kofi Annan and the European Union announced that they also endorsed the conclusions of the report.

Sharon felt that he did not have much of a choice if he wanted to head off a crisis with the United States. He thus ordered the IDF to suspend all preventative operations against the Palestinians, "except in cases posing a real threat to human life." During a press conference, he spoke at length on the issue of the settlements: "In our government program, we are concerned not with building new enclaves in Judea-Samaria, but we will continue to meet the needs of their natural growth. If it is necessary to pave a road circumventing [Palestinian enclaves], we will do it. . . . We do not speak of freezing." For the Palestinian leaders, this statement indicated that Ariel Sharon only intended to selectively implement the recommendations of the Mitchell commission.

The cease-fire was only partially observed. On May 23, an Israeli was shot during an ambush near Ariel, a settlement situated in the center of the West Bank. South of Jerusalem, Palestinians fired in the direction of Gilo, an Israeli neighborhood constructed in a sector occupied during the 1967 war. The IDF responded by spraying Beit Jalla with machine gun fire. This Palestinian enclave north of Bethlehem was supposedly the source of fire. An Israeli was seriously wounded. In Rafah, in the south of the Gaza Strip, exchanges of gunfire resulted in forty-five wounded on the Palestinian side.

That evening, George W. Bush telephoned the two leaders to ask their support for William Burns's mission. It was the first time Arafat had spoken to the new president of the United States. Guessing that the diplomatic process was about to begin yet again, Islamic movements took action. In Hadera, north of Tel Aviv, early in the afternoon of Friday, May 25, a car driven by two Palestinians exploded next to a bus. Sixty-five Israeli civilians were wounded. Islamic Jihad claimed responsibility for the attack in a statement broadcast in Lebanon by Hezbollah television. A few hours earlier, another attack had failed near a Gaza checkpoint. Soldiers had opened fire on a truck packed with explosives. The daylight hours of Saturday, May 26, were relatively peaceful. But at midnight, and then at nine o'clock on Sunday morning, two car bombs exploded in Jerusalem. Thirty Israelis were lightly wounded.

William Burns arrived that evening and immediately opened his series of talks. Sharon and Binyamin Ben-Eliezer played along and presented the Israeli plan for implementing the Mitchell report. First, a formal proclamation of a cease-fire and, within the context of cooperation on security, a return to calm for two months followed by confidence-building measures. And then three months later, a resumption of peace negotiations, anticipating the freezing of construction in the settlements. During the interim period, Israel would execute its third withdrawal from the West Bank, envisioned by the Wye River accords concluded by Benjamin Netanyahu and Arafat in October 1998. In exchange, the Palestinian Authority would honor its promises from that time and arrest terrorists and collect illegally obtained arms. But "if terrorist attacks continue, we will not be able to stand around for long with our arms folded," warned Sharon. And Ben-Eliezer added that, since Israel's announcement of a unilateral cease-fire, the Palestinians had committed ninety-six attacks.

On Monday, Burns traveled to Ramallah. His Palestinian interlocutors explained that it would be difficult to establish calm without at the very least a declaration of the freezing of construction in the settlements. That squared the circle! Burns then began a round of shuttle diplomacy between Arafat's headquarters and the Israeli prime minister's office. Simultaneously, so-called security meetings were taken up again near Ramallah and the Erez checkpoint, north of Gaza.[23]

PALESTINIAN MOURNING

On May 31, a man passed away who, more than any other, symbolized Palestinian national combat in Jerusalem. Faisal Husseini died at the age of sixty from a heart attack suffered in his hotel room in Kuwait, where he was attending a conference. He was the son of Abdel Kader Husseini, the leader of the Arab revolt against the British during the 1930s, who was killed near Jerusalem during combat with Jewish forces during the Israeli war of independence in 1948. Husseini had been one of the main Palestinian leaders to engage in dialogue with Israeli Zionists to whom he prophetically insisted: "If you do not conclude an agreement with Palestinians like me, you will find yourself with Hamas for an interlocutor." In 1991, he had negotiated with Secretary of State James Baker for the participation of a Palestinian delegation in the Madrid peace conference. However, Arafat saw him as a potential rival, and the relations between the two men were tense.

Palestine was in a state of mourning. The Orient House, where Husseini had his office and which had become the unofficial headquarters site of the PLO in Jerusalem, was draped in black flags. The corpse of the deceased leader was transported to Amman by plane and then by helicopter to Ramallah.

The funeral took place the next day. An immense crowd gathered: young Palestinians, who saw in him a charismatic and respectable leader, veterans who had fought at his father's side, and many thousands of East Jerusalem inhabitants, who saw him as their protector. The police and

Israeli army did not intervene. The coffin, covered with a Palestinian flag, was carried onto the esplanade of the al-Aqsa Mosque, where it was placed in a vault. Husseini received a funeral worthy of a great Arab leader.

HAMAS STRIKES

Hamas, which was not concerned with the three days of mourning declared by the PLO, decided to torpedo the negotiations that appeared to be getting under way. At Qalqilya, Abdel Rahman Hamad, the head of the local Ezzedin al-Qassam cell, took charge.[24] He chose a twenty-two-year-old visitor to play the role of human bomb. Sayid Hassan Hutri was unknown to Israeli security services, and his family had left the city for Amman, Jordan, several years before. On June 1 at 11:30 p.m., he approached a line of people waiting at the entrance to the Dolphinarium, a beachfront nightclub in Tel Aviv, packed with a Friday-night crowd. He activated his explosive-lined belt. Twenty-one Israelis were killed, and eighty-three were wounded. Most of the victims were high school students of Russian origin.

Joschka Fischer, the German foreign minister who arrived in Israel that morning, was one of the principal witnesses to the horror as a guest at the hotel across from the Dolphinarium. Profoundly shaken by the scene of destruction, he decided to stay in the region to try to restore control. During that night and the next morning, fearing a violent Israeli reaction, Colin Powell, Javier Solana, and several European leaders telephoned Sharon to offer their condolences and to advise him not to react. Sharon decided to let images speak for themselves: the suffering families of the young Russian immigrants opened all of the televised news programs. The IDF abstained from all actions in the West Bank and Gaza, but security around all Palestinian cities was tightened. Palestinians were no longer authorized to travel to Israeli territory.

Fischer went to Ramallah to meet with Arafat. True to form, the Palestinian chairman explained the recent events in his own way: "I did what I could . . . I gave orders . . . I tried to take back control . . . But what can I do if those who committed the attack were driven by Israeli agents? I have evidence that these men [the perpetrators of the attack] had collaborated in the past with the Israeli security services . . ." The German minister listened patiently. He had been informed of Arafat's wild imaginings by European emissaries who had already experienced this kind of performance. On several occasions during the last few months, Arafat had formulated accusations of this sort in the presence of his clos-est advisors, who tried to dissuade him. To embarrassed foreign visitors, they discreetly explained that Arafat's behavior was an attempt to cam-ouflage his incapacity to retake control of the streets of Palestine.[25] Fischer feigned to ignore the Palestinian president's fanciful explanations and continued the discussion. Arafat announced that he gave a written order to all of his security services to observe a total cease-fire in all sec-tors under their control. He explained that he had no confidence in the Israeli army and demanded international supervision for the cessation of hostilities. Javier Solana, the European Union's senior representative for foreign policy, rushed to offer Fischer his assistance. Sharon declared to his visitors that Arafat had to immediately implement three measures if he wanted to achieve a cease-fire: put a stop to all incitements to vio-lence in the Palestinian media (the Israelis blame public Palestinian tele-vision in particular), put an end to acts of terrorism and violence, and again incarcerate all prisoners liberated from Palestinian prisons. He also insisted that the Autonomous Authority was responsible for "murders and terror-ism," and that Arafat was "a murderer and a pathological liar." He ex-plained to the press that, for Israel, restraint was a component of force.

Could the Palestinian security services act against terror? Brigadier General Ilan Paz did not think so: "They did not control terrorism for two reasons. Their motivation to do so was very low, and also because we did not let them do it. We controlled the territory. Everything that moved needed our permission. For a long period, we did not let Pales-tinian policemen wear uniforms or bear weapons in their own towns. Even to guard an official building with a pistol they needed our permis-sion. . . . Or a few pistols to guard a court house or a jail. . . . Most of the time we did not allow them to bear even such weapons. This is the rea-son it did not happen. The policy was dictated from above."[26]

ARAFAT'S ROLE

On June 5, Binyamin Ben-Eliezer adopted Sharon's position during a speech before Labor Party members: "Yasser Arafat has completed his historic mission. Perhaps the next generation of Palestinians will be more pragmatic, and will choose to turn to the peace process. Arafat is incapable of coming to an agreement with Israel."

In fact, the Israeli security cabinet had just made a crucial decision: Arafat would no longer be considered a credible partner with whom to pursue the peace process. The ministers had adopted a resolution proclaiming that "Arafat supports and directs terrorism." Moshe Yaalon, the deputy chief of staff, was satisfied. His vision of the conflict triumphed in the end: "We have finally succeeded in explaining, when all is said and done, that Arafat is the origin of the war against Israel. Sadly, I found myself in opposition to the minister of foreign affairs, who is not of the same opinion."[27] During a meeting of the Labor members of Parliament, Shimon Peres, the minister of foreign affairs, responded to Ben-Eliezer and Yaalon: "Arafat is not the problem. The problem is the Palestinian people, and whoever waits to see what will happen after Arafat will find themselves dealing with Hamas!"

TENET ARRIVES ON THE SCENE

The Europeans gave the impression that they were taking responsibility while the Russian minister of foreign affairs embarked on a visit to the region. All this activity started to create quite a crowd on American turf. And George Bush, who until that point did not want to get his administration embroiled in the seemingly insoluble conflict, decided to send George Tenet to the region and charged him with the mission of calming things and relaunching Israeli-Palestinian cooperation on matters of security. The CIA chief, who at the beginning of the year had already attempted to negotiate a cease-fire, arrived forty-eight hours later. He immediately met Ariel Sharon in Tel Aviv, where the heads of Shin Bet and Mossad participated in discussions. The Israeli prime minister informed him of his conditions: a total cessation of Palestinian violence and terrorism, and the arrest of militants from Hamas and Islamic Jihad by the Autonomous Authority. Sharon stated that attacks and incitements to violence had not stopped, contrary to Arafat's assertions. Tenet persuaded Sharon to permit the immediate resumption of meetings between security officials from both camps. Then he left for Ramallah, where Arafat and his advisors were waiting. The Palestinians explained to their interlocutor that it would be difficult to act to restore calm if the Israelis continued to seal off the principal cities in the West Bank. They demanded the withdrawal of the IDF to the positions they had occupied on September 28, 2000, before the start of the intifada, but agreed to hold new security meetings.

The first took place the next evening in Jerusalem, under Tenet's aegis. Amin al-Hindi, head of Palestinian intelligence, was present, as well as Jibril Rajoub and Mohammed Dahlan. Despite American pressure, they had boycotted the previous meetings with the Israelis as a sign of protest against the attacks to which they had been subjected. A long, stormy discussion ensued. Avi Dichter, Ephraim Halevy, the head of Mossad, and the generals present reiterated their condition: the Autonomous Authority must apprehend thirty-four militants accused of terrorism, the identities of whom were known by the Israelis. The Palestinians demanded the end of incursions of the IDF into zone A (autonomous) and "a halting of attacks by settlers and the army" against the Palestinian people. The CIA chief submitted a timetable for the implementation of the Mitchell commission's recommendations, and requested a response within twenty-four hours.

The proposals were greeted with suspicion by both camps. At the prime minister's office in Jerusalem and at Arafat's headquarters in Ramallah, each side held discussions to strategize how to proceed in order to receive favorable modifications. The Americans, meanwhile, made moves to accelerate the political process. On June 9, while Tenet was pursuing his security mediation, William Burns met with Ariel Sharon, who reaffirmed his position: no political negotiations without a total cessation of all forms of violence. It was the opposite of what Arafat told the American emissary, namely, that politics and security are linked. A return to calm would only be possible if the Palestinian public was persuaded that an agreement was within reach.

This diplomatic activity unfolded against a background of violence. The previous day in Gaza, an eleven-year-old child was shot and killed, and another seriously wounded. The IDF spokesman did not deny it but explained that, in this sector, soldiers had to respond to shooting and grenade attacks. In addition, two soldiers had been wounded. The following day, near the settlement at Netzarim, the army committed a bloody error: a tank had fired a mortar shell on a Bedouin tent. Three women were killed, and four other members of the family wounded. Sharon would express his apologies for this "error." Thousands of Bedouins attended the funerals for the victims.

YES TO TENET

On June 11, negotiations reached an impasse. The Israelis had accepted Tenet's plan, but on the absolute condition that the Palestinian Authority succeed in putting a stop to all forms of violence—including stone throwing—and in apprehending Hamas and Islamic Jihad militants. They also wanted to create buffer zones in the autonomous sector. In Ramallah, the Palestinians presented a cool reception to the CIA chief, who came with the final version of his proposal. Their answer was no. They also rejected the latest Israeli amendments: no buffer zones! And they said it was impossible under the present circumstances to arrest the thirty-four militants as Israel demanded.[28] Tenet's entourage made it known that he could leave for Washington and the responsibility for failure would fall on Arafat's shoulders.

In fact, the dice were loaded. Israeli security had been informed of everything that had transpired in their adversary's headquarters—it was completely bugged. Ariel Sharon and Avi Dichter followed the discussions between Arafat and his advisors hour by hour. They were convinced the Palestinians would not accept Tenet's proposals, or that, even if they agreed in the end, they would not—or could not—ultimately implement them.[29] On June 12 Saeb Erekat, Arafat's principal negotiator, presented the aging leader with the slightly improved final version of the plan. Arafat asked him if he believed the Israelis had the intention of implementing it on the basis of the elements that they had introduced into the agreement. Erekat responded in the negative. He would explain later: "The game was played as follows: I know and you know, but we act like we didn't know. If you follow the sequence of attempts at de-escalation, that was the common denominator." The Palestinian leader thus concluded that if no one had the intention of implementing the plan, then they could accept it.[30]

The scene that followed took place the evening of June 12 at the Muqata, Arafat's headquarters in Ramallah.[31] The Palestinian security officials, Rajoub, Dahlan, and Arafat's closest advisors, examined the proposals made by Tenet, who was waiting in a nearby room. After two hours of discussion, Arafat grabbed the document and went to meet the CIA chief. He found him lying on the floor. Tenet explained that he was suffering from back pain and asked whether he could stay where he was. Arafat suggested that he call a doctor ("We have excellent ones, you know!"). Tenet replied, "Thanks, it'll be OK." So, bending toward his guest, Arafat announced that he accepted the plan and dictated a letter to Erekat announcing his agreement. Arafat then attached a letter in which he reiterated his refusal to allow buffer zones to be set up and pledged to undertake efforts to prevent anti-Israeli attacks. Specifically, he promised to apprehend likely perpetrators of future attacks, but excluding those who had committed them in the past.

The plan, which recapitulated the Mitchell report in its broad outlines, would be published twenty-four hours later:

> . . . The GOI [Government of Israel] and PA [Palestinian Authority] will immediately resume security cooperation. A senior-level meeting of Israeli, Palestinian, and US security officials will be held immediately and will reconvene at least once a week, with mandatory participation by designated senior officials. Israeli-Palestinian District Coordination Offices (DCOs) will be reinvigorated. . . . As soon as the

security situation permits, barriers to effective cooperation —which include the erection of walls between the Israeli and Palestinian sides—will be eliminated and joint Israeli-Palestinian patrols will be reinitiated. U.S.-supplied video conferencing systems will be provided to senior-level Israeli and Palestinian officials to facilitate frequent dialogue and security cooperation.

Both sides will take immediate measures to enforce strict adherence to the declared cease-fire and to stabilize the security environment. . . .

Israel will not conduct attacks of any kind against the Palestinian Authority's Ra'is facilities: the headquarters of Palestinian security, intelligence, and police organization; or prisons in the West Bank and Gaza.

The PA will move immediately to apprehend, question, and incarcerate terrorists in the West Bank and Gaza and will provide the security committee the names of those arrested as soon as they are apprehended, as well as a readout of actions taken.

Israel will release all Palestinians arrested in security sweeps who have no association with terrorist activities. In keeping with its unilateral cease-fire declaration, the PA will stop any Palestinian security officials from inciting, aiding, abetting, or conducting attacks against Israeli targets, including settlers. . . . Israeli forces will not conduct 'proactive' security operations in areas under the control of the PA or attack innocent civilian targets. The GOI will reinstitute military police investigations into Palestinian deaths resulting from Israeli Defense Forces actions in the West Bank and Gaza in incidents not involving terrorism. . . . The PA will undertake preemptive operations against terrorists, terrorist safe houses, arms depots, and mortar factories. . . . Palestinian and Israeli security officials will identify and agree to the practical measures needed to enforce 'no demonstration

zones' and 'buffer zones' around flash points to reduce opportunities for confrontation. . . . Palestinian and Israeli security officials will make a concerted effort to locate and
confiscate illegal weapons, including mortars, rockets, and
explosives, in areas under their respective control. In addition, intensive efforts will be made to prevent smuggling and
illegal production of weapons.

On June 13, 2001 at three o'clock in the afternoon, at the close of
the final security meeting, Tenet proclaimed the start of the cease-fire.
The timetable, based on the Mitchell report, provided for a two-day period in which the first measures for a restoration of calm would be put
in place, followed by a cooling-off period with the purpose of setting the
stage for the next step, three months during which the parties would
adopt measures to reestablish mutual trust, including the halting of construction in the settlements. Political negotiations would follow in due
form.

The first few hours were promising. The border post at Rafah, between Egypt and Gaza, was reopened. Several military checkpoints, at
the entrance to Ramallah and at the Netzarim crossroad, in the Gaza
Strip, allowed Palestinian vehicles to pass through. In Jerusalem, the
prime minister's office published a statement following a security cabinet meeting. Ariel Sharon again dotted the i's: "Each stage of the Tenet
plan must be completely executed before passing on to the next stage.
The Palestinians will be judged based on their actions. Security forces
and the army will act according to the principle that there will be no al-
leviation of measures in sectors where terrorist attacks are perpetrated,
but, on the whole, will do their best to allow the Tenet plan to succeed."
He also stated that the cooling-off period would last six weeks, but would
not begin until after a complete restoration of calm. Meanwhile, late that
night, on the road near a settlement south of Ramallah, a Palestinian was
shot and killed, and the following morning an Israeli colonel in the intelligence service was killed in turn by his Palestinian contact near Jerusalem. Fatah, in Bethlehem, explained that he had intended to avenge the

assassination of Hussein Abayat, one of his leaders, which had occurred in November 2000. That afternoon, General Giora Eiland, the IDF chief of operations, met with the press:

> Twenty-six hours after the start of this new beginning, I cannot say that we are satisfied with the results. To this point, we have counted sixteen violent incidents. Thirteen [Palestinian] shootings at Israeli targets in the West Bank and three mortar attacks in Gaza. These statistics are no different from those that had been collected over the past two weeks.

On June 16, Arafat's opposition organized protests against the cease-fire in several towns in the West Bank and Gaza during which approximately thirty Palestinians were wounded by gunfire. Twenty-four hours later, soldiers beat a Palestinian "suspect" near Ramallah, while two Israeli settlers were shot and killed near Nablus and Tulkarm. Several dozens of settlers mounted a punitive raid on a Palestinian town, burning cars and uprooting dozens of olive trees. Furious, officials of the settlement movement and Likud hardliners demanded the cessation of the cease-fire and the resumption of military operations.

PERES SEEKS A MEETING WITH ARAFAT

On June 16, Kofi Annan arrived to offer his support to the Middle East peace effort. He met with Ariel Sharon at his home in Jerusalem. The prime minister reiterated that he had accepted the Tenet plan, but that it was first necessary to reestablish total calm. Israel alone would decide when the cooling-off period would begin. He also warned the secretary-general that the Israeli government would not accept any international diktat on this matter. After having been briefed by Terje Larsen, his emissary in the Middle East, Annan—who personally had contact with close advisors to Shimon Peres—suggested to Sharon that he authorize Peres to accompany him that same afternoon to Ramallah to meet with Yasser Arafat. "It's important," he said, "it will allow him to feel as if he was less under pressure and will give him the impression that there is a role for him to play!" "No," Sharon immediately responded, "not under the current state of affairs, while Arafat is not observing the cease-fire." Kofi Annan asked his interlocutor to make a gesture that would send a message to the region, namely, to evacuate a settlement—Netzarim, for example, which was located in the middle of the Gaza Strip, literally surrounded by Palestinians, and which did not serve any purpose in the security framework. Absolutely not, Sharon responded, "From Netzarim, it will be possible to control a future port in Gaza!"[32]

Annan left for Ramallah, accompanied only by his advisors. Arafat then accused the Israelis of not observing the cease-fire. Their army, he said, was not obeying government orders. Nothing had changed on the ground: the few checkpoints that the Israelis had opened had been sealed again. The Palestinian chairman asked his interlocutor to deploy international observers in the West Bank and Gaza. Annan responded that he would examine this proposal and left the region with the impression that things were going very badly.

The following day in Jerusalem, the weekly meeting of the Israeli government unfolded in a stormy atmosphere. Peres, who did not appreciate Sharon's refusal, took the podium and described the situation in the Palestinian territories. The poverty. The hunger. The unemployment, which was nearing 40 percent. The wait, which could be as long as two hours, at the military checkpoints. And, he added: "The American administration will stop involving itself in the region if its efforts don't produce any results. If the Mitchell plan fails, what will happen? It is also necessary to fight terrorism using political means!" Sharon explained the reasons he had not authorized Peres to go to Ramallah in the company of Annan: "I am opposed to any meeting between Israeli persons and Arafat as long as he does not implement the Tenet plan . . ." The prime minister concluded the session by confirming that the Oslo Accords were a total failure, which provoked another reaction from Peres, who raised his voice and threatened: "I cannot serve in a government where decisions are adopted unilaterally! In a national unity government, it is necessary to be two. I am not here to implement your decisions . . ." Several Likud ministers, as well as the minister of tourism Rehavam Zeevi, on

behalf of his extreme right-wing party, criticized Peres by recalling that
Sharon had been elected with 63 percent of the vote. Sharon closed the
meeting. He realized that he would have to mollify his foreign affairs
minister: the Nobel Peace Prize lent international legitimacy to his
government.

The two men had already had a quarrel that made its way into the
press. During a closed meeting of the security cabinet, Sharon had announced that he required 100 percent success from Arafat in the struggle
against terrorism. Peres had responded that a 100 percent effort would
have to suffice. Two days later, the two men reconciled during a dinner
held at the prime minister's official residence. Sharon promised to take
proper measures to improve the everyday lives of Palestinians, and Peres
promised to coordinate all his diplomatic initiatives with the head of the
government.

ISRAEL-USA

It was high time, because George Bush decided to seize the initiative. He
announced on June 20 that he was rushing Colin Powell to the Middle
East to "reinforce the cease-fire" negotiated the previous week by George
Tenet. Bush then revealed that he had telephoned Hosni Mubarak, the
Egyptian president, Ariel Sharon, and Yasser Arafat, to inform them of
his decision. Bush ended by hearing out the arguments of Powell and
several of his advisors: the Israeli-Palestinian conflict threatened to de-
generate and to endanger American interests in the region, notably its
isolationist policy toward Iran and Iraq.

The next day, Powell declared that he believed the beginning of an
improvement of the situation on the ground was underway, notably in
the area of coordination between Palestinian and Israeli security forces.
In fact, during that week, security officials from both camps met four
times, and a joint patrol passed around Netzarim for the first time since
the beginning of the intifada in September 2000.

But Sharon was under pressure from the extreme Right. On June 18
two Israeli settlers had been killed in the West Bank. The hardliners in the
government coalition demanded an end to the cease-fire. The prime min-

ister issued a statement: "Israel will not wait indefinitely with its arms folded in the face of an unacceptable situation." On June 20 another settler died in an ambush. The security cabinet met that same evening and decided to reject a plan that should have been presented to the Palestinians concerning the redeployment of forces in the West Bank, "until terrorism ceases." Military officials made it known that they had received a green light for the resumption of so-called targeted killings. Fifteen Knesset members and two ministers called on the government to unleash "total war until the Palestinian Authority is destroyed."

On June 22 settlers protested throughout the West Bank, blocking roads, throwing stones at Palestinian cars, setting fire to crops. The army stopped two settlers and confiscated their weapons. In the north of Gaza, two soldiers were killed by a suicide bomber. Hamas claimed responsibility for the attack. Around fifteen Palestinians were wounded in various incidents. The next day in Gaza, three Palestinians tried to infiltrate Israel. Soldiers opened fire, killing one and wounding the other two. A tank unit then made an incursion into Gaza, destroying around twenty houses.

William Burns was in the region at the time. He met Arafat, who reiterated his demand for international observers in the Palestinian territories. That evening, Sharon told him that Israel required a period of total calm for at least ten days before declaring the beginning of a cooling-off period of six weeks, as outlined in the Tenet plan. Two days later, in Nablus, Osama Jawabri, a member of the al-Aqsa Martyrs Brigades, was killed in the explosion of a telephone booth he had just entered. The Palestinians accused the Israelis of the assassination.

Sharon decided to fly to Washington and explain to George Bush that acts of violence were continuing and that the American administration should not declare the beginning of the period of "appeasement." He reaffirmed his position: Israel would not negotiate under fire. The Israeli prime minister knew that Colin Powell and the State Department diplomats were convinced that the Palestinians would not stop their attacks in the absence of any diplomatic opening.

The meeting took place at the White House on June 26. Sharon could only draw attention to their incompatible viewpoints. Bush began the brief press conference that, traditionally, precedes an interview in the Oval Office by bidding the Israeli prime minister welcome: "A leader who has faced extraordinary circumstances in the Middle East . . ."

Sharon thanked him and presented his position:

> Israel is committed to peace, will make every effort to reach peace. Peace should be peace for generations and peace should provide security to Israeli citizens. The Jewish people are having one tiny, small country, that is Israel . . . [they should] have the right and the capability to defend themselves by themselves. And that, of course, we have to preserve and we have to thank God for that every day. . . . We adopted the Mitchell report and we received the . . . Tenet plan. And we'll be willing to continue. The one thing that we are looking for is, first of all, it would be full cessation of hostilities, of terror and incitement. If that would happen, I am fully convinced that the day will come and we'll have peace in the Middle East.

The differences between the two men came to light when they responded to journalists' questions.

> **Bush**: But progress is being made in [the Middle East]. Is it as fast as we'd like? No, it's not. But the fundamental question my administration makes is, are we making progress? Is peace closer today than it was yesterday? We believe that the answer is: Yes! And, therefore, the secretary of state leaves tonight to try to advance the process, to make peace more real. And he's going to meet not only with the Israelis, he'll be meeting with the Palestinians as well . . . urging the cycle of violence to be broken.
>
> **Sharon**: Israel's position is that we can negotiate only, and we would like to negotiate only when it will be full cessation of hostilities, terror, violence, and incitement. Otherwise, I

don't think we'd be able to reach a peace which will really make all of us committed to. One must understand that if last week we had five dead, it's like the United States, Mr. President, having 250 killed, or maybe even 300 people killed by terror. And that is saying that one should not compromise with terror. . . .

Bush: Any terror is too much terror. Any death is too much death. We recognize that. And we recognize the pressure that the prime minister is under. And we condemn terror. We condemn violence. We condemn death. We also believe progress is being made. . . . Yes, there's violence; yes, there's terror, but it's being isolated . . . contained. Can the parties do more? Absolutely! And that's what the secretary of state is going to do, is to urge Mr. Arafat to do more, to take better control of his security forces. We're going to talk to the prime minister about his attitudes. We're friends, and I believe that what's important from this perspective is not to let the progress that's been made so far to break apart. We cannot let violence take hold. And that's why I've said I admire the prime minister's restraint and patience. I understand the difficulties and the pressures. As he just said, five Israeli lives lost is [for us] equivalent of 250—five is too many. But, nevertheless, progress is being made. And it's essential that we continue the process and continue the progress that's being made. We're gaining by inches, I recognize. Progress is in inches, not in miles! But, nevertheless, an inch is better than nothing!

When the press conference was nearly over, Sharon decided to drive the point home, answering in Hebrew to a question from an Israeli radio reporter while his statement was translated for Bush: "Yesterday, we had sixteen terrorist attacks, and it included side bombs, it included shooting and sniping. We had ten wounded. So, all together, generally speaking, maybe there are less, but terror is still going on. And by now, though

I would very much like to hear that Chairman Arafat instructed to rearrest those terrorists who are planning and sending and mobilizing those suiciders, he has not done it yet. He has not instructed to arrest them and they were not arrested. . . . And that, of course, he could do—I would say he could have done it immediately because he controlled the [inaudible] completely!" In short, Bush and his secretary of state were forced to understand that in Sharon's eyes, there had been no improvement on the ground.

The journalists left the room and the meeting got underway. Bush asked about the halting of construction in the settlements. Sharon reiterated that he was committed to creating no new settlements, but he had never renounced his support for natural growth within existing settlements. He then presented his peace plan: "a Palestinian state with limited sovereignty" on a part of the West Bank, without East Jerusalem, but constructed following the principle of territorial continuity. Israel would preserve security zones in the Jordan Valley and in certain sectors along the 1967 line of demarcation. This plan was published by the Israeli press several days later. The Palestinians definitively rejected it. The notion of a temporary Palestinian state would, however, resurface several years later by the authors of the famous "roadmap" of the Quartet: the United States, the European Union, the United Nations, and Russia. George Bush concluded by reaffirming that his administration would not impose any agreement upon Israel, but offered assistance to the parties to help them to achieve peace.

POWELL IN THE MIDDLE EAST

Colin Powell arrived in Jerusalem on June 27. His meetings kept returning to the same key question: What was the timetable for the implementation of the Mitchell and Tenet plans? How long did the period of calm have to last before "appeasement" could begin? After his talks with Shimon Peres, Powell stated: "[The Mitchell committee report] is a package, and no part of that package can be separated from any other part of the package. It begins with the ending of the violence, it begins with the cease-fire, it begins with the cooling-off period where confidence can be restored. . . . The whole thing is a package, but we can't start opening the package until we end the violence, until we have a period of quiet for a number of days where we can let the wounds begin to heal, let the passions begin to drop."

Someone asked Peres: "The region has just experienced three or four days of calm . . . is it necessary to wait another six days in order for the cooling-off period to begin?" Peres answered:

> Even if we are talking about a 100 percent of effort, we can see three missing links. One is: clear orders to the different police or several military organizations under the authority of the Palestinian Authority. Our feeling is that not all of the commandos understood that there is one clear policy given by Chairman Arafat, and we can see variations on the ground where some give different interpretation to what is permitted and what is not, and we think there is an immediate need for clear instructions and orders to stop the shooting and the violence. The second is, both in the Mitchell report and the Tenet report, there is a call to arrest people who carry a potential of explosives or bombs or shooting. This again was not done. And, the third is really the cessation of the incitement.

Powell traveled the next morning to Ramallah, where Arafat was impatiently awaiting him. The Palestinian chairman accused the Israelis of not observing the cease-fire and of provoking incidents. He again demanded the deployment of international observers in the West Bank and Gaza, on the model of the dozen European security agents discreetly placed in the Bethlehem sector, who had succeeded in imposing a cease-fire by preventing automatic weapons fire on the Israeli neighborhood of Gilo, south of Jerusalem.[33]

During a joint press conference, Arafat announced from the outset (and in Arabic) the arrival of a commission of international observers from several countries, presided over by the United States, Europe, and the United Nations. A journalist asked for clarification.

> **Colin Powell:** I think as we get into the confidence-building measure, confidence-building phase—there will be a need for monitors and observers to see what's happening on the ground, to serve as interlocutors to go to points of friction and make an independent observation of what has happened. Now what the nature of that monitoring or observer regime might look like, who might be members of it, we have not yet come to any conclusion on that. But I think there is clear understanding of the need for some kind of monitoring observer function performed by some group.

International observers? These two words made Israeli officials jump out of their seats. This could mean an internationalization of the conflict, which they always vehemently rejected. The question would be clarified during a meeting between Sharon and Powell. To the press, the Israeli prime minister repeated that he was opposed to such a measure:

> No, we never supported . . . United Nations observers, with all our respect to the United Nations, and we never accepted European observers, not because we think professionally they are not good, but because I don't think they are needed mostly when there is no balanced approach [to the conflict] of some European countries, and we don't expect that they are preferring us. . . . I think that the arrangement that we have now fits the situation.

> **Powell:** May I just add a P.S. on that? Earlier today, when we were talking about monitors or observers, I had it in the context of what the two sides might decide to do within their own resources or whatever resources might be appropriate by mutual agreement. Not some outside group or forces com-

ing in. The word 'force' was used in one of the reports. No such thought, no such consideration, and we had spoken against that kind of intervention previously.

Powell left the region having accomplished one thing: persuading Sharon to reduce his demand for a total cessation of Palestinian violence by three days. Henceforth, he only demanded seven days instead of ten. In fact, Israeli security services knew perfectly well that calm could not be established in a week. That was practically an impossible mission, especially since the Palestinian police were still not authorized to bear arms and their bosses were not authorized to transfer units from one sector to another.[34] In short, no one could exert total control over the Palestinian population.

ESCALATION

The same evening, Yasser Abed Rabbo, the Palestinian minister of culture and information, persuaded Arafat to reach out and communicate. An international group of journalists was invited that evening to Ramallah to have a discussion (off camera) with the PLO leader. An American correspondent asked him what he thought of Ariel Sharon's proposal to create a Palestinian state over 56 percent of the West Bank.[35] His response: "How much? 50? How much? 56? That's too much! That's too much!" And he let out a low whistle. Conclusion of the press: "Arafat knows how to whistle!"

On June 29, Shimon Peres was in Lisbon at a meeting of the Socialist International. Sharon authorized him to meet with Arafat there, but on the condition that their exchange be completely devoid of any mention of negotiations and that it not take place behind closed doors. The dinner, held at the home of the Portuguese prime minister in the presence of several prominent figures, proceeded smoothly. Arafat turned on the charm, talking of the cessation of violence and the need for reconciliation between the two peoples. However, the next day the tone shifted. In a speech given before the Socialist congress, the president accused Israel of attacking Palestinians using jets, tanks, and helicopters:

"Our economy is destroyed and our children can no longer go to school because the tanks prevent it." To which Peres responded: "Give us one week without ambulances, tears of mourning mothers. We pray that there will be no bombs planted near discotheques, schools, or malls, and that people will be able to move about without the fear of being killed. If you give us security, you will have freedom!"

During this time, the tension was mounting in south Lebanon. Hezbollah attacked the Israeli position at Shebaa Farms using mortar shells and anti-tank missiles, wounding two soldiers. In Beirut, the Shiite militia released the following statement: "The cell of martyrs of the al-Aqsa intifada conducted this operation as a sign of support for the Palestinian uprising." The IDF responded with a series of bombings on the Shiite militia's positions. Forty-eight hours later, warplanes destroyed a Syrian radar base in Rayak, in the Bekaa valley. It was the second raid of this kind in two months. In London, the daily *al-Hayat*, citing Lebanese governmental sources, confirmed that Syrian leaders were furious. The Hezbollah operation occurred at a bad moment, the day after a successful visit of President Bachar el-Assad to Paris.

The month of July thus got off to a very bad start. Near Jenin, helicopters launched eight missiles at a vehicle transporting three Palestinian militants, who were killed in the attack. Several hours earlier, two Palestinians had been killed by the Israeli army. The soldiers explained that they were about to plant a bomb. On July 2, two car bombs exploded in Israel without causing any serious injuries. Later that afternoon, soldiers observed a taxi driver leaving a bag on the side of a road in Nablus. Believing that it contained explosives, they opened fire and killed him. When a bomb disposal expert examined the package, it was found to be full of vegetables. Near Tulkarm, an Israeli civilian was killed by Palestinians, and the corpse of a settler was discovered on a hill near Hebron. That evening, a meeting of security officials from both camps ended without results.

The security cabinet met on July 4 and decided to increase "targeted killings." Henceforth, the IDF had the green light to assassinate "known terrorists," even if they weren't on the verge of committing an attack.

Until that point, the army was only authorized to strike when "the bomb was on the point of exploding."

Sharon decided to make a European tour of his own. He left for Berlin, where the Syrian head of state was due to visit three weeks later. The discussion with Chancellor Gerhard Schroeder opened first on the issue of a possible exchange of prisoners with Hezbollah.

The German intelligence service served as an intermediary. Israel wanted the return of three soldiers kidnapped by Hezbollah in October 2000. Next, Sharon raised the issue of the crisis with the Palestinians and accused Arafat of inciting violence against Israel: "We must apply pressure," he said, "on the PLO leader to make that stop!" The leader of the German government responded that Israel had to implement the Mitchell report and advised him to reduce (if not halt) settlement activity. That evening, the Israeli prime minister was in Paris, where he was invited to dine with Jacques Chirac. The discussion with the French was identical to that which occurred in Berlin.

THE TWO JAMALS

While Palestinian attacks and "targeted [Israeli] killings" continued to take place almost daily, Omri Sharon made a secret trip to Ramallah to pass on a message from his father, the prime minister, to Arafat: Israel does not intend to assassinate the PLO leader, but will respond to all acts of violence. In July, ten Israelis were killed in ambushes or attacks with explosives, and thirty-one Palestinian militants were killed by the army, three others by settlers. The heads of security from both sides met six times without reaching any kind of agreement.

Sharon put pressure on the chief of staff. He demanded a pinpoint operation that would allow him to show the Israeli public that he was intensifying the struggle against terrorism. Military officials proposed a target in Nablus, a town that had been the source of so many attacks. Their proposal involved two Hamas sheikhs, Jamal Mansur and Jamal Salim. On July 31, a helicopter gunship fired three missiles on an office building where the men were reported to be. They were killed on the spot, along with three of their assistants, a Palestinian journalist who had come to interview them, and two children playing in the street. The IDF released a statement announcing that "the leaders of the military command of Hamas in Samaria have been killed. The operation took place while they were busy planning future operations . . ."

In Tel Aviv, military intelligence analysts—along with Matti Steinberg, the special advisor for Palestinian affairs to the head of Shin Bet—heard the news first on the radio. They had not been consulted before the raid. "As soon as I heard about it," Steinberg said, "I asked: 'Why did you do that?' Mansur was, all things being equal, one of the most moderate members of the Hamas leadership. He was not planning an attack and to say that he corresponded to the definition of 'a terrorist on the point of executing an attack' was unthinkable. Several days earlier, he had publicly [and in writing] taken a position against suicide attacks. Earlier he had even published a book[36] in which he affirmed that Hamas must support the Palestinian people during the process of negotiations with Israel. We have just erased the difference that had existed between the political and military levels. The reaction will be harsh . . ."[37]

The next day in Nablus, all armed organizations and a crowd of one hundred thousand attended the funeral for the victims, crying for vengeance.

This would be accomplished August 9. Late in the morning, a young couple walked up Jaffa Road, Jerusalem. She spoke English to her companion. Nearing the intersection at King George Road, they separated. The man, a guitar case in his hand, entered a Sbarro pizzeria. The explosion killed fifteen people and wounded 110. The terrorist, Izzedin Masri, was twenty-two years old. Recruited by Hamas, he was from a village near Tulkarm.

At two o'clock the following morning, police raided the Orient House in East Jerusalem. The Israeli flag was raised on the three-story building that had been, since the 1991 Madrid conference, the official seat of the PLO in Jerusalem. It was a major victory for the nationalist Right, which demanded the closing of this symbol of the Palestinian claim on the eastern portion of the city. Nine other institutions linked to the Autonomous Authority were also closed.

Marwan Barghouti, the secretary general of Fatah on the West Bank, declared soon after: "This is a declaration of war against the Palestinians. Does Israel's occupation of the building where the peace process began also signify its end?"

The measure, however, provoked very little protest in East Jerusalem. Most of its inhabitants feared being transferred to Arafat's authoritarian regime, and especially did not want to lose the social advantages—social security, health insurance—that were granted to them by Israel, and that did not exist in the Palestinian territories.

CHAPTER 3

9/11

After the murders of Jamal Mansur and Jamal Salim, the hunt for informants collaborating with the Israeli security services intensified in the West Bank. It was prolonged, in this case, by sham trials. On August 9, 2001, while events in Jerusalem dominated the front page, one such trial was being held in Nablus. A bearded man, his eyes wide with terror, stood accused of collaborating with the Israeli enemy. Mundher al-Hafnawi, a forty-three-year-old businessman, had allegedly given Shin Bet information that led to the assassination of Mahmoud al-Madani, a Hamas activist, on February 12. The two men had been friends. Family and members of the al-Madani clan were present in the courtroom, clamoring for vengeance.

The hearing began:

> **The prosecutor:** "Your testimony yesterday . . . Was it the truth?"
> **Mundher al-Hafnawi:** "I said something under pressure."
> **The prosecutor:** "Are you a faithful Muslim?"
> **Hafnawi:** "Yes."

The prosecutor: "Do you fast? Do you pray five times a day?"

Hafnawi: "Yes!"

The prosecutor: "Five times a day?"

Hafnawi: "Yes!"

The prosecutor: "You are a sheik and a faithful Muslim, you read the Koran. . . . And at the same time you are loyal to the Israeli secret services!"

Hafnawi: "I have never been loyal to the Israeli secret services!"

The prosecutor: "How can you live with both? With religion and with Israeli security?"

In the audience, a woman yelled: "He met the agent two weeks before! He was sitting with him!"

The prosecutor: "You met the Israeli agent two weeks before Mahmoud was killed! You showed him a photo of Mahmoud, of his store! His house!"

Hafnawi: "That's not true!"

The prosecutor: "Did he give you money?"

Hafnawi: "No! He did not give me money! None of that took place!"

This kangaroo court continued for three days. No witnesses were called to testify. In the absence of material evidence, the prosecutor built his case entirely upon Hafnawi's interrogation and testimony that was obtained earlier under pressure. The lawyer for the defense did not plead his case and seemed content to read a simple statement. The trial concluded with the following exchange:

The prosecutor: "The indictment states that the accused is guilty. Mundher al-Hafnawi is a traitor. I call upon the court to apply its most severe punishment to Mundher al-Hafnawi: that he be put to death by firing squad."

The public yelled: "Long live justice!"

The judge: "The verdict: under the authority of law 1911 and Jordanian law 16/1960, we, the majority, decide upon . . . the death penalty for Mundher al-Hafnawi."

The accused would escape on March 9, 2002, after an Israeli helicopter bombed the prison in which he was incarcerated. But he would later be found and killed in the middle of the street by a group from the al-Aqsa Martyrs Brigades. According to B'Tselem, the Israeli organization for the defense of human rights in the Palestinian territories, 117 Palestinians suspected of collaborating with Israel had been executed by firing squad or assassinated by armed groups since the beginning of the al-Aqsa intifada.[1]

Palestinian leaders were powerless in the face of this major crisis shaking their society. Salah Taamri, a legendary Fatah fighter, today governor of Bethlehem, explained:

> The Israelis targeted the moral structure of Palestinian society. . . . In turning brother against brother . . . neighbor against neighbor . . . teacher against students . . . everyone against everyone. Each time that an assassination occurred, that a Palestinian was murdered, people began to speak of collaborators while in fact [the Israelis] could have used high-tech . . . planting bugs . . .
>
> Sometimes, at checkpoints, for example, if they know that you are Christian, the soldier will say to you: go to the head of the line! Meanwhile, when most Muslims see that, they resent it, and they think, maybe he collaborates. . . . In this situation, the Palestinian individual is weak. . . . Everyone needs work. . . . They need to be able to move about freely, they need to earn a living. . . . And the Israelis give that in exchange for collaboration.[2]

On August 12, Islamic Jihad decided to act, sending a suicide bomber to set off explosives near Haifa, on a café terrace, wounding twenty-one

Israelis. The bomber, who came from Jenin, was a former Palestinian policeman. The government in Jerusalem blamed Arafat for the attack and revealed that three members of Hamas arrested by the Palestinian police after the Dolphinarium attack had been released.

IMPASSE

Increasingly worried, Colin Powell wanted to return to the region, but Vice President Dick Cheney persuaded George Bush to limit American intervention in the conflict to a minimum. It was instead David Satterfield, the assistant undersecretary of state charged with Middle Eastern affairs, who left for Jerusalem with a message for Ariel Sharon. The latter was informed that the closing of the Orient House was detrimental to Israel's interests because it shifted attention from the principal problem of terrorism. Instead, Satterfield told Sharon that this incident had become, in Arafat's hands, a means of exercising pressure. The Israeli prime minister responded that Israel "would not allow the Palestinian Authority to violate agreements by infringing upon its sovereignty over Jerusalem." The American diplomat did not remind Sharon that the United States failed to recognize Israel's annexation of East Jerusalem.

In Ramallah, Arafat informed Satterfield that he would not discuss a cease-fire while Israel occupied the Orient House, and he refused to renounce his claim to East Jerusalem. They had reached an impasse. At his Texas ranch, George Bush interrupted a golf game to address the press: "And the United States is doing everything in our power to convince the parties—but I want to remind people there must be the will. The people in the area must make the conscious decision to stop terrorism. . . . I think [Arafat] can do a lot more to be convincing the people on the street to stop these acts of terrorism."

Meanwhile, Shimon Peres was becoming more rebellious, speaking out about the humanitarian crisis unfolding in the Palestinian territories. He described the situation to the central committee of the Labor Party thus: "It is inconceivable that three million people live under lock and key, while unemployment and poverty grow." In the West Bank and Gaza, more than a half million Palestinians were going hungry; 270,000 workers had lost their jobs, and, on August 14, the World Food Program began to distribute food; 250,000 Palestinians had already been benefiting from WFP aid since December 2000.

Sharon gave in and decided to compromise. He needed his minister of foreign affairs, winner of the Nobel Peace Prize, now more than ever, as he was facing pressure from the international community in the wake of the closing of the Orient House. He authorized Peres to meet with Palestinian leaders, but only to discuss a cease-fire and on the condition that he be accompanied by a superior officer, General Giora Eiland, director of the department of strategic planning. The general was nicknamed by the Israeli Press as Peres's "babysitter."

On August 14, forty-eight hours after the Haifa attack, a tank unit moved into Jenin. The soldiers made it as far as the seat of the city's Palestinian governor and destroyed the neighboring police station with a bulldozer. It was the deepest incursion into autonomous Palestinian territory since the beginning of the intifada. For the leaders of the IDF, it was a test. They wanted to evaluate the intensity of the reaction provoked by such an operation. From Beit Jalla, south of Jerusalem, Palestinians opened fire in the direction of the Gilo neighborhood.[3] The Israeli army responded, and skirmishes broke out in areas around several checkpoints.

There was a massive buildup of tanks and armored troop transports near Bethlehem and Beit Jalla. Binyamin Ben-Eliezer issued a warning: "There will be no more shooting in Gilo!" From a distance Jibril Rajoub, head of preventive security for the Palestinians on the West Bank, tried to calm the Fatah militants responsible for the attacks. He gave orders to his men to intervene and deploy themselves on site. That evening, he asked his Israeli interlocutors to allow him to leave Ramallah in order to go to Beit Jalla. (I was an eyewitness to this telephone conversation, and heard the Israeli respond by saying, "You may go on foot through the Kalandia checkpoint!") For several days, a tense calm reigned in the area around Bethlehem.

The next day, a Fatah militant was killed by a special Israeli unit in Hebron. The army accused him of being a terrorist. On August 17, Shimon Peres, after having met secretly with Abu Ala, the president of the Palestinian parliament, proposed a new plan for a cease-fire by sector. Measures would be taken by both parties, first in Bethlehem and Nablus, in order to quiet the tension. The Palestinians would make an effort to assure security, and Israelis would then progressively open the barriers. Sharon did not oppose the plan and allowed Peres to present it to David Satterfield and Dan Kurtzer, the United States ambassador in Tel Aviv.

FISCHER FAILS

Meanwhile, Joschka Fischer, the German foreign minister, returned to the Middle East to try his luck, but the situation was strained. In Rafah, on August 20, in the south of the Gaza Strip, a thirteen-year-old was killed by the Israeli army, meeting the same fate as a thirty-nine-year-old Palestinian who was trying to bypass a checkpoint near Nablus. The IDF announced that an investigation was under way. The next day, Fischer met Sharon who told him that he had authorized Peres to meet with Arafat, but only to discuss a cease-fire and the improvement of living conditions for the Palestinian people. Sharon insisted that the PLO leader was doing nothing to halt terrorism. The German minister suggested that the meeting should be held the following week in Berlin. The idea gained ground and Fischer traveled to Ramallah twice. Arafat, all smiles, declared to the press that he agreed. He did not mention, however, that his guest had relayed a warning from Sharon, namely, that the IDF would occupy Beit Jalla if firing on Gilo resumed. They would respond "in such a way that cannot be imagined."

Arafat's advisors accorded the German initiative little hope for success: didn't the Israeli prime minister declare to a delegation of Jewish Americans that he demanded 100 percent results from Arafat in the struggle against terrorism, and not only 100 percent effort, and that he would not reduce, by even a second, the period of total calm which had to precede the implementation of the Tenet plan?

The IDF accused Atef Abayat, a Fatah militant, of organizing terrorist attacks in the region of Bethlehem, and demanded that he be arrested by Palestinian security. Abayat was ultimately imprisoned by a unit led by Haj Ismail, a rival of Jibril Rajoub, but his "jailers" allowed him to come and go from the prison as he pleased. Other Palestinian officials made a real effort. In Gaza, Al'Ali, the head of the local security council, described the impracticality of the situation to *Haaretz*: "Israel is preventing us from acting against armed groups on the ground. For example, on July 31, one of my officers was killed by Israeli soldiers when he was trying to stop militants who were launching a mortar on the settlement at Netzarim. In the West Bank, we only control small, discontinuous portions of land. It is the same situation in the Gaza Strip. Israel demands that Arafat control the population without giving him control over territory. How can I keep my promise to restore calm if every officer I send to stop the shooting [against Israeli targets] risks being exposed to Israeli fire?"[4]

SHARON DID NOT BRING SECURITY

On August 22, a helicopter fired a missile at the car of a Fatah militant in Gaza, killing him on the spot. Near Nablus, four Palestinians were killed during a skirmish with an IDF patrol. The Israeli soldiers claimed that the Palestinians were preparing to set off an explosive. The governor of Nablus contradicted this explanation, claiming that the militants were trying to retrieve one of their own, who had been wounded the previous night. On the 23rd, the second-in-command of the police in Nablus was lightly wounded while escaping a targeted assassination. According to Israel, he was responsible for numerous attacks against Israeli civilians. *Yedihot Aharonot* published a poll: 66 percent of Israelis questioned believed that Ariel Sharon still had not resolved the security problems their country was facing, while 59 percent felt it was impossible to arrive at a peaceful agreement with the Palestinians.[5]

On the evening of August 25, two Palestinians succeeded in infiltrating a military post near the Atzmona settlement in Gaza. An officer and two soldiers were killed, and seven other soldiers were injured. The two Palestinians were killed in the ensuing battle, which lasted around fifteen minutes. They had resigned from the Palestinian security forces at the beginning of the intifada. As soon as the attack was announced, there were demonstrations of joy in the streets of Gaza. The next day, the Israeli air force launched reprisal raids. F16 jets and combat helicopters pulverized buildings in the Gaza Strip, primarily police posts and offices of the security service, which had been evacuated the previous day by their occupants who had cleared out fearing such a response. In several locations, tanks fired on Palestinian positions. The casualty toll: three Palestinians killed, including a fourteen-year-old, and around thirty wounded.

FIRST ASSASSINATION OF A LEADER

Sharon gathered his security cabinet that evening. Officially, a decision was made: "As in the past, Israel will respond immediately to each Palestinian attack and will pursue the 'targeted killing' of those who commit terrorist attacks." In fact, the leader of the government had decided to launch an important operation, and on the morning of August 27 at 9:30 a.m., an Israeli helicopter launched a missile onto the third story of a house in a neighborhood in north Ramallah. Mustafa Zubari, known as Abu Ali Mustafa, head of the Popular Front for the Liberation of Palestine, was killed. He was sixty-three and had just succeeded George Habash, the historic leader. It was the first time Israel assassinated the head of a Palestinian organization. Until this moment, the Palestinians and Israelis had observed a tacit agreement whereby their leaders were considered to be off-limits.

Israel justified the operation by accusing Abu Ali Mustafa of having personally authorized an attack on an Israeli kindergarten in Jerusalem on September 1. Despite the government's position, General Amos Malka, the head of military intelligence, took a stand against "targeted killings," believing that they exposed the political wing to vengeful reprisals from the PFLP. Once again, Matti Steinberg, the Shin Bet analyst, had not been consulted. Along with other specialists, Steinberg issued a warning: Israel had just crossed a new red line, and the Palestinians would intensify the fighting.[6] Amos Malka and Dan Meridor, the cabinet minister charged with intelligence oversight, adopted identical positions.

In Beit Jalla, several Palestinian police officers attempted to prevent the resumption of shooting on Gilo. Lacking reinforcements, they were unable to control the area and the Jewish neighborhood was subjected to bursts of machine-gun fire. The next day, the IDF launched a large-scale operation in Beit Jalla and in the suburbs of Bethlehem. Fighting also broke out in Aida, a nearby refugee camp. Around fifteen Palestinians were wounded. On the Ynet Web site of the weekly *Yedihot Aharonot*, Ofer Shelah, the political commentator, wrote:

> According to an opinion poll, three-quarters of Israelis approve of the operation in Beit Jalla and of the liquidation of Abu Ali Mustafa. In spite of all that, they are not convinced that [these operations] will damage the ability of the PFLP to execute attacks. In fact, that this will only reinforce terrorism and lead to new military operations. The conclusion of the [Israeli] leaders is the following: the public is frustrated, tired, suffers for the victims [of attacks], and supports any offensive, whether or not it is conducted successfully. When the [public] supports the use of force by the government, it makes use of it.[7]

The Israeli army pulled back from Beit Jalla forty-eight hours later under American administration pressure as well as a verbal agreement concluded by telephone between Shimon Peres and Yasser Arafat, and an intervention by Miguel Moratinos, the European emissary, whose security advisor, Alistair Crooke, and several other of his men were on site. Discreetly, they managed to skirt Ariel Sharon's refusal to pull back his troops. And some European observers even took up positions on the ground.

ANTI-SEMITISM AND THE CONFERENCE AGAINST RACISM
If winds of optimism were beginning to blow in the Middle East, in Durban, South Africa, the atmosphere was noxious. The third global

conference against racism and racial discrimination was getting under way in a virulent atmosphere that was sinking into pure and simple anti-Semitism. During an official dinner, Mary Robinson, United Nations high commissioner for human rights and a good Catholic, hurled "I am a Jew!" when a delegate showed her a pamphlet published by the Arab Lawyers Union containing anti-Jewish caricatures. Yasser Arafat gave one of the opening speeches, and those underlying strains were also present: "The Israeli occupation, its racist practices, its laws founded on racism. . . . " Several pro-Palestinian organizations drove the point home by having the forum of NGOs vote on a resolution that also contained anti-Semitic rhetoric. The official delegations sent by the United States and Israel walked out of the conference, slamming the door shut behind them. Under European pressure, the conference ended by accepting a resolution excluding any accusation of racism against Israel. But the damage had been done. The amalgamation of Judaism, Zionism, and Israel, as well as the anti-Semitic demonstrations taking place on the sidelines of the conference, reinforced the feeling of isolation of Israel and numerous Jewish communities.

On September 1, in Gaza, a colonel in the Palestinian intelligence service was killed when his car exploded. The Israelis claimed that it was an accident, that the officer had been manipulating an explosive device. But few were satisfied with this explanation. Three days later, at eight o'clock in the morning, a Palestinian disguised as an orthodox Jew activated his explosive belt in front of a French school in Jerusalem. The terrorist's head was hurled into the school's courtyard. Since November 2000, forty Palestinian militants had been the object of "targeted killings," which had also killed twenty bystanders as "collateral damage."

THE IDF AGAINST PERES

Shimon Peres continued his talks with the Palestinians. During a visit to Jerusalem, Javier Solana, the European Union's senior representative for foreign affairs, presided over a meeting that included, in addition to the Israeli foreign minister, Abu Ala, the president of the Palestinian parliament, as well as Saeb Erekat. The main topic of discussion was the proposed meeting between Arafat and Peres. Theoretically, it was to take place after Ariel Sharon's return from an official visit to Moscow. But to the Israeli military officials, the meeting was a mistake. Shaul Mofaz, the chief of staff, asserted in private and to a few journalists hovering in the wings that such a meeting "would be offering Arafat a reward for violence." Short of canceling the meeting, they suggested holding it far from the reach of the press, at the military base of the Erez checkpoint or at Taba instead of in Berlin as Joschka Fischer had initially suggested.

The IDF opposed Peres's plan, which consisted of negotiating a local cease-fire in places like Beit Jalla. Instead, they wanted the PLO leader to proclaim a general cease-fire. But, above all else, the generals intended to set their own plan in motion, which consisted in creating security zones in designated sectors of the West Bank. It entailed most notably the prohibition of any movement of Palestinians without permits between Qalqilya and the nearest Israeli city, Kfar Saba, and between Tulkarm and Taibeh, the Arab-Israeli border town. This plan had been presented a month earlier to the security cabinet. The ministers had decided that the details would be ironed out later in coordination with the security agencies concerned. In Moscow, where he was on an official visit, Ariel Sharon was stunned to learn that, during a break between meetings, Shaul Mofaz had called for a press conference in Tel Aviv to announce— without the prime minister's agreement—the creation of security zones. He had it canceled. On September 6, during his flight home, the prime minister met with the journalists who had accompanied him to Russia and proceeded to harshly criticize the IDF. He declared: "In Israel, we do not have an army that has power over the country . . . but rather a government responsible for defense!" As soon as he arrived, Ariel Sharon summoned Binyamin Ben-Eliezer and Shaul Mofaz in order to reprimand them.[8]

The same day, near a kibbutz to the east of Hadera, some Palestinians opened fire on a jeep, killing a young officer. A female soldier was also seriously wounded. In Tulkarm, two Fatah militants were struck down by a missile in a "targeted killing." They were the bodyguards of Raed Karmi, the local leader of the al-Aqsa Martyrs Brigades, who was only lightly wounded. The IDF had its eye on him for he had planned and executed several attacks against Israelis, including the murder of two restaurateurs on January 23, 2001.[9]

September 9 was a particularly bloody day. That morning, in the Jordan Valley, members of Islamic Jihad with automatic weapons attacked a minibus transporting teachers. Two were killed. The IDF responded by firing missiles on offices near Arafat's headquarters in Ramallah. Earlier that afternoon, a Hamas suicide bomber set off explosives near the station in Nahariya, in northern Israel, killing three and wounding close to ninety. For the security services, it was a very bad omen. This time, the perpetrator was not a young Palestinian, desperate for revenge, but rather a forty-eight-year-old Israeli Arab and father of six children! Once again, after these two attacks committed by Islamists, Israeli spokespeople accused Arafat and the Autonomous Authority, while Miguel Moratinos and Terje Larsen, the envoy of the secretary-general of the United Nations, were still trying to organize the meeting between Peres and the PLO leader. Raanan Gissin, Ariel Sharon's press secretary, set the tone: "What's the use of such talks when Arafat is speaking of peace at the same time he is instigating terrorism?"

That night, tanks took up positions outside Jenin where, according to the military, dozens of attacks had been planned. The city was to be besieged. Arafat called the governor and gave the order to resist. Within forty-eight hours, nine Palestinians were killed.

SEPTEMBER 11

Arafat was under pressure and in a bad mood. He still refused to meet with Peres if his conditions were not satisfied. He wanted the Israeli minister to get approval from Sharon to conclude an agreement, and for the meeting to address not only conditions for a cease-fire, but also deeper questions concerning the final status of Palestine. He demanded two confidence-building measures from the Israelis: first, that they proclaim a halt to the "targeted killings" of Palestinian activists and second, that they transfer to the Autonomous Authority all the money collected from customs duties imposed on goods delivered to the West Bank and

Gaza. The money in question, several hundreds of millions of dollars, was frozen in an Israeli bank. After Abdullah of Jordan, Hosni Mubarak called to advise him to accept the summit with Peres, obviously following the intervention of Miguel Moratinos! The latter had arrived from Cairo that morning, and Arafat told him by telephone that he could not receive him. "I'm coming anyway!" the European emissary responded, who, while waiting for the hypothetical meeting, settled down at a seaside restaurant with his advisors.

Around 2:30 p.m., the customers gathered around a television. The images were being transmitted live from New York. An airplane had smashed into the side of a World Trade Center tower. Several minutes later, a second plane appeared. Everyone realized that it was an unprecedented terrorist attack. Moratinos's cell phone rang. Arafat had changed his mind and asked him to come immediately.

In Israel, Shlomo Harari, a reserve colonel, formerly of military intelligence, immediately grasped the importance of the event. He telephoned several superior officers and recommended that they make certain that television crews filmed the reaction in the Palestinian territories.[10] The spokesman for the Israeli army sent a cameraman to East Jerusalem where a dozen Palestinians were applauding and giving out sweets to celebrate the blow delivered to America.[11] Reuters also filmed the scene, as well as brief demonstrations of joy in Nablus and Gaza. From his home in Ramallah, Yasser Abed Rabbo was shattered to see the images broadcast by satellite. Even worse, Leila Odeh, a correspondent for Abu Dhabi television, mentioned that the attacks were claimed by the DFLP. Abed Rabbo called to protest. She answered that she had received an anonymous call. He replied: "And you didn't verify. . . . I can also call correspondents and say that I personally directed the attack."[12]

In Gaza, Arafat and Moratinos watched the collapse of the two towers on CNN:

> **Yasser Arafat:** "It's incredible! I'm shocked! Civilians don't have enough experience to pull off an attack like that. . . . They must certainly be military!"

Moratinos explained that after such an attack, America would turn to the Middle East: "It is all the more important to make progress here. The meeting with Shimon Peres can take place in a neutral place. In Cyprus, for example."

Arafat: "No. But why not Europe? Maybe next Thursday."

Moratinos: "Peres wants it to be discreet. A discussion without publicity!"

Arafat sniggered: "On the contrary! Peres wants publicity!"

Nabil Aburdeineh, the head of Arafat's cabinet: "Only yesterday, Peres revealed thirty elements that were to remain confidential."

Arafat, turning toward the television: "It's a war!"

Before separating, the two men spoke of Arafat's next trip to Syria.

Yasser Abed Rabbo arrived in Gaza at the end of the afternoon. Arafat was busy constructing theories: "I'm an engineer. For the towers to fall like that, it would be necessary for explosives to be placed inside."

Abed Rabbo interrupted him: "We must take immediate measures to block the images of a few kids celebrating in the streets. They are being broadcast to the United States and throughout the entire world, as if the Palestinians, all Palestinians, are celebrating these criminal attacks in New York and Washington."

Arafat: "We're going to issue a statement!"

Abed Rabbo: "That's insufficient! The image is too powerful; we cannot oppose it with simple words."

Saeb Erekat, who had just arrived from Cairo, joined the conversation. Arafat presented a theory concerning the collapse of the towers, to the dismay of Rabbo.

Abed Rabbo: "Whoever did it, from the inside, from outside, or from the sky. . . . it's the beginning of a new era. America has never been attacked like this, on its own territory. . . . It's a war that is going to reach us. . . . We have to change. If not, it will be the Americans who will change us!"

Arafat: "How?"

Abed Rabbo: "In declaring a cessation of violence! In stopping the intifada! But it's necessary to send as clear a message as possible, to affirm that we stand at America's side during their difficult hour. . . . We, Palestinians, who have been victims of terrorism, condemn such acts."

Erekat: "I agree! The Middle East begins a new chapter in its history!"

Someone proposed an idea: Yasser Arafat can launch a blood donation campaign for the victims of the attack to set an example. The head of state hesitated: "At my age? Isn't it dangerous?"

His advisors explained that he did not run the slightest risk. But nothing worked. He refused to allow himself to be pricked by the needle. The problem was solved by staging a little drama at Shifa Hospital in Gaza, starring Chairman Arafat. Stretched out on a bed, Arafat had a needle on his arm. A doctor, summoned for the occasion, was holding a bag of blood in front of the cameras. No one knew that it wasn't Arafat's blood.[13] The chairman, meanwhile, had given orders to his police force to prevent Palestinian cameramen from filming any further jubilant demonstrations in the West Bank and Gaza. In Nablus, the representative of the Associated Press received threats to not show, at any price, the images that he had filmed.

THE MEDIA EQUATION CHANGES

Thus, in the Middle East, the initial reactions to the 9/11 attacks fed the battle of images. Arafat tried to show his support for America by the symbolic gesture of giving blood, while the Israelis emphasized the Palestinian rejoicing—as limited as it was—over the dramas unfolding in New York and Washington.

In Jerusalem, Sharon, who had just met with his security cabinet, gave instructions to his ministers. They were ordered to content themselves with sending their condolences to the Americans. But above all they were told not to use the mourning taking place in the United States for the purposes of propaganda. Everyone sensed that the media environment had changed. Until this moment, Western public opinion viewed Israel as an occupier which, by means of its tanks, repressed the uprising of Palestinian freedom fighters. Few from abroad were persuaded by the Israeli argument that the intifada was directed against the very idea of the existence of a Jewish state. The attacks in New York and Washington would make Arab terrorism, and thus Palestinian terrorism, appear in a new light. Very quickly, the international press barely mentioned the ongoing Israeli operations in the West Bank and Gaza, and the IDF took advantage of this media blackout to increase pressure on the Palestinians.

On September 14, Binyamin Ben-Eliezer could state with satisfaction:

> It is a fact that we have killed fourteen Palestinians in Jenin, Qabatya, and Tammun, with the world remaining absolutely silent. For Arafat, it's a catastrophe. Once he has lost international legitimacy, it will be over for him. All that we can do is get Arafat's back up against the wall: either he engages in negotiations, or the world will see him as a chief terrorist. In the latter case, we will be free to respond to any attack.[14]

The next day, Ben-Eliezer approved new air and tank raids in the Gaza Strip. Three Palestinians were killed and thirty injured. That evening, north of Jerusalem, Palestinians opened fire from a car and killed an Israeli.

On September 16, Avi Gil, the head of Shimon Peres's cabinet, met with Sharon at his ranch in the Negev. He explained to him that he had nothing to lose in authorizing his foreign minister to meet with Arafat. Sharon allowed himself to be persuaded, but decided that first a firm message would be sent to the PLO leader. His son, Omri, and Gil would deliver it that very evening.

Miguel Moratinos had returned to Gaza, where he found a furious Arafat. An Israeli incursion was taking place in Ramallah and the PLO leader said, "the Israelis are using what happened in the United States against me. Shimon Peres said: 'Arafat has become bin Laden!'"

> **Moratinos:** "I spoke to Shimon Peres and to Avi Gil: they told me that Shimon is under a great deal of pressure. Sharon is against a meeting between Israelis and Palestinians, but we will have an answer later."
>
> **Arafat:** "Get control of the situation! Get a move on! Make proposals! Europe can be present!"
>
> **Moratinos:** "We can prepare proposals! Meanwhile, you can give a speech that will surprise everyone. Instead of waiting for the implementation of the proposals made by Mitchell and Tenet, take the initiative!"

OMRI SHARON MEETS WITH ARAFAT

At eleven o'clock that evening, Arafat received Omri Sharon and Avi Gil in a room at the Erez checkpoint, in the north of the Gaza Strip. Saeb Erekat was also present at the meeting. The son of the Israeli prime minister explained his father's position: "You will not gain anything through violence. You must do everything possible to stop the violence if you want to return to the path towards a political agreement."

> **Arafat:** "We are doing everything possible, but you continue [targeted] assassinations, and that complicates things."
>
> **Avi Gil:** "You now have, after the attacks in the United States, a historic opportunity. If you want to, you can stop the violence. Control the situation in Gaza. Make the suicide attacks stop! Silence the gunfire in the West Bank!"
>
> **Saeb Erekat:** "What do you mean by a historic opportunity?"
>
> **Avi Gil:** "If you make the decision now, it will make it possible for us to move to a political process. We can convince the prime minister of a global political solution that would take into account our demographic needs and your geographic

needs. . . . We will be able to hold [Palestinian] elections. . . .
We will have peace!"

Ariel Sharon had other concerns. The echoes emanating from Washington disturbed him. Didn't Israel risk paying the price for the vast coalition the Bush administration intended to create in order to fight international terrorism? His old suspicions toward America gained the upper hand. He remembered the American pressure he was forced to endure in 1982 during the war in Lebanon. Ronald Reagan had feared the reactions of Arab oil-producing nations. This time, the old general decided to make the first move. He declared to the *Jerusalem Post*: "I let it be known to the American administration, as well as to several European nations, that it is not because stability in the Middle East is important to them—and it is equally important to Israel—that we will be made to pay the price for it. Quite simply, we will not pay the price for it."[15]

The same day in *Yedihot Aharonot*, Sharon intensified his rhetoric: "Terrorism is terrorism! . . . What difference is there between what happened in New York and the murder of twenty-one teenagers at the Dolphinarium in Tel Aviv? . . . [A]nd the attack by a car bomb in front of the Russian church in Jerusalem? Or near a school? Or two car bombs near the kindergarten in Yehud? These are inhuman murders, and there is no difference!"[16]

Arafat seized every opportunity to send his best wishes to the Israelis and their leaders on each Jewish holiday. On Rosh Hashanah, the Jewish New Year, he sent a letter to the members of the Israeli government to wish them a happy new year. He added: "I gave strict orders that a cease-fire be respected. I hope that my call for peace will be repaid in turn, and that the Israeli army will stop the shooting. . . . I am ready to meet Mr. Peres when the Israeli government decides in order to implement all the agreements that have been signed for the safety of your children and ours."[17]

CEASE-FIRE?

September 18, 2001 got off to a bad start. At dawn, Israeli armored vehicles made an incursion on the seaside in the center of the Gaza Strip.

They destroyed the offices of French and Dutch companies that were planning the construction of the future Palestinian port. According to the IDF, it was a response to a mortar attack that targeted the neighboring settlement of Netzarim!

Terje Larsen and Miguel Moratinos were in Ramallah and exerted tremendous pressure on Arafat, from whom they demanded a public statement concerning the cease-fire. That afternoon, Arafat gathered around thirty diplomats in Ramallah, the few Arab ambassadors accredited by the Palestinian Authority, and the consuls general based in East Jerusalem. He read the text of the statement, which was carefully scrutinized by Larsen and Moratinos. He said that he had given "the order to officials of all Palestinian security forces to work with the utmost resolve to observe a cease-fire and to abstain from responding to Israeli attacks, even if it be in a situation of legitimate defense." And he added these words which the mediators wanted to hear: "We, Palestinians and Israelis, must work together to break this vicious cycle of violence. Israel has the right to exist within secure boundaries." Several hours later, Binyamin Ben-Eliezer, the Israeli minister of defense, gave IDF units the order to halt all offensive operations, and to only open fire if they were attacked. The army was also ordered to withdraw from the autonomous zones that it was occupying. That evening, this would be accomplished in Jenin.

The meeting between Arafat and Peres was planned for September 23 at 5 p.m. in Dahaniya, in the V.I.P. terminal of Gaza International Airport, closed since the beginning of the intifada. The IDF got what it wanted. The site was sufficiently remote to reduce media coverage to a minimum.

The number of skirmishes diminished considerably, but on September 20, an Israeli was killed in an ambush near his settlement, Nokdim. His three children, who were in his car, were not injured. The al-Aqsa Martyrs Brigades claimed responsibility for the attack.

SHARON WAVERS ON DAHANIYA

September 23 was a Sunday. The weekly meeting of the Israeli government had been delayed several hours. Ariel Sharon had summoned

Shimon Peres at 7:30 a.m. to discuss his meeting with Arafat. The previous evening and into the morning, the ministers on the Right and on the extreme Right had violently criticized Peres's initiative. Avi Gil, Omri Sharon, Avi Dichter, the head of Shin Bet, and General Giora Eiland attended the meeting. From the outset, the prime minister declared that the Dahaniya meeting would not take place because the Palestinians were not observing the cease-fire. Indeed, mortar shells had been launched on Israeli settlements in Gaza, and in Bethlehem, Atef Abayat, who had been arrested a month before, had been set free once again. Although Dichter confirmed that his services had observed a significant decrease in Palestinian violence, the army's position did not waver: "Arafat has not renounced his strategy of creating tension through terrorism."

Peres was furious. This was the third time he had to cancel the meeting with Arafat. He decided to boycott the government meeting and announced that he was going to take a few days of vacation to "think." Would the Labor Party return to the opposition? Several hours later, Omri Sharon had a long discussion with Peres, who subsequently canceled his vacation. Binyamin Ben-Eliezer called his Palestinian contacts and asked them to ensure that Abayat was returned to prison, and that mortar fire was put to a stop.

Late in the afternoon, Colin Powell telephoned Sharon to tell him the American administration wanted the Peres-Arafat meeting to take place. The prime minister responded that he demanded, as a prerequisite, forty-eight hours of total calm, and he would only give his approval on that condition. The secretary of state also contacted Ben-Eliezer to explain to him that George Bush would be furious if the Israeli government continued to resist a meeting.

Would the Fatah leaders succeed in controlling their armed cells? Certain groups no longer had any contact with the hierarchy. As for the secretary general of the organization in the West Bank, Marwan Barghouti, he couldn't even leave Ramallah: the IDF accused him of having ordered several anti-Israeli attacks. That day, an extradition request was sent to the Palestinian Authority.

On September 24, Islamic Jihad decided to break the cease-fire. An Israeli woman was killed when she was getting behind the wheel of her car in the Jordan Valley. Later that day, the Palestinians were outraged to learn that the IDF had declared a sixty-kilometer area along the former armistice line, between Tulkarm and Jenin, where 24,000 Palestinians were living, "a prohibited military zone." Only these inhabitants and those in possession of special authorization were permitted to move about in the area. In spite of these developments, the Peres-Arafat meeting was rescheduled for September 26, the day before Yom Kippur.

TERMIT AND FAILURE IN DAHANIYA

Very early that morning, a powerful explosion resounded not far from the airport in Dahaniya, near Rafah, where the meeting was to take place a few hours later. Some Palestinians had dug an underground tunnel in which they had placed explosives under an Israeli post named Termit, situated a few dozen meters from the Egyptian border. Three soldiers were lightly injured. The IDF retaliated against a neighboring refugee camp. Palestinian militants struck back with Kalashnikovs, as tanks rolled into action. Peres's security officials advised him to cancel the meeting because his convoy had to pass near where there had been exchanges of fire. The minister's cabinet contacted Ben-Eliezer and asked him to try to restore calm in the area. Perhaps Israeli reprisals could wait. The IDF's response to this request is not known, but on the way to Dahaniya, Peres was able to see the tanks in action with his own eyes. Avi Gil would later recount that at that moment he understood the meeting was meant to fail.[18] Hamas claimed responsibility for the attack, but the army attributed it to the "Popular Committees" of Rafah, in which Fatah participated, and accused Mohammed Dahlan's preventative security team of foreknowledge of the plans.

The meeting began under an extremely tense atmosphere. General Giora Eiland was there. He had in his possession a timetable for the implementation of a cease-fire, as well as a list of ten Palestinians among the approximately one hundred that the IDF and Shin Bet wanted the

Autonomous Authority to arrest. It was a test for Arafat. Avi Dichter and Amos Gilaad were certain the PLO leader would not be able to order arrests—or that he wouldn't want to. This would prove that he did not want to restore calm.[19]

> **Shimon Peres:** "This is a complicated matter. It is difficult. I am here to lay the groundwork, to eliminate obstacles to an honorable peace between us and the Palestinians. It is no secret that a huge debate is raging in Israel. . . . I am here for peace, and the world has changed. . . . The world has changed since September 11. At the present moment, Mr. Chairman, the menace of terrorism is fundamental. We are facing up to risks without an army and to armies without risk. We must immediately begin to take September 11 into account."
>
> **Yasser Arafat:** "We have a problem in Rafah. You are attacking at this very moment in Rafah."
>
> **Peres:** "We will be able to rebuild what has been destroyed in Rafah. We want to rebuild our credibility. We are going to restore confidence. I propose a meeting between the generals and security officials within the next twenty-four hours."
>
> **Arafat:** "We have spoken of American observers in Rafah. A dozen!"
>
> **Peres:** "Yes, it has been a question. That would facilitate the implementation of the Mitchell report. We have to implement two documents."
>
> **Erekat interrupted:** "The Mitchell and Tenet plans: they have to be implemented simultaneously."

Peres proposed a timetable calling for one week of total calm before the period of "appeasement," which would last for four weeks. Erekat put forth the Palestinian position: one week of calm, two weeks of appeasement. Then he inquired about the status of the transfer of the Autonomous Authority's funds that had been frozen in an Israeli bank since the beginning of the intifada. He also asked the reason for the arrest of the mufti of Jerusalem the day before. Peres explained that it apparently concerned a simple interrogation. From time to time, an explosion resounded from afar. Outside, the IDF was pursuing its operations.

Abu Ala, Yasser Abed Rabbo, and Mohammed Dahlan entered and, as so often when he was in the public eye, Arafat raised his voice: "We want to open a new chapter. . . . We have taken numerous measures. . . . You yourself recognize that there has been an improvement. . . . The intensity of the violence has decreased. . . . We have arrested someone who wanted to commit a suicide attack. . . . But towns are sealed off. . . . The siege of our cities. . . . the shortage of food. . . . And why do you compare me to bin Laden? Ninety percent of our factories have been destroyed. . . . I have 130,000 unemployed. . . . Gaza fishermen cannot go out to sea. . . . Why have you closed the Orient House? We call it the House of Peace! You arrest the mufti."

> **Abu Ala interrupted:** "We expect a lot from this meeting. We must walk away from here with results!"
>
> **Shimon Peres:** "You know, bombs explode in Haifa, in Jaffa! Women and children have been killed."
>
> **Arafat:** "And our children?"
>
> **Peres continued:** "I applaud your call on September 18 for a halt to violence. We appreciate this position and we know that you have renounced all violence . . . but we hope that you are going to arrest ten people who are planning terrorist attacks. You arrest ten people, and everything will change."
>
> **Arafat:** "What?"

Peres answered that he was talking about suspects who represented a real threat to the peace process. Next, Giora Eiland presented the timetable: "After an initial period of forty-eight hours of calm, we will take unilateral measures for five days. Next, we will open one or several cities in the West Bank, as well as checkpoints on major roads and on the Saladin Road, in the Gaza Strip. Our forces will redeploy in order to permit the passage of workers. Your security forces may once again circulate between the West Bank and Gaza."[20] The Israelis had made significant concessions.

Another meeting was set to occur forty-eight hours later on Friday, September 28, the day after the Yom Kippur fast. The Israelis were in a hurry to leave Dahaniya since the holiday was to begin in a few hours. In two days, the casualty toll was five Palestinians dead and around forty wounded. A dozen homes were destroyed in Rafah, including the one containing the opening to the tunnel used by the assailants of the Termit military post.

As planned, for the first time since July 25, security officials from both camps met in Tel Aviv. The Israelis agreed, beginning Sunday, to reopen the Rafah border post between Gaza and Egypt, and to permit free movement between Palestinian cities. The Palestinians pledged to act against groups that shot mortars at Gaza settlements and at neighboring military bases. But September 28 was also the anniversary of the intifada. Thousands of Palestinians demonstrated in areas throughout the West Bank, Gaza, and East Jerusalem, and skirmishes occurred at military checkpoints. The toll included five Palestinian deaths and dozens more wounded. There were new clashes the next day. Four more killed. Yasser Abed Rabbo, the Palestinian information minister, spoke out: "Since the Arafat-Peres meeting on the twenty-sixth [of September], fourteen people have died. If that's a cease-fire, what do you call a war?"

Peres accused the IDF of doing too much. He had still not digested the pursuit of Israeli operations in Rafah during his meeting with the PLO leader. He was convinced the army wanted to sabotage the meeting, and that Moshe Yaalon, the deputy chief of staff, wanted Arafat dead. Some of those close to Peres told the press: "The IDF cannot stand the idea of a cease-fire and will not accept the political wing assuming control." The soldiers were not easily taken in, and superior officers, who preferred to remain anonymous, accused the minister of foreign affairs of indiscipline. They would not implement the decisions made by the security cabinet.

BUSH SPEAKS OF A PALESTINIAN STATE

On October 2, receiving congressional leaders at the White House, George Bush took the plunge and added a new term to his personal dictionary: "The idea of a Palestinian state has always been part of a vision, so long as the right of Israel to exist is respected." This was the first time a United States president took such a clear position in favor of a Palestinian state, and Colin Powell, the secretary of state, knew the Israelis and their allies in the Senate and the House of Representatives were going to react. During an improvised press conference, he stated: "As the president said this morning, there has always been a vision in our thinking, as well as in previous administrations' thinking, that there would be a Palestinian state that would exist at the same time that the security of the state of Israel was also recognized, guaranteed, and accepted by all parties. That vision is alive and well, and we hope that it will come about as a result of negotiations between the two sides. So, in that regard, there is nothing new." At the prime minister's office in Jerusalem, all warning lights were flashing red. Ariel Sharon was convinced the Americans intended to impose a new peace plan upon Israel. George Bush was perhaps planning to divulge the details in the speech he was to give to the United Nations General Assembly on November 10.

Early in the evening on October 2, two Palestinians succeeded in infiltrating the Alei Sinai settlement on the northern edge of the Gaza Strip. They killed two young soldiers on leave. And, during a long exchange of gunfire with soldiers who had arrived to reinforce the settlers, they further wounded fourteen Israelis before being killed themselves. In Lebanon, al-Manar, the Hezbollah television channel, announced that Hamas had claimed responsibility for the attack. At midnight, Ariel Sharon gathered his cabinet and authorized the IDF to resume operations in the autonomous Palestinian zone. Early the next morning, tanks and bulldozers destroyed plantations and houses, as well as eight Palestinian police posts near Alei Sinai. Six Palestinian policemen were killed. Arafat's entourage accused Israel of neutralizing the security forces of the Autonomous Authority, which was supposed to be acting against

Hamas. Meanwhile, Ariel Sharon called Colin Powell in Washington and told him Arafat wasn't doing anything to prevent terrorism, attacks, and incitation to violence. The secretary of state then told him that the United States would demand that the PLO leader do more to combat terrorism.

BUSH IN CHAMBERLAIN'S CLOTHES

On October 4, after another bloody attack in Afula during which a Palestinian disguised as a soldier opened fire on a bus station, killing three Israelis and wounding around twenty, Ariel Sharon refused to accede to the demands of his advisors, who suggested that he await more precise information concerning the plans being developed in Washington. According to press reports, the Saudis had allegedly persuaded George Bush that, as part of the U.S. struggle against al-Qaeda, he needed to find a solution to the Palestinian problem in order to calm the Arab world. And now more than ever, Sharon feared Israel would be called upon to pay the price for the large coalition being created by the American administration. He called a press conference at the Journalist House in Tel Aviv. After having evoked the attack in Afula, he declared:

> All attempts to achieve a cease-fire have been thwarted by the Palestinians. The fire has not ceased. . . . Starting today, we can only count on ourselves. We are facing a difficult political battle. I am addressing Western democracies, and especially the leader of the free world, the United States, so that they avoid committing the same error that was made in 1938, when European democracies decided to sacrifice Czechoslovakia in exchange for a simple and temporary solution. Do not try to appease the Arabs at our expense. Israel will not be Czechoslovakia!

Sharon refused to respond to journalists' questions and left the room.

Dan Kurtzer, the United States ambassador in Tel Aviv, was not informed of Sharon's outburst. Along with a representative from the CIA, he was busy coordinating with Palestinian security the rescue of two

Israelis lost in a West Bank town. In the middle of the night, the White House woke him up. Bush's entourage had learned of Sharon's statements in the press, and the president was furious. Kurtzer was asked to immediately call the prime minister in order to tell him to retract his accusations by the next morning. Sharon's direct line was busy, but finally the ambassador succeeded in getting the message through. As soon as Kurtzer finished speaking, Sharon started yelling. For twenty minutes he accused Kurtzer of being the source of Washington's anger.[21] The following evening in Jerusalem, the government issued a statement: "The prime minister called Colin Powell to tell him that he appreciated the efforts of the American president." The secretary of state insisted that it was unacceptable to compare George Bush to Neville Chamberlain. "Israel," he said, "does not have a better ally than the United States."

ARAFAT AND BIN LADEN

On the ground, the cease-fire was but a mirage. In Hebron, Palestinians regularly opened fire on Israeli settlers around the Tomb of the Patriarchs. The day before, two Israelis had been killed, and responsibility for the attack had been claimed by the al-Aqsa Martyrs Brigades, of Fatah. The IDF had been given approval to reoccupy the neighborhoods from which the shots originated, and six Palestinians paid for the operation with their lives. Meanwhile, Saeb Erekat met Shimon Peres for one hour in Jerusalem without result. In Ramallah, the central committee of Fatah met under Arafat's chairmanship and issued an appeal for a cease-fire, threatening "those who violate the law and undermine the national interest with draconian measures." The movement, whose political leaders were becoming more and more cut off from their base, reiterated its condemnation of the September 11 attacks in the United States and of "all forms of terrorism." This statement was not only destined for the Bush administration, but also for Palestinian Islamists, at a moment when in both Gaza and the West Bank the popularity of Osama bin Laden was at its zenith. After the launching of the American offensive in Afghanistan, while aerial bombings were multiplying, the al-Qaeda leader appeared on the satellite network Al-Jazeera, defying Bush and comparing his own "holy war" to the fight of the Palestinian people.

On October 8, students organized a demonstration in front of the Islamic University in Gaza. Posters of bin Laden were brandished at the head of the procession. Arafat gave the order to the police to intervene. The demonstrators threw stones at the police, who responded with tear gas grenades and then by shooting real bullets. Two Palestinians were killed, a thirteen-year-old and Yusef Akel, a member of the commando unit Ezzedin al-Qassam. Hamas held Colonel Rajeh Abu Likhyah, who directed the police repression that day, personally responsible for the death of its militant. A year later, the Akel family would kidnap the colonel and assassinate him. Palestinian security never succeeded in arresting his murderers.

Two days later, in Doha, Qatar, speaking before the Islamic Organization Conference, Arafat drove his point home by once again condemning the attacks committed by al-Qaeda. This assumption of such a position and the skirmishes with Hamas in Gaza were very welcome signs in Washington, where Sharon's speech comparing Bush to Chamberlain had still not been forgotten. According to Dan Kurtzer, American leaders believed that Arafat had chosen the Western camp in the struggle against global jihad. He said: "He let us know that he had understood. That he wanted to participate in the solution to the problem. Sharon's argument that Arafat was precisely a part of the problem was badly understood by the administration."[22] On October 11, several newspapers published the details of the peace initiative being planned by Colin Powell. It was a question of a "viable Palestinian state," which implied territorial contiguity in the West Bank as well as the rejection of Ariel Sharon's proposal to give 40 percent of the territory to the Palestinians. Jerusalem would be the capital of both states and would maintain its national characteristics. Israel would remain Jewish, and Palestine would be Palestinian. But it was understood that the solution to the problem of Palestinian refugees would not be found on Israeli territory. The secretary of state envisioned sending a new mediator to the Middle East: General Anthony Zinni, whom he knew well.

Arafat's entourage was enchanted. His advisors applauded an "American proposal that is not simply an Israeli document bearing an American seal of approval." On the ground, the number of violent incidents was consistently decreasing, but on October 14, several hours before Arafat's arrival in London where he was to meet with Bush's principal ally, Tony Blair, a Hamas leader was killed on the roof of his home in Qalqilya by an IDF sharpshooter. Israel accused him of being one of the planners of the Dolphinarium incident. The Islamic organization swore revenge. Meanwhile, the British prime minister announced in front of his guest that he was also favorable to the formation of a viable state, with Jerusalem as the capital of both states.

Under American pressure, and due to the calm that began to spread in the West Bank, the Israeli security cabinet decided on October 15 to evacuate the Palestinian neighborhoods in Hebron that it had occupied for twelve days. For the settlement movement, this was unacceptable. It meant that the settlers would once again be exposed to Palestinian fire. Two ministers on the extreme Right, Avigdor Lieberman, who had a portfolio in national infrastructure, and Rehavam Zeevi, the tourism minister, resigned. That day in Nablus, another member of Hamas became the object of a "targeted killing," the second in twenty-four hours. He died in a car explosion.

Several London newspapers asserted that Ariel Sharon was trying to torpedo the Anglo-American initiative.

CHAPTER 4

HAMAS

On October 17, 2001, shortly before seven in the morning, Yael Zeevi returned to her room on the eighth floor of the Hyatt Hotel in Jerusalem. In the hallway, she discovered her husband, Rehavam, unconscious after being shot in the head. Rushed to Hadassah Hospital, he was pronounced dead on arrival. He had just resigned from his post as tourism minister. But as a leader in the extreme right-wing National Union Party, he advocated the transferring of Palestinians and Israeli Arabs to Arab countries. Also a former general, he had fought alongside Ariel Sharon in several wars.

The Popular Front for the Liberation of Palestine (PFLP) claimed responsibility for the assassination, stating: "The combatants of the brigades of the martyr Abu Ali Mustafa confirm that they assassinated the Zionist terrorist Rehavam Zeevi in order to avenge the death of our leader." In Ramallah, a spokesman for the organization confirmed the claim for the press: "Everyone knew that, sooner or later, we were going to avenge our leader. It's done!" Arafat gave the order to arrest the PFLP spokesman and promised to apprehend the assassins.

During an internal debate, Dan Meridor, the Israeli chairman of the foreign affairs and defense committees, stated: "Zeevi is also the victim of our mistakes. By assassinating the leader of the PFLP last August, we changed the rules of the game. Until that point, we avoided attacking major leaders. Now, the conflict has become an affair of individuals, and in that case, we do not have the advantage."[1]

At one that afternoon, Ariel Sharon gave a speech to the Knesset: "This morning Rehavam Zeevi, minister and member of the government, was assassinated in Jerusalem by Palestinian terrorists. . . . This was a great loss for the people of the state of Israel. It was also a personal loss. He was above all else a friend, a comrade in arms who shared our belief in the inalienable right of the Israeli people to their historic homeland. Only criminal terrorists could imagine assassinating an elected official in a democratic state. Only a regime working for the destruction of the state of Israel and profoundly opposed to peace would protect such murderers. The responsibility for this murder falls entirely to Arafat, who fomented—and still foments—terrorism and has not taken a single measure to this day to put a stop to terrorism. And he does so even though he knows that in not acting against organizations like the Popular Front, he is authorizing horrible murders."

That evening, the security cabinet decided to suspend all diplomatic contact with the Palestinian Authority and gave Arafat an ultimatum to apprehend the leaders of the PFLP, as well as the assassins, and hand them over to Israel. If he failed to do so, the statement read: "Israel will have no choice and will have to consider the Palestinian Authority a hostile regime that supports terrorism." This was the equivalent of a bona fide declaration of war. And, for the first time, a personal measure against Arafat was adopted: under no circumstances would he be permitted to take off from the Palestinian airport in Dahaniya.

Meanwhile in Washington, the White House spokesman condemned the assassination and asked Arafat for "vigorous action: to apprehend and bring to justice the assassins and all those working against a return to calm and security for the Palestinians and Israelis." The head of the

PLO immediately called Shimon Peres and told him that he would do everything within his power.

NO AMERICAN PRESSURE

In Bethlehem the following day, Atef Abayat was once again free. Alongside two of his cousins, he was behind the wheel of a top model 4 x 4 that, he believed, had been stolen in Israel. In reality, the vehicle was rigged. The explosives planted inside were activated by remote control from a helicopter and the three Abayat cousins were killed instantly. Jibril Rajoub was furious. He had been called out: he and Arafat had confirmed on several occasions that Abayat was under lock and key. It was true, however, that Abayat's jailers operated under the services of his rival, General Haj Ismail.[2] That evening, militants from the al-Aqsa Martyrs Brigades took revenge by turning automatic weapons on Gilo. Several hours later, however, tank units assumed positions in Bethlehem and Beit Jalla, killing three Palestinians during the ensuing skirmishes. Similar operations took place in five other cities in the West Bank, including Ramallah. All of these locations were hermetically sealed.

On October 20, the fatality count rose to eight. In Washington, the State Department was concerned about the breadth of the Israeli operations. A State Department spokesman asserted: "The Israeli Defense Forces should be withdrawn immediately from all Palestinian-controlled areas, and no further such incursions should be made." An official Israeli source in Jerusalem rejected this appeal, stating: "We will only halt the operations when we have attained our objectives: to protect the citizens of Israel." Ariel Sharon and Binyamin Ben-Eliezer departed, under the ever-watchful eye of the cameras, to inspect the headquarters in the central military region.

The prime minister was not too worried about the State Department's reaction. Sharon mentioned to several Likud members of Knesset that he was not feeling any pressure from the United States. In fact, his neoconservative allies in Vice President Dick Cheney's entourage at the National Security Council, at the White House, and in the Pentagon, informed him that there would be no American sanctions against Israel. At most, there would be a public expression of discontent. But it was important that the Israeli operations not go wrong, last too long, or result in too many Palestinian victims.[3] This was confirmed by Shimon Peres and several Israeli leaders sent to Washington to present the Israeli position. They returned bearing a message of appeasement: America was absorbed in its war against al-Qaeda and did not have time to deal with local Israeli problems. The Bush administration did not intend to "offer Israel to the Arabs." The connection between the two countries was solid. The president had allegedly promised Peres: "Even if you wanted to, you could not succeed in destroying our relationship."[4]

At the same time, the so-called Quartet (Terje Larsen, the emissary of the secretary-general of the United Nations; Miguel Moratinos, of the European Union; Andrei Vdovin, Russia's Middle East envoy; and Ron Schlicher, the U.S. consul general in Jerusalem) came to Arafat's office in Gaza to warn him. The Palestinian chairman had to arrest Zeevi's assassins, as well as the ten men Israel considered to be the most dangerous terrorists. He also had to shut down the offices of the incriminated organizations. Meanwhile, Schlicher relayed a personal message from George Bush asking Arafat to act as swiftly as possible. A Palestinian official explained that the Autonomous Authority was paralyzed in the West Bank by the Israel incursions. In Bethlehem, thousands of the faithful, led by the heads of the thirteen Christian churches in the Holy Land, demonstrated "for justice and for the end of the occupation."

In Tulkarm on October 24, three armed Palestinians were killed during an IDF ambush. Later that night, the army launched a major operation in Beit Rima, a village near Ramallah, killing six Palestinians and apprehending eleven militants, including those close to Rehavam Zeevi's assassins. In Washington, the State Department spokesman corrected his statement. The White House was no longer asking for the "immediate," but rather, "the soonest possible" withdrawal of Israeli forces. Four days later, Sharon's cabinet announced the implementation of a progressive withdrawal plan from the occupied cities in the West Bank.

The withdrawal from Bethlehem would begin that evening, despite an attack on Hadera, north of Tel Aviv, where a Palestinian had shot into a line of people, killing five before being killed himself by a policeman.

ARAFAT EQUIVOCATES

The investigation into the assassination of Zeevi was making progress—two accomplices had been caught in Israel. Shin Bet supplied the Palestinian Authority with a list of the other members of the PFLP who had participated in the murder, but they were not arrested. Arafat knew perfectly well that these suspects risked being captured by the IDF as soon as they were placed in a Palestinian detention site. He especially did not want to give the impression that he was extraditing militants to Israel. Besides, even if the army was maintaining positions in Ramallah and in four other West Bank towns, it had withdrawn from Bethlehem and Beit Jalla, where a preventative security team under Jibril Rajoub had taken up a position to prevent further shooting on Gilo. Mohammed Dahlan's relations with Arafat were poor, and he had resigned from his position as head of preventative security in Gaza. Dahlan had regularly advised Arafat not to make promises to the Americans or the Israelis if he couldn't keep them. In fact, he even advised him to announce publicly that there was little chance the Palestinian public would obey a call to end the violence in the absence of a political agreement. Dahlan also suggested that Arafat make gestures that would, in effect, act as subtle messages addressed to the White House. These gestures would include arresting leaders from Islamic Jihad or Hamas. But Arafat did not respond. He was playing it by ear, and his closest advisors, who demanded a coherent strategy, distanced themselves from him. Abu Mazen, the second-in-command of the PLO, stayed away from Ramallah and would no longer leave his home in Gaza, while Abu Ala declared, during private conversations, that he no longer understood the intentions of his chairman.

Ariel Sharon was fully informed of these proceedings. The Israeli security services listened to everything that was said in Arafat's offices and in those of his advisors.[5] When, on November 2, Shimon Peres left for a European economic conference in Palma de Mallorca that also included Yasser Arafat and Hosni Mubarak, Likud officials warned Sharon: "Peres is going to negotiate behind your back!" The prime minister answered: "There will be no negotiations! I know when there will be negotiations. . . . A prime minister always knows, and in detail, all that he wants to know." Shimon Peres had himself been head of the government, and was thus knowledgeable of Shin Bet's work. Nevertheless, he soon had two meetings with Arafat, enough time to briefly discuss the difficulties of the cease-fire. The two men did not know it at the time, but these were to be their final meetings.

In Jerusalem on November 4, a Palestinian terrorist from Islamic Jihad opened fire on Israelis at a bus stop, killing two people and wounding around twenty more before he was gunned down by police.

NO WHITE HOUSE FOR ARAFAT

The White House announced that George Bush would not meet with Yasser Arafat during the United Nations General Assembly on November 10. The president was swayed by the arguments of Dick Cheney (which were the equivalent of Israeli arguments) and believed that he could not trust the PLO leader. General Amos Malka had gone in person to Washington to present the "evidence" on the Abayat affair (where, he said, Arafat had been caught red-handed in a lie), and to enforce the fact that none of Rehavam Zeevi's assassins had been arrested by the Palestinian police. Condoleezza Rice, the head of the National Security Council, stated "that Arafat should break his ties to international terrorism."

Arab leaders, and notably the Saudis, did not appreciate Washington's boycott of Arafat. Since his election, Bush had not once shaken the hand of the Palestinian chairman. Four sentences in his speech were supposed to calm the critics:

> The American government also stands by its commitment to a just peace in the Middle East. We are working toward a day when two states, Israel and Palestine, live peacefully together within secure and recognized borders as called for by the Security Council resolutions. We will do all in our power to

bring both parties back into negotiations. But peace will only come when all have sworn off, forever, incitement, violence, and terror.

In the auditorium, Arafat applauded. The president of the United States had uttered the words "state" and "Palestine." That evening, the secretary-general of the United Nations presided over a gala dinner. George Bush turned to Kofi Annan, gestured toward the PLO leader with a movement of his head and whispered: "I will never shake that guy's hand!" It was the first time he found himself in Arafat's presence.

On November 15, Shimon Peres was also scheduled to speak before the General Assembly. As a precaution, he decided to submit the text of his speech to Ariel Sharon at his ranch on the Saturday prior to his departure. The prime minister gave his approval, but it was understood that any last-minute changes were to be submitted to the head of his cabinet. Despite this supervision, the extreme Right protested violently against the speech. Here are some extracts:

> Yesterday, for example, it would have been difficult to find an Israeli in favor of a Palestinian state. While it is not officially the policy of the Israeli government, there does exist [in Israel] support in favor of Palestinian independence. We do not want to dominate the Palestinians; we want them to breathe liberty, to build a new economy, to preserve their traditions, to benefit from the best education while insuring the security of all parties. From Israel's point of view, we are convinced that good neighbors are worth more than good guns. . . . But the new solution must confront terrorism.

As Peres was giving his speech, the IDF was pursuing operations in the West Bank and the Gaza Strip. A militant from Islamic Jihad was killed; the Israelis blamed him for the murder of two settlers. A skirmish in the Khan Younis refugee camp resulted in one death and the wounding of fifteen Palestinians. In Washington, eighty-nine senators sent a petition to George Bush asking him not to prevent Israel from using all its force against Palestinian terrorism.[6] It was an initiative of the pro-Israelis, a warning addressed to the administration on the eve of an announcement by Colin Powell regarding a new diplomatic initiative in the Middle East.

POWELL SENDS ZINNI TO THE MIDDLE EAST

On November 19, the secretary of state gave a speech to the professors and students of the University of Louisville:

> President Bush and I are convinced that the Arab-Israeli conflict can be resolved, but that that will only happen if all of us, and especially Israelis and Palestinians, face up to some fundamental truths. To begin with, the Palestinians must accept that, if there is to be real peace, Israelis must be able to live their lives free from terror as well as war. The Palestinian leadership must make a 100 percent effort to end violence and to end terror. There must be real results, not just words and declarations.
>
> Terrorists must be stopped before they act. The Palestinian leadership must arrest, prosecute, and punish the perpetrators of terrorist acts. The Palestinians must live up to the agreements they have made to do so. They must be held to account when they do not. Whatever the sources of Palestinian frustration and anger under occupation, the intifada is now mired in the quicksand of self-defeating violence and terror directed against Israel. Palestinians need to understand that however legitimate their claims, they cannot be heard, let alone be addressed, through violence.
>
> And as President Bush has made clear, no national aspiration, no remembered wrong can ever justify the deliberate murder of the innocent. Terror and violence must stop and stop now. Palestinians must realize that the violence has had a terrible impact on Israel. The lynching of Israeli soldiers in Ramallah, the assassination of the cabinet minister

and the killing of Israeli children feed Israelis' deepest doubts about whether Palestinians really want peace. The endless messages of incitement and hatred of Israelis and Jews that pour out of the media in so much of the Palestinian and Arab worlds only reinforce these fears. . . .

Palestinians must accept that they can only achieve their goals through negotiation. That was the essence of the agreements made between Israelis and Palestinians in Madrid, and again in Oslo in 1993. There is no other way but direct negotiation in an atmosphere of stability and nonviolence.

At the same time, Palestinians must also be secure and in control of their individual lives and collective security. In the absence of peace, Israel's occupation of the West Bank and Gaza has been the defining reality of Palestinians' lives there for over three decades. . . . The overwhelming majority of Palestinians in the West Bank and Gaza have grown up with checkpoints and raids and indignities. Too often they have seen their schools shuttered and their parents humiliated.

Palestinians need security as well. Too many innocent Palestinians, including children, have been killed and wounded. This, too, must stop.

The occupation hurts Palestinians, but it also affects Israelis. The sad truth is that it is the young people who serve on the front lines of conflict who are at risk. Embittered young Palestinians throw stones, and young Israeli soldiers on the other side learn only that Palestinians are to be feared, seen as enemies.

One thing I've learned in my life is that treating individuals with respect and dignity was the surest path to understanding. Both sides need to treat the other with respect. Humiliation and lack of respect are just another path to confrontation.

Israeli settlement activity has severely undermined Palestinian trust and hope. It preempts and prejudges the outcome of negotiations and, in doing so, cripples chances for real peace and security. The United States has long opposed settlement activity. Consistent with the report of the committee headed by Senator George Mitchell, settlement activity must stop.

Colin Powell announced that he was sending a new American mediator to the Middle East: General Anthony Zinni. His mission was to help the parties conclude an enduring cease-fire. Powell declared: "Get that cease-fire in place, and other things can start to happen. Without that cease-fire, we are still trapped in the quicksand of hatred."

In Jerusalem, Ariel Sharon welcomed the American initiative. His entourage was satisfied, especially with the fact that the Americans were applying special pressure on the Palestinians, and that they were demanding that the start of negotiations depend upon the halting of the intifada. In addition, Colin Powell did not ask Ariel Sharon to renounce his demand for seven days of total calm before the Tenet plan could be implemented. As for the halting of construction in the settlements, the Israeli government would not construct any new ones, and would only provide for the "natural growth" in the interior of existing ones. The government press office issued a statement insisting that "the end of all acts of violence is the prerequisite for any diplomatic progress."

ZINNI IS WELCOMED

Anthony Zinni arrived in Tel Aviv on November 26, and he immediately participated in a series of briefings at the United States embassy. On the ground, things were going badly. Very badly, in fact. On November 22, five Palestinian children were killed in an explosion near the Khan Younis refugee camp in the south of the Gaza Strip. An Israeli unit in that sector ultimately admitted that it had planted explosives at the site in an attempt to trap Palestinian militants who had been firing upon a neighboring settlement the previous day. The army pursued its operations throughout the West Bank. On November 23, a helicopter fired a missile on a vehicle moving along a road north of Nablus. Mahmoud Abu Hanoud, the man who had escaped all assassination attempts since the month of August 2000, was killed along with two members of the military branch of Hamas. In response, the Islamic organization authorized its militants to launch attacks using automatic weapons. Until that moment, this type of attack was primarily used by the al-Aqsa Martyrs Brigades, affiliated with Fatah. The following day, in a settlement in Gaza, a soldier was killed by a mortar shell. The commando unit Ezzedin al-Qassam circulated a pamphlet announcing that this was only the beginning of its revenge for the death of Abu Hanoud.

The first meeting between Sharon and Zinni took place on November 27. Zinni was taken on a helicopter tour so that he could see with his own eyes the strategic problems Israel was facing. Suddenly, while the helicopter was hovering over Galilee, the pilot learned by radio that an attack had just occurred in Afula. The helicopter changed course and headed for the town. From the air the American general was able to see the ambulances, the emergency rescue organizations, etc. Two Palestinians had opened fire on passersby near the bus station. Before being killed by a policeman and a reservist, they had killed two Israelis. There were also around fifty wounded. Sharon and Zinni turned back and landed in Jerusalem where the American general had meetings with Shimon Peres, Binyamin Ben-Eliezer, and Shaul Mofaz.

That evening, he was invited to dinner at the home of the prime minister. After a brief meeting in the garden with the press, they returned to the dining room. At that same instant, General Moshe Kaplinsky, the prime minister's military advisor, received details of the attack by telephone. Sharon asked him to report aloud to General Zinni. General Kaplinsky reported: "Islamic Jihad claimed responsibility for the attack in Afula. The two terrorists are from Jenin, and one of them is a Palestinian police officer and the other belongs to Arafat's intelligence services." Sharon, smiling, replied: "That's terrible. Terrible! It's an example!"[7] Dan Kurtzer, the United States ambassador to Israel, took Zinni, who seemed completely shocked, off to the side. He later explained: "One of the things we were trying to avoid was for Zinni to become a kind of intermediary dealing with everyday problems. We tried to keep Zinni's mission focused on its major objective, which was both to stop terrorism and to restart bilateral negotiations, and to avoid letting him become embroiled in problems concerning who hit whom."[8]

In fact, the terrorists were *former* Palestinian police officers. One of the two belonged to Islamic Jihad, and the other to the al-Aqsa Martyrs Brigades. In Jenin, as in other towns in the West Bank, some Fatah armed cells had been infiltrated by Islamists.

The next day, Zinni started the day by touring the West Bank in order to grasp the settlement question more clearly. That afternoon, he went to Ramallah to meet with Arafat, who pledged his cooperation. At the time, however, the American general thought that the head of the PLO "could never look at concluding a deal that risked his own place in history and his personal legacy."[9]

As Zinni attempted to gain information and establish contacts with the key players, the Islamists took it upon themselves to torpedo his mission. On November 28, in the north of the West Bank, a soldier was shot and killed. Several hours later, a suicide bomber sent by Islamic Jihad exploded on a bus in Galilee, killing three and wounding nine. Early in the morning, Sharon flew to the United States. His objective was to prove to the American public that Israel and the United States were fighting an identical battle against terror, and to persuade George Bush that his demand for seven days of total calm before the implementation of the Tenet plan be maintained.

On December 1, soon after his departure, Hamas commited two suicide attacks right in the center of Jerusalem. Eleven Israelis were killed, and 188 were wounded. A car bomb exploded at the same moment rescue services arrived, without resulting in any victims. On December 2, an Israeli physician was killed in a Gaza settlement.

Ariel Sharon was in New York touring Ground Zero, the site of the September 11 attacks, accompanied by Mayor Rudy Giuliani. He asserted his solidarity with the victims' families and added: "There is no good or bad terrorism. I am waiting for the United States to put pressure on the Palestinians in order that they put a stop to all forms of violence. I am convinced that the United States and Israel will both win in this war on terror." Giuliani praised Sharon ("a great leader!") and confirmed that he was certain Yasser Arafat "participated in the worst acts of terrorism in the course of the last twenty years. I am certain of it because I investigated these issues when I was Manhattan prosecutor." Sharon invited him to travel to Jerusalem the following week.

Ariel Sharon was satisfied. His visit had gotten off to a good start. Things would go still better in a few hours at the White House. However, just as he was getting ready to meet with Bush, he received a horrible message from Israel: Hamas had struck again. A suicide bomber exploded in a bus in Haifa, killing fifteen and wounding forty. There had been a total of twenty-six deaths and 220 wounded in less than twenty-four hours.

Sharon shortened his trip and planned to leave for Tel Aviv immediately after his meeting with Bush. The situation in the Middle East was deteriorating. As he was disembarking from a helicopter, George Bush addressed journalists:

> In a couple of minutes, I'll have the honor of receiving the prime minister from Israel. . . . I will tell him that I strongly condemn the acts of murder that killed innocent people in Israel. I will tell him our nation grieves for those whose lives have been affected by the murderers. . . . Chairman Arafat must do everything in his power to find those who murdered innocent Israelis and bring them to justice. . . . Clearly, there are some that, every chance they have, they will use violence and terror to disrupt any progress that's being made. We must not allow them to succeed. We must not allow terror to destroy the chance of peace in the Middle East. . . . May God bless the Israeli citizens who lost their lives, and their families!

The meeting proceeded in the same vein. Sharon said to his host: "Since Arafat won't do it, Israel will attack the problem of terrorism alone." The chief executive reminded him of his promise not to kill the head of the PLO. Sharon replied that he would keep his word. Condoleezza

Rice and Colin Powell then arrived to participate in the discussion, for it was crucial that the scope of the Israeli reaction not provoke widespread disorder in the region or tensions with Arab countries, whom the United States needed in its struggle against global jihad.

On December 2, in the company of Moshe Katsav, the president of the Israeli parliament, Zinni visited the site of the double attack on Ben Yehuda Street, in the center of Jerusalem, in order to lay a bouquet. He made a short speech: "This is the worst gesture of inhumanity imaginable. . . . To attack young people and children, and the emergency teams who were trying to reach this spot! . . . It is important to fight that, together, and to not stray from our objective of peace." A portion of the crowd was not convinced. Cries of "*go home!*" were heard.

Clashes continued to occur in the West Bank. Near Jenin, five armed Palestinians were killed the day before during a fight with an Israeli patrol. Yasser Arafat declared a state of emergency in the Palestinian territories, and prohibited the bearing of arms as well as demonstrations and strikes in the schools and universities. The police force of the Autonomous Authority began to capture Islamic militants, especially in Ramallah.

FOR SHARON, ARAFAT IS RESPONSIBLE FOR EVERYTHING

As soon as he returned on December 3, Ariel Sharon had a preliminary meeting on matters of security with leaders in the army and Shin Bet in the military zone of the Tel Aviv airport. The speech he delivered was in fact an accusation against Arafat:

> A war has been inflicted upon us. A war of terrorism. A war which, every day, results in innocent victims. A war of terrorism led systematically, organized systematically. The objective of this war, of those who help the terrorists and send them [to attack us], the objective of those who permit them to commit these acts without preventing them, is to expel us from here. Their objective is to lead us to total despair, to hopelessness, to a loss of the national vision that guides us, a free people, in our land, the land of Zion and Jerusalem. We

know who imposes it upon us. Arafat is responsible for everything that happens here. Arafat has made strategic choices:
his strategy is that of terrorism, he is trying to make political
gains through murder, by permitting the brutal assassination
of innocent civilians. Arafat chose the way of terrorism. For
a long time, the world did not see Arafat for what he is, but,
recently, we have witnessed a significant change. A greater
comprehension of our position. Everyone has come to see
who the true Arafat is. Arafat is the greatest obstacle to peace
and stability in the Middle East. We already observed that in
the past, we see it now. . . . But Arafat will not fool the government. This time, Arafat will not fool this government. . . .
The Palestinian people must know that if it is the principal
victim of the current situation, this has been fomented by
Arafat. I say it to you now: we will pursue those responsible,
the perpetrators of terrorist attacks and those who support
them. We will pursue them until we have captured them and
they pay the price. . . . And while the United States pursues a
war against international terror by mobilizing all of their
power, we will do the same.

Not a word was spoken about Hamas, who was responsible for the
attacks. That evening, the Israeli government met in a special session and
adopted a series of unprecedented resolutions. It marked a break. The
Autonomous Authority was declared "an entity supporting terrorism."
Fatah and its armed branch, as well as Force 17, the Praetorian Guard of
the PLO chief, joined Hamas and Jihad on the list of organizations designated "terrorist" by Israel. And, in particular, the web was spun more
tightly around Yasser Arafat: he was no longer authorized to leave the
autonomous territories.

The next day, the IDF unleashed its response on the Autonomous
Authority. In Gaza, four combat helicopters destroyed Arafat's three
helicopters with machine-gun fire. F16s bombed the offices of the Palestinian chairman, the police headquarters in Jenin, and the government

center in Bethlehem. In the south of Gaza, bulldozers destroyed the landing strip of the airport in Dahaniya. George Bush made his own contribution by announcing that in Texas, the FBI had closed charity organizations affiliated with Hamas by freezing their bank accounts.

The Israeli initiative continued the next day. Helicopters fired missiles on police stations and Fatah offices in several towns in the West Bank and Gaza Strip. In Ramallah, a commissariat was bombed within Arafat's headquarters, whose building trembled under the impact.

Arafat called Shimon Peres to request a twelve-hour respite, enough time to allow his security services to make some arrests. The Israelis had given him a new list of thirty-eight suspects. But those close to Arafat did not believe such an operation was even possible. Outside Ramallah, in the West Bank, the Palestinian police were powerless. Saeb Erekat declared to anyone willing to listen: "The Israelis demand that the Authority do certain things, then, they tie Arafat's hands and feet, put a blindfold over his eyes, throw him in the sea, and demand that he swim! And, they add: If he does not swim, he is not a credible partner!"[10] December 4 was relatively calm. During the morning, a suicide bomber exploded in front of a hotel in Jerusalem without harming anyone.

Arafat decided to act where he felt he still had some capability of doing so. In Gaza, Sheik Ahmed Yassin, the founder of Hamas, was placed under surveillance at his home. Palestinian police barricades blocked his access. His telephone line was cut. Other leaders of the organization entered clandestinely. But, in no time, hundreds of militants and partisans of Hamas poured out into the street, throwing stones at police, who began firing their guns into the air. Several attempts to apprehend one of Yassin's bodyguards failed, one after another. The crowd resisted it. In Gaza as well, Arafat was growing increasingly powerless.

For better or worse, Anthony Zinni pursued his mission and brought together—without significant results—the heads of security of both sides. These men, who had known each other for years, spoke in a completely amicable way during coffee breaks, but resumed a stern tone as soon as serious discussions began. The Palestinians complained of having received a contradictory list of people to arrest. Finally, exhausted by the bickering between the two sides, the American general, with the help of a representative of the CIA, concocted a definitive list of thirty-three terrorist suspects.[11] On December 7, in an interview on an Israeli television station, Arafat proudly announced that seventeen of the thirty-three were under lock and key. The problem was that it was not possible to incarcerate them either in a prison or in a police station because such sites risked being bombed by the Israelis.

To a journalist from one of the main Israeli television stations, who made the observation that the Americans viewed these arrests as a farce, an extremely irritated Arafat responded: "Enough! What are the Americans doing there? The Americans are on your side and give you everything. Who gave you your planes? The Americans. Who gave you your tanks? The Americans. . . . Your leaders won't stop their campaigns against us. You say that I'm bin Laden, and the Autonomous Authority the Taliban. Am I bin Laden?" Israeli sources made it known that only ten of the thirty-three suspects had been arrested.

Rudy Giuliani arrived in Jerusalem accompanied by Michael Bloomberg, his successor to the mayoralty in New York. Applauded during his trip, he visited the site of some attacks on December 9. "We feel," he said, "a kinship with the people of Israel. We have been close and I think that, since September 11, we are even closer!" The visit received a great deal of coverage from the American press. Israel-New York: both were involved in the same fight.

In Jerusalem, another American was at the end of his rope. Anthony Zinni was threatening to throw in the towel. During another meeting of the Israeli and Palestinian heads of security in the King David Hotel in Jerusalem, he threatened to return to Washington if neither side presented tangible ideas that would allow progress to be made toward a cease-fire. And then he left the room. The American mediator decided to base his own plan on the premise of a progressive cease-fire. As such, a superior security committee composed of political leaders and principal military leaders would meet regularly under his supervision in order to oversee the implementation of agreements. The next day, Zinni regained some of his optimism. The Palestinians had submitted a plan of action "against extremist organizations" that was broader, they said, "than that which had been implemented in 1996 when hundreds of Islamic militants had been placed behind bars."

On Tuesday December 11, Zinni asked the Israelis to reduce their operations in the West Bank and Gaza as much as possible for forty-eight hours. Ariel Sharon and Shaul Mofaz agreed. The IDF would only act in situations of legitimate defense, to respond to mortar fire or to kill a terrorist on the point of committing an attack. The number of attacks appeared to diminish during the day on December 12, but the situation deteriorated again before six in the evening. There were two explosions next to a bus one kilometer from the entrance to Emmanuel, an ultra-orthodox community. Several passengers were killed on the spot. Those who were lightly wounded tried to get out through the windows, but one of the three attackers from Hamas threw grenades on the survivors while the two others opened fire on the emergency and rescue workers arriving from the settlement. The toll: eleven Israelis were killed, and twenty-three wounded. One of the terrorists was killed, and the two others managed to escape to Nablus.

ARAFAT IS OUT OF PLAY

Once again, Israel did not blame Hamas, but pointed the finger at the Palestinian Authority, which had nevertheless hastened to condemn the attack. According to a statement released in Ramallah:

> [T]he Palestinian leadership continues to work energetically to stabilize the situation despite the escalation perpetrated by Israel, its bombings, its assassinations in Hebron, Anabta, Tulkarm, and Khan Younis, and the siege inflicted upon all of the villages, the towns, and the sectors inhabited by the Palestinians. The Palestinian Authority rejects the Israeli accusations that it is responsible for the escalation and that it

did not respond positively to Anthony Zinni's proposal for a forty-eight hour cease-fire.

This had no effect. Following Sharon's lead, the Israeli government broke off all contact with the Autonomous Authority and declared Arafat "out of play." The following day, tanks moved into Ramallah, destroying Palestinian radio antennas several hundred meters from the Muqata, Arafat's headquarters. In the Gaza Strip, Israeli units occupied buildings near the Netzarim settlement while in the Khan Younis refugee camp bulldozers destroyed fifteen houses. Zinni immediately asked for a meeting with Sharon. Did his mission still make sense after the decision of the Israeli government to burn all bridges with the Palestinian Authority? The Israeli prime minister had absolutely no intention of changing his mind. The Bush administration confirmed that an impasse had been reached and recalled the American envoy to Washington "for consultations." While he was in the United States, seven attacks occurred, resulting in forty-five Israeli deaths. The toll for the IDF operations in the West Bank and Gaza was forty-nine deaths for the Palestinian side.

In an interview with Tim Russert on NBC's *Meet the Press,* Colin Powell explained:

Arafat is not irrelevant, because he is the head of the Palestinian Authority, and made head of the Palestinian Authority through a process that came out of the Oslo Accord of 1993, and it is somebody that we recognize as the head of the Palestinian Authority, and he is seen by the Palestinian people as the leader of the Palestinian people. . . . We created the circumstances as recently as just a month ago, when I gave my speech in Louisville, when President Bush spoke at the United Nations General Assembly announcing a vision for a Palestinian state as an American position. We then created a way for the two sides to talk to each other. We sent General Zinni over to try to get that dialogue going. And all of that was blown up by these terrorist organizations on the Palestinian side. They are attacking Mr. Arafat just as surely as they are attacking the people of Israel and the state of Israel. And Mr. Arafat has to act against them.

While the Israeli army pursued its strikes throughout the Gaza Strip and the West Bank, Arafat, after stormy discussions with Miguel Moratinos and Terje Larsen, issued the order to close all institutions linked to Hamas and Islamic Jihad. On the evening of December 16, the day before the Muslim feast of Idr Fitr, he made a speech that was broadcast on radio and television:

> I repeat today my call for a total and immediate halt to all military operations. I repeat my call to stop all operations, especially suicide attacks. We will punish all those who do not respect this order, we will punish the organizers of these attacks and those who execute them, and will pursue them. We will only allow the existence of a single authority; we will not allow the credibility of the Palestinian leadership and its decisions to be weakened. . . . I know what the Israelis are plotting. They are preparing for military aggression and to use attacks against their civilians as a pretext. We must not give Sharon and his military institutions the pretext to intensify their aggressions against our people and allow them to qualify our legitimate resistance as terrorist.

Arafat concluded by proposing the resumption of negotiations with Israel.

The organizations in question responded, in tracts distributed in the West Bank and Gaza, that they were not interested in Arafat's cease-fire. Furthermore, they accused him of submitting to the diktats of America and Israel. Hamas and Jihad swore to continue the struggle until the liberation of all occupied territories was achieved. On December 18, in Herzliya, in the context of a conference on national security, Shaul Mofaz observed with satisfaction: "The painful attacks that we have endured have resulted in Arafat losing a large part of his legitimacy and have, by contrast, legitimized Israeli responses, which permits us greater freedom of action."

THE VIOLENCE SUBSIDES

Arafat gathered the decision-making bodies of Fatah in order to obtain their help in imposing a cease-fire. Marwan Barghouti, the secretary general of the organization for the West Bank, called militants—over whom he still had some influence—on their cell phones. Notably, he had a long conversation with Raed Karmi, the head of the al-Aqsa Martyrs Brigades in Tulkarm, who decided to give in and prohibit an anti-Israeli attack that had been planned by one of his subordinates. All of this was heard in real time by Shin Bet, who observed that Arafat was at least making an effort.

In Gaza, things were going much worse. Palestinian police tried to arrest Abdel Aziz Rantisi, one of the most virulent Hamas leaders. His bodyguards opened fire on police while dozens of militants, most of them armed, took up positions within the neighborhood. Seven of the badly wounded were taken to Shifa Hospital, in the city center. The Autonomous Authority had less difficulty apprehending fifteen of its officers who, in the south of the Gaza Strip, refused to respect the cease-fire.

Under such conditions, it was necessary for Israel to make a gesture. Binyamin Ben-Eliezer authorized 5,800 Palestinians to return to their jobs in Israel, while 6,000 others were authorized to return to work in the industrial zones in the settlements. In Ramallah, Terje Larsen, the emissary of the United Nations secretary-general, revealed during a press conference that the unemployment rate in Gaza exceeded 50 percent. During the first twelve months of the intifada, the IDF imposed checkpoints in the West Bank for 240 days, and in Gaza for 342 days.

In Bethlehem, preparations for the traditional Christmas mass were in full swing. But in Saint Catherine's Basilica, one chair would remain empty: that of Yasser Arafat. Ariel Sharon had in effect decided against allowing him to travel. He could not leave Ramallah. The Palestinian chairman let it be understood that he would attend midnight mass no matter what, even if he had to get there on foot. The IDF reinforced its checkpoints between Ramallah and Jerusalem, and soldiers searched every vehicle in which Arafat was capable of hiding.

Meanwhile, Shimon Peres was pursuing his talks with Abu Ala, the chairman of the Palestinian parliament. He was on a quest for a magic formula that would give Palestinians the hope for a political solution. Persuaded that these meetings would lead nowhere, Sharon gave Peres free rein to do this. At least they would keep his minister of foreign affairs busy.

The new year 2002 got off to an optimistic start. Shin Bet observed a significant decrease in security alerts—sometimes fewer than twenty per day—as opposed to a hundred only a month before. The Israeli government announced that it anticipated a progressive withdrawal from autonomous sectors occupied by the IDF in the West Bank and Gaza. That meant a withdrawal of tanks which, in Ramallah, were still stationed a hundred meters from Arafat's headquarters. This announcement—which the Palestinians did not believe—was made the day before Zinni restarted his mission.

THE *KARINE A*

Accompanied by Aaron Miller, the American emissary arrived in Tel Aviv on January 2. Sharon was impatiently waiting for him. He believed that he was finally in possession of definitive proof of Arafat's duplicity. Several weeks earlier, Mossad had located, from the island of Kish (off the Iranian coast of the Persian Gulf), the departure of a ship commanded by an official of the Palestinian navy. The *Karine A* had been purchased in Beirut in November 2001 by the holder of an Iraqi passport: Ali Mohammed Abbas, the leader of the Palestinian organization responsible for the terrorist attack against the cruise ship *Achille Lauro* in 1985. Kish Island was administered by the Iranian Revolutionary Guard. On December 14, the Israelis asked the American navy to track the boat. The Pentagon accepted the mission, and a destroyer, the *USS John Young*, followed it from afar. It appeared that the *Karine A* had made a stop in the port of Hodeida in Yemen, where it took on supplementary cargo, apparently a shipment of arms. Then it departed on December 29, 2001, apparently in the direction of the Suez Canal.

Zinni and Miller were led to an out-of-the-way terminal where Avi Dichter, the head of Shin Bet, Ephraim Halevy, the head of Mossad, and General Aharon Zeevi-Farkash, chief of military intelligence, were waiting for them. The Israelis informed the Americans that an operation would take place within the next twenty-four hours involving the interception of the *Karine A*, a ship loaded with arms destined for the Palestinian Authority.[12]

On January 3, Zinni started his day by having breakfast with Sharon at his ranch in the Negev. The American general asked the prime minister if he would authorize him to give Arafat the news: "I want to see," he said, "the expression on his face when I tell him."[13] Sharon agreed, but asked Zinni not to reveal anything before noon, the time when the navy commandos were to act.

Zinni traveled to Ramallah. In Arafat's office, the discussion was interrupted at 11:45 a.m. when his advisors suddenly burst into the room and whispered in his ear. Zinni grasped that the Palestinians had just learned of the capture of the *Karine A*. Zinni looked Arafat straight in the eye and demanded: "What is going on?"

> **Arafat:** "It's nothing!"
> **Zinni:** "I know what's happening. I know that this is about the *Karine A*. I know that it is carrying arms. . . . I know that the Israelis were close to intercepting it. Obviously, they succeeded!"
> **Arafat:** "It's not our boat. . . . No! No! It's an Israeli plot. We have nothing to do with this!"[14]

He assured Saeb Erekat that it was an Israeli plot. Nervous throughout the rest of the day, Arafat paced up and down his office repeating: "It's a manipulation! It's a manipulation!"[15]

The ship was seized in international waters, on the coast of the Saudi port of Djedda. To their American colleagues, the Israeli intelligence services attested to the presence of Hezbollah officials during the loading of the boat on Kish Island. In Washington, Dick Cheney and his neoconservative team at the White House drove the nail into the coffin: Arafat wants war.

The Israeli intelligence services prepared for a press conference in the southern Israeli port town of Eilat, on the very dock where the cargo of the *Katrine A* was revealed: 122 millimeter Kaytusha rockets; mortar shells made in Russia, China, North Korea, and Iran; antitank missiles and rockets, scuba equipment, night vision goggles, etc. In addition, the captain of the ship was Omar Akawi, a colonel in the Palestinian navy. When Akawi appeared on television, he swore that the arms were destined for the Palestinian Authority and that he was under the orders of Abdel Awadallah, an advisor to Arafat. Arafat promised an investigation in due form. Palestinian spokesmen asserted that their boss had nothing to do with the *Karine A*.

In Cairo, President Hosni Mubarak expressed doubts concerning the actual destination of the boat, which would have necessarily had to pass through the Suez Canal to arrive in Gaza. There, the *Karine A* would have been subjected to an obligatory search, without even taking into account that the head of Egyptian intelligence had an excellent relationship with Shin Bet. To many experts, it seemed strange that such a ship carrying illegal weapons would travel through the Persian Gulf and the Red Sea, especially given that the United States intensely monitors and boards such ships in search of al-Qaeda terrorists and smuggled goods. At the headquarters of military intelligence in Tel Aviv, officials shook their heads. They had found no formal evidence implicating Arafat personally in the *Karine A* affair. And moreover, everything that occurred at the Muqata was totally transparent to the Israeli intelligence services.[16] They also recalled that the PLO had, in the past, earned some juicy profits engaging in arms trafficking. In Washington, for the first time, the State Department avoided taking a position. Later, after receiving "proof" from Israeli intelligence and a confused letter from Arafat, the White House concluded that the Palestinian chairman was lying.

Zinni was worried. Did the Israelis want to suspend negotiations? "After the capture of the *Karine A* and after all of its arms had been exposed, and with all the publicity surrounding this affair, I asked the Israelis: 'Good, where are we? I mean to say, should I leave now?' Are you going to say: 'Look what Arafat did. We are not going to negotiate'? And, they surprised me when they said: 'No, let's continue. . . . We're going to negotiate. We're ready to work with you.'"[17]

Two meetings on the coordination of security took place without result. Binyamin Ben-Eliezer, the defense minister, revealed that the number of attacks had diminished for the third consecutive week. He let it be understood that at this pace the seven days of total calm demanded by Israel prior to the implementation of the Tenet plan could soon be in sight. But Hamas was watching. Two Palestinians disguised as Israeli policemen attacked an IDF position near the Kerem Shalom kibbutz close to Gaza, in Israeli territory. The assailants were killed during an exchange of gunfire, but only after they had killed an officer and three Israeli soldiers. The next day, tanks and bulldozers destroyed approximately thirty houses in the Rafah refugee camp. According to the army, these were Palestinian positions.

THE DEATH OF RAED KARMI

In the West Bank, relative calm continued until January 14. On that day, Raed Karmi was killed in an explosion in the street when he was on his way to the home of his mistress. Shin Bet had finally figured out his itinerary, but it was crucial to avoid the appearance that it was a targeted assassination—the execution of the leader of the al-Aqsa Martyrs Brigades threatened to completely obliterate the cease-fire. That is why, while a special unit had indeed planted explosives along his route, Israeli officials asserted it was a "work accident" by claiming that Karmi was killed by explosives he was transporting. Military correspondents learned the truth: it was a successful operation resulting in the liquidation of the assassin of a dozen Israelis and the perpetrator of numerous attacks.

General Moshe Yaalon, the deputy chief of staff, explained his thoughts at the time: "I thought it would work if we had a situation that resembled a work-related accident. We could get rid of the threat [that Karmi represented] without suffering the consequences. But, to my great regret, as always in Israel, whether something is done openly or covertly, there is always someone who very quickly tells his friends. Arafat uses that to escape pressure."[18]

The al-Aqsa Martyrs Brigades reacted immediately and the cease-fire collapsed. Near Nablus, that evening, an Israeli was assassinated. The next day, an American was kidnapped near Beit Jalla. His bullet-ridden body was discovered later. The next day, another Palestinian member of the al-Aqsa Martyrs Brigades opened fire on a religious ceremony organized in honor of young girls in Hadera, north of Tel Aviv, killing six and wounding thirty.

Arafat nevertheless tried to make promises to the Americans and the Israelis. In Ramallah, Ahmed Saadat, the successor to Abu Ali Mustafa to the leadership of the PFLP, was arrested and taken to the Muqata. The Israelis accused him of being the instigator behind the assassination of Rehavam Zeevi, which occurred on October 17. But PFLP militants threatened to attack Arafat if Saadat was not freed.

THE FIRST SUICIDE ATTACK BY FATAH

For its part, the IDF continued its operations against the Autonomous Authority and destroyed the building occupied by the national radio station, Saut el Falastin, in Ramallah. On January 22 near a bus stop in central Jerusalem, a Palestinian shot and killed two women and wounded forty in the name of the al-Aqsa Martyrs Brigades. On January 25, a suicide bomber from Islamic Jihad exploded in Tel Aviv: thirty-four wounded. And then, on January 27, Wafa Idris activated her explosives on Jaffa Road, right in the center of Jerusalem. One woman was killed and 150 people were wounded. This marked the first time that Fatah had committed a suicide attack. It was also the first time that a woman played the role of suicide bomber. She was twenty-four years old, a native of Bethlehem, divorced, and working as a nurse at the Palestinian Red Crescent in Ramallah. Saeb Erekat, the negotiator, also a Fatah militant, henceforth felt alienated from his own movement: "I was truly shocked when Fatah began to send suicide bombers. I spoke to people, and they looked at me with surprise.

Pointing at me, they asked, why is this guy stuck on something called a 'peace process' that doesn't exist?"

Anthony Zinni returned for consultations in Washington. The American administration believed that given the current circumstances, the chances of achieving a cease-fire were slim. And so Zinni did not return to the region for the moment. Matti Steinberg, the Shin Bet analyst, thought that all of this was perfectly predictable: "It would have been necessary to view the situation as a whole, not only the immediate results but also the long-term consequences. It was obvious that the assassination of Karmi would lead to the end of the cease-fire."[19]

During the next few weeks, the region slid once again into violence. Israeli retaliations followed Palestinian attacks. Palestinians responded to IDF operations with new attacks. On February 8, 2002, Binyamin Ben-Eliezer was in Washington, where Vice-President Cheney told him: "From my point of view, you can do what you want to Arafat, even hang him!"[20]

On February 11, hand-made rockets and mortar shells were fired from Gaza onto Israeli settlements. In response, the air force unleashed a series of strikes on Palestinian security bases in Gaza City. Militants of Islamic Jihad and Hamas who were imprisoned there were released during the bombing. Thirty-seven Palestinians were wounded, including schoolchildren who were just getting out of class.

HEZBOLLAH

Only a few politicians were paying attention to the reinforcement of Hezbollah, the Shiite militia in south Lebanon. Several military intelligence officers decided to sound the alarm. They contacted Ron Leshem, from *Yedihot Aharonot*, who published a lengthy article describing the danger facing Israel:

> The huge weapons shipments that continue to flow with variable regularity from Tehran to Damascus, and from there via convoys to Hezbollah command centers in Lebanon, provide the organization with an arsenal of weaponry

of an extent that no other terror organization has in the world—from 5.56 mm bullets to long-range missiles. On the strategic side, Hezbollah has 107 mm Kaytushas with a range up to 10 km, upgraded Kaytushas of 122 mm with a range up to 20 km, Fagr missiles with a range of 45 km, and the advanced Fagr 7 with a range of 70 km. These missiles can reach all of northern Israel to Haifa and Tiberias, and threaten a population of close to 1.5 million Israelis. They also have 130 mm cannon with a maximum range of 27 km, and mortars compared to which Palestinian weaponry is like an improvised firecracker. There are advanced anti-tank missiles.[21]

This article passed almost unnoticed. Nothing was done to prepare the IDF and Israel's civilian population for a potential war with Lebanon.

THE SAUDI INITIATIVE

On February 17, 2002, Thomas Friedman, columnist for the *New York Times*, published a scoop. On a visit to Saudi Arabia, he was invited to dine with Prince Abdullah, the designated heir. That evening, he suggested that the prince propose a new peace plan to the Arab League: in exchange for a total withdrawal of Israel to the June 4, 1967 lines, and the creation of a Palestinian state, the twenty-two members of the Arab League would establish diplomatic and commercial relations with Israel by offering security guarantees. The prince responded that he had exactly the same idea in mind, and explained to the *New York Times* envoy: "I wanted to find a way to make clear to the Israeli people that the Arabs don't reject or despise them. But the Arab people do reject what their leadership is now doing to the Palestinians, which is inhumane and oppressive. And I thought of this as a possible signal to the Israeli people."[22] These major statements were published with the assent of the Saudi leader. The news was welcomed in Jerusalem with surprise. Ariel Sharon decided not to react. The Saudi initiative was not official and his advisors believed it was only a gimmick.

February 19, 2002 was a particularly bloody day. Nine Palestinians were killed during aerial strikes, bombings, and exchanges of gunfire. On the road to Nablus, six Israelis, soldiers and settlers, were killed by a Palestinian gunman. The next day, nine Palestinians were killed in Nablus, two others in Ramallah, and four in Gaza. There were a dozen wounded. On February 21, the offensive continued. A missile exploded near Arafat's office in Ramallah. That evening, for the first time since the beginning of the month, representatives of Israeli and Palestinian security met and came to an agreement. The Palestinians promised to do all they could to try to calm the streets in the West Bank and Gaza, and would make a serious effort to prevent attacks. The Israelis, for their part, would work to cease operations in autonomous zones, to open military checkpoints near several Palestinian towns, and to limit "targeted killings" to terrorists on the verge of committing an attack. On the occasion of the Muslim feast of Idl Atra, inhabitants of the West Bank would be permitted to come pray at the al-Aqsa mosque in Jerusalem: at least, Binyamin Ben-Eliezer gave instructions along these lines to the IDF.

On February 24, the Israeli government authorized Arafat to leave his headquarters but not the municipal boundaries of Ramallah. The PFLP militants responsible for the assassination of Rehavam Zeevi were arrested and held in Ramallah. Tanks that had been positioned next to the Muqata left the area.

The Israeli government did not officially react to the Saudi initiative, and pressure was mounting. Ariel Sharon made it known that he would try to find channels of communication with the Saudis in order to "clarify" the Israeli position. Several ministers, including Shimon Peres and Meir Sheetrit, showed some enthusiasm, and Moshe Katsav, the president of the state, announced that he was willing to fly to Saudi Arabia. This proposal was immediately condemned by the Arab press which proceeded to accuse Israel of trying to reap the benefits of normalization without paying the price. While Arafat and his advisors were enthusiastic (Saeb Erekat even called this initiative "an historic endeavor"), the Islamists were leading the charge against the Saudi peace proposal. On February 25, in Gaza, Hamas leader Mahmoud Zahar said that "talking about the Saudi idea at this time has a negative impact on the Arab path because none of the Arab nations accepts Israel . . . Arabs and Palestinians in particular are against normalization and recognition of the so-called Israel."[23]

On February 26, White House spokesman Ari Fleischer announced that President Bush called Prince Abdullah to praise his ideas regarding full Arab-Israeli normalization once a comprehensive peace agreement was achieved. He added that "while the president welcomed the Saudi ideas as a 'note of hope,' Saudi statements had not changed anything on the ground in the Middle East."[24]

The same day, *Haaretz* published an editorial titled "An Important Saudi Initiative," calling on Sharon, "who promised to bring peace and security, to undertake a sincere and serious examination of the significance of the Saudi initiative and its ramifications."[25] The prime minister would react one month later.

But on March 1, the IDF resumed operations in the West Bank. Tanks and armored troop transports occupied the refugee camps in Jenin and Balata, next to Nablus. The following day in Jerusalem, a suicide bomber from the al-Aqsa Martyrs Brigades exploded in the ultra-orthodox neighborhood of Mea Shearim killing eleven people, including six children and an entire family. On March 3, a lone Palestinian gunman attacked an IDF roadblock north of Ramallah. He killed seven soldiers and three settlers, and wounded six others. Israel retaliated by bombing Palestinian police targets. Two members of the Palestinian intelligence services were killed. In Jerusalem, Ariel Sharon found a way to respond to the Saudi initiative. He said that it was "unacceptable and dangerous for the security of Israel, for it calls for a total withdrawal from all occupied territories, which would be contrary to resolutions 242 and 338 of the Security Council, which call for a withdrawal from territories."[26]

On March 4, Binyamin Ben-Eliezer made apologies: a tank had made an identification error and fired on a vehicle in Ramallah, killing a woman and five children. In all, throughout the day, seventeen Palestinians were killed. On March 5, a terrorist from the al-Aqsa Martyrs Brigades sprayed the patrons of a Tel Aviv restaurant with machine-gun fire: three dead, twenty-five wounded. On March 8, after a new round of suicide attacks and Israeli responses, the death toll came to twenty-nine Palestinians—the heaviest in a single day since the start of the intifada. The following Saturday evening, a Hamas suicide bomber exploded in front of the Moment restaurant, 30 meters from Ariel Sharon's residence in Jerusalem: eleven dead, fifty wounded. The air force again did not retaliate against Hamas but destroyed instead Arafat's presidential headquarters in Gaza City.

ZINNI'S PROPOSAL

On March 13, 2002, Anthony Zinni returned. Ariel Sharon informed him at the outset that an agreement could be achieved. The last meeting of the joint security commission had been promising: the Palestinians were working to assume control of the autonomous zones from which the IDF forces could then withdraw. Five days later, Dick Cheney himself arrived in Israel for an official visit. His entourage announced that he would only meet with Arafat if the latter made real progress in the fight against terrorism. Finally, Zinni was charged with informing the head of the PLO that he could travel to Cairo to meet with Dick Cheney, but only if Arafat made an effort to track illegal arms and made a certain number of arrests. Given the current climate, the task seemed impossible, for it would take just another attack to throw everything into question. And, indeed, just such an attack occurred on March 20, when a suicide bomber from Islamic Jihad exploded on a bus in Galilee, killing seven Israelis. Twenty-four hours later, a member of the al-Aqsa Martyrs Brigades committed suicide under the same conditions in Jerusalem, killing three and wounding ninety.

On March 23, in response to the Saudi prince's proposal, Ariel Sharon suggested that he go to Beirut in person to present his own peace plan at the Arab League summit, a proposal that was immediately rejected by all interested parties, who viewed it as a provocation. Arafat also wanted to make the trip. And George Bush, following the advice of the Saudis, asked Sharon to authorize him to travel to Beirut. But the Israeli government imposed such stringent conditions that Arafat decided to stay behind in Ramallah after all.

Anthony Zinni wanted to reach an agreement before the start of the Arab summit. Such a statement would be difficult to ignore as the Arab world prepared to adopt a resolution proposing the recognition of Israel after a withdrawal from the occupied territories. On March 24, 2002, Zinni submitted his proposal for compromise to the Israelis and the Palestinians. It consisted of a new timetable for the implementation of the Tenet plan, which in turn would set the stage for the implementation of the Mitchell report. Arafat had first to arrest Palestinian security officers accused of terrorism. In exchange, Israel would withdraw from specified sectors. The superior security committee would be resuscitated in order to oversee both the arrest of suspects by the Palestinians and the simultaneous Israeli withdrawal.

Sharon's entourage studied the proposal and concluded that it was favorable to Israel by 80 percent because the Palestinians had more obligations than the Israelis.

Finally, on March 26, Sharon gave the green light. Avi Dichter and the other Israeli security officials then met with Zinni and informed him: "The prime minister agrees: Israel accepts your proposal for compromise." The American general was dumbstruck: the Israelis had not asked for any amendments! He thought that was fantastic, and said as much to his interlocutors.[27] He thought that the Palestinians would give their own green light the next day. Avi Dichter recounted Zinni's impending disappointment at the time: "Zinni told us that a new day was dawning . . . We answered: 'Don't start dreaming too soon.' Zinni asked: 'What do you mean? The Palestinians are going to respond negatively?' We told him: 'They won't give you any response at all!'"[28]

Thanks to its surveillance, Shin Bet knew that Palestinian officials were extremely divided on the proposal, and did not want to run the risk of replying too quickly.[29] Mohammed Dahlan pushed Arafat to accept the American proposals: "If we do nothing, if you do not give me the order to arrest the heads of Hamas in Gaza, the Israelis will unleash a major operation in the West Bank after a particularly bloody suicide attack."[30] Arafat hesitated and replied that he was going to think about it.

March 27 dissipated in Palestinian-American quibbling. Zinni received the impression that his interlocutors would never agree to his plan.

All the less so since Arafat was extremely preoccupied: he was trying to intervene in the debates at the Arab summit via satellite-video hookup. The system was not working: his Syrian adversaries, who controlled the Lebanese ground station, were blocking the transmission. By the time he finally succeeded in making his speech by webcam, most of the Arab leaders had already left the room.

That evening, the Israelis invited Zinni to the Passover seder, while in the Muqata, in Ramallah, the Palestinians continued their discussions. Not for long, however, for the Hamas leadership decided to put an end to what could have marked the beginning of an agreement. In Tulkarm, Abbas el-Sayyd, the leader of one of the organization's cells, equipped Abdel Basset Odeh with a belt packed with explosives. At twenty-five years of age, the young Palestinian from Qalqilya volunteered to commit the suicide attack. Driven to Netanya, he entered a ballroom of the Park Hotel, where a number of families were seated for the seder. In what was to become known as the "Passover massacre," thirty Israelis were killed and 144 wounded.

Zinni telephoned Arafat to tell him to condemn the attack immediately and to accept his proposal. The head of the PLO cooperated and decided to accept the American plan. Shortly after midnight, Saeb Erekat left Ramallah to deliver a letter from Arafat to a chauffeur at the United States consulate in Jerusalem. He crossed an immense convoy of tanks, ambulances, buses, and soldiers. On his return to the Muqata, he told Arafat that something very important was going to happen.[31] Arafat called Mohammed Dahlan and gave the order to arrest the heads of Hamas in Gaza. "Too late! The Israelis are going to reoccupy the West Bank," the head of preventative security in Gaza told him.[32] Early the next day, March 28, al-Manar, Hezbollah television, broadcast from Lebanon the video recording made by Abdel Basset Odeh, the suicide bomber. At the same time in Beirut, the Arab League adopted the Saudi initiative:

Emanating from the conviction of the Arab countries that a military solution to the conflict will not achieve peace or provide security for the parties, the council:

1. Requests Israel to reconsider its policies and declare that a just peace is its strategic option as well.

2. Further calls upon Israel to affirm:

I-Full Israeli withdrawal from all the territories occupied since 1967, including the Syrian Golan Heights, to the June 4, 1967 lines, as well as the remaining occupied Lebanese territories in the south of Lebanon.

II-Achievement of a just solution to the Palestinian refugee problem to be agreed upon in accordance with U.N. General Assembly Resolution 194.

III-The acceptance of the establishment of a sovereign independent Palestinian state on the Palestinian territories occupied since June 4, 1967 in the West Bank and Gaza Strip, with East Jerusalem as its capital.

3. Consequently, the Arab countries affirm the following:

I-Consider the Arab-Israeli conflict ended, and enter into a peace agreement with Israel, and provide security for all the states of the region.

II-Establish normal relations with Israel in the context of this comprehensive peace.

4. Assures the rejection of all forms of Palestinian patriation which conflict with the special circumstances of the Arab host countries.

5. Calls upon the government of Israel and all Israelis to accept this initiative in order to safeguard the prospects for peace and stop the further shedding of blood, enabling the Arab countries and Israel to live in peace and good neigh-

borliness and provide future generations with security, stability, and prosperity.

6. Invites the international community and all countries and
organizations to support this initiative.[33]

In Israel, this resolution went practically unnoticed in the media.
Foreign Minister Shimon Peres welcomed it and said: "[T]he details of
every peace plan must be discussed directly between Israel and the Palestinians, and to make this possible, the Palestinian Authority must put an
end to terror, the horrifying expression of which we witnessed just last
night in Netanya."[34] But a spokesman for his ministry declared that the
Saudi initiative ultimately anticipated the destruction of the state by stipulating the return of Palestinian refugees to Israel. This interpretation was,
at the very least, inexact. In fact, the text provided for a "just solution" to
the refugee problem "to be agreed upon in accordance with resolution 194
etc.," and did not claim "the right of return," which would in turn pave
the way for negotiations. In addition, the Arab League resolution did not
mention the Islamic holy sites in Jerusalem, the Dome of the Rock and the
al-Aqsa Mosque, only that the capital of a future Palestinian state should
be East Jerusalem. Matti Steinberg and several other Israeli analysts considered this a major turning point, for the Arab League had de facto recognized and proposed fully normalized relations with the Jewish state.

But the Israelis had other concerns. The IDF was on the brink of war.
Thousands of reservists were mobilized. The army prepared to unleash
operation "Rampart" in the West Bank. Tank units and infantry were
to reoccupy all of the towns and refugee camps, and the institutions of
the Palestinian Authority were to be partly destroyed. The Muqata was
to be completely surrounded, and Chairman Arafat would henceforth
be isolated, cut off from the rest of the world.

Saeb Erekat described his troubled thoughts at that crucial moment:
"Here is the father of the Palestinian national movement, the symbol of
our independence and our freedom, and I was wondering: Is this the end?
Are they going to kill him?"[35]

CHAPTER 5

A STRONG HAND AND
AN OUTSTRETCHED ARM

Preparations for the occupation of autonomous zones in the West Bank had begun in July 2001. At that time, the code name for the operation was "Different Field" because its primary purpose was the eradication, by military means, of the very concept of an autonomous Palestinian zone. On March 29, 2002, after the government gave the army the go-ahead, the military staff bestowed a new name upon the operation that was just as evocative: "Necessary Order." Several days later, Colonel Gal Hirsch told military leaders that yet another name was needed that was even more meaningful, one that was consistent with the policy of low-intensity conflict and that, more importantly, could win the war of "perception," or public opinion. In the end, the operation was named "Homat Magen" or "Defensive Shield."[1] The message was broadcast far and wide: the purpose of this "shield" was to protect Israeli civilians from terrorism. The military received the approbation of the Israeli press which, with few exceptions, had shown its patriotism since the beginning of the intifada. *Maariv*, a daily paper, stood out for its militancy and forty-eight hours after the Netanya attack, its headline—"A Strong Hand and An Outstretched

Arm"—was very clear. It was a citation from the Haggadah, the text read the night of the Passover seder referring to the exodus of the enslaved Israeli people from Egypt with divine assistance. In this context, the phrase read like a demand for a widespread military operation. On page three, another citation from the Haggadah—"Every generation, they rise against us to destroy us"—was illustrated by a photograph of the bloody scene at the Park Hotel.

Twenty thousand reservists were called into emergency service, but were only operational after a number of days. There were problems: most of the units had not participated in any form of training for years and their equipment, including bullet-proof vests, combat belts, and night-vision goggles, was extremely outdated. The infantry brigades, reinforced by tank units, were deployed on March 28.

In Ramallah, which was under curfew, the Muqata government compound was completely surrounded. Tanks destroyed company cars and 4x4's parked in front of the building. Two armored bulldozers began to destroy the perimeter wall. Arafat, under siege, feared the Israelis wanted to kill him, and said as much on Arab satellite television broadcasts: "God is great! I am ready to become a martyr, and may God honor me as a martyr in death!" Led by José Bové, the French labor activist, a group of foreign anti-globalization activists entered the building to act as human shields for Arafat.

The army faced little resistance—a few combatants armed with Kalashnikov rifles opened fire—and occupied the city relatively easily. Nevertheless, that evening Palestinian emergency services found the bodies of five members of Force 17, Arafat's Praetorian Guard, on the fourth floor of the Cairo-Amman Bank, a few of whom had been shot in the head. The final toll for the day would only become known later: 700 people had been arrested.

The army cut off access to Palestinian towns, but they were far from hermetically sealed, and several television news teams managed to circumvent blockades and get inside. They captured the images of destruction on film—the Palestinian victims, the arrests, the destruction caused by tanks—and broadcast them worldwide, instigating a virulent reaction in the Arab world. In Cairo and Amman, police dispersed thousands of protesters demonstrating against the violence. The opposition press in Jordan and Egypt demanded that diplomatic relations with Israel be severed. Demonstrations in support of the Palestinians also occurred in several European capitals, where Jewish communities also reported a troubling increase in anti-Semitic incidents, especially in France. Fearing the destabilization of moderate Arab governments, the American administration took a stand. George Bush declared:

> I fully understand Israel's need to defend herself; I respect that. . . . As she does so, I urge that their government, the Israeli government, makes sure that there is a path to peace as she secures her homeland. . . . I think Mr. Arafat could have done more three weeks ago and can do more today. I know I have been disappointed in his unwillingness to go 100 percent toward fighting terror.

The next day, the United States refrained from using its veto to oppose a Security Council resolution demanding the withdrawal of Israel from Palestinian cities, as well as condemning both suicide attacks and Israel's siege of Arafat's headquarters.

RAJOUB IS NEUTRALIZED

In Beitunia, a southern district in Ramallah, around fifteen tanks and armored troop transports surrounded the headquarters of Jibril Rajoub, the head of preventative security in the West Bank. By loudspeaker, officers threatened to bomb the building if those inside refused to come out. They had received orders from Shaul Mofaz and his deputy, Moshe Yaalon, to seize Hamas militants who were detained inside. The military leadership was convinced that Marwan Barghouti was among the 400 people who had sought refuge in the headquarters. At the start of the siege, Palestinian officers had brought their families there, thinking it would be a safe place. Rajoub, who had not been able to leave his home north of Ramallah due to the curfew, telephoned his Shin Bet contacts and assured them that Barghouti was not being held in his headquarters. They responded that they were unable to interfere and that the affair was entirely under the supervision of the military. General Dov Sedaka, the head of civil administration in the West Bank, who was present at this exchange, was incredulous. In his view, there could be no possible justification for the destruction of the main Palestinian security service, for it did not participate in any way in the intifada.[2] In *Boomerang*, journalists Raviv Drucker and Ofer Shelakh speculated that Mofaz and Yaalon were out to destroy the very idea that a Palestinian organization like Rajoub's preventative security service could contribute to Israel's security.[3] General Yossi Kuperwasser, head of the department of analysis of military intelligence, and Yitzhak Eytan, commander of the military region, asserted that there was no justification for the operation. Mofaz fired back: "I don't give a damn! I hope Rajoub kills himself!"[4]

While the army was continuing its incursions into Palestinian cities, Israel was subjected to a barrage of suicide attacks. During the afternoon of March 29, an eighteen-year-old Palestinian killed two Israelis in a Jerusalem supermarket. The next day, in the center of Tel Aviv, thirty people were wounded by a human bomb sent by the al-Aqsa Martyrs Brigades. Anguish was palpable in the Israeli streets. Restaurants and cafes emptied. Families forbade their children and teenagers to go out at night.

On March 31, yet another suicide attack took place in Haifa in a popular restaurant owned by a Jew and managed by Israeli Arabs. Both Muslims and Christians were counted among the fifteen dead and thirty wounded. Two hours later, another human bomb exploded in the Israeli settlement of Efrat in the West Bank, wounding four. The Efrat attack brought the toll to five suicide attacks in five days. Ariel Sharon appeared on national television and threatened:

> We are at war. And it is a war that reaches into our homes. The government of Israel, under my direction, has made all possible efforts to achieve a cease-fire. . . . And in reply, we have gotten terrorism. Terrorism! And still more terrorism!

We must fight terrorism, uproot these [savages], [and] dismantle their infrastructure, for there is no possible compromise with those who are prepared to die in order to kill innocent people and spread fear, terror, like the suicide attackers of the Twin Towers in New York!

From the Israeli-Lebanese border, Hezbollah fired rockets on Galilee without causing any casualties. This was the first time since the Israeli withdrawal from Lebanon in May 2000 that Kaytusha rockets had been launched at Israeli territory. In the West Bank cities of Tulkarm and Qalqilya, masked men belonging to the al-Aqsa Martyrs Brigades broke into prisons and assassinated a dozen Palestinians suspected of collaborating with Israel. On April 1, a soldier was shot and killed at a military checkpoint near Bethlehem. In Jerusalem, a Palestinian detonated his car bomb when a policeman tried to capture him, killing both men. Qalqilya was now occupied, and in some neighborhoods soldiers were attempting to conduct door-to-door searches. In Bethlehem, tanks rolled toward Manger Square.

The bombing of preventative security headquarters in Beitunia began the following night at two o'clock in the morning. Combat helicopters launched dozens of missiles on the building, followed by tanks firing mortar shells at point blank range. Rajoub insisted that his men would not surrender: "If the Israelis try to attack, there will be a massacre!" he warned. CIA representatives offered to mediate the conflict. Mohammed Dahlan, the head of preventative security in Gaza, and Mohammed Rashid, Arafat's financial advisor, participated in the negotiation by telephone since they, too, had been unable to leave Ramallah due to the curfew. Rajoub finally gave the order to his men to surrender late that morning. He claimed that he had received, through Dahlan, American assurances that the Israelis would not attempt to enter his headquarters. Dahlan denies ever having transferred such a message. The two men ceased speaking to one another. This silence would last for many years. Meanwhile, one hundred eighty-four people exited the building with their hands raised in the air. Around thirty were held, including members of Hamas,

Islamic Jihad, and the al-Aqsa Martyrs Brigades, most of whom had been sought by Israel. The others belonged to preventative security. All were handcuffed, blindfolded, and transported to Ofer, the neighboring detention camp. The next morning, Shin Bet officials came to meet with the Palestinian officers with whom they had cooperated only a few days before. Rajoub's men refused to shake hands with the Israelis: "Nothing," they said, "will ever be the same as it was before. You have betrayed us! There will no longer be any trust between us!"[5]

Jibril Rajoub was harshly criticized by the Palestinian public and various armed organizations for having turned his prisoners over to the Israelis. In their eyes, this was just more proof that any attempts at pragmatism, or even just cooperation with Shin Bet, only rewarded the Palestinian initiator with punishment by Israel. To anyone willing to listen, Rajoub asserted: "It is all the easier for Israel to proclaim that there is no one with whom to negotiate and that we are all terrorists."[6] A list of the terrorists captured in Beitunia and of the arms seized in the building was published by the IDF information services and the foreign affairs minister. The soldiers also found, hanging in plain sight in Rajoub's office, a wooden plaque bearing the Shin Bet insignia inscribed with the words: "To Jibril Rajoub, with thanks, from Avi Dichter."[7]

BETHLEHEM

On Tuesday April 3, in the middle of the night, while combat helicopters were firing missiles on several targets in Bethlehem, armored vehicles were taking the city, which was under curfew. Soldiers began to comb through some neighborhoods. The leaders of all the Christian churches made an appeal to George Bush to persuade him to put an immediate stop to "the inhuman tragedy that is taking place in the Holy Land." The Vatican issued a statement containing a similar message. The president of the United States responded the next day:

> The storms of violence cannot go on. Enough is enough! When
> an 18-year-old Palestinian girl is induced to blow herself up,
> and in the process kills a 17-year-old Israeli girl, the future

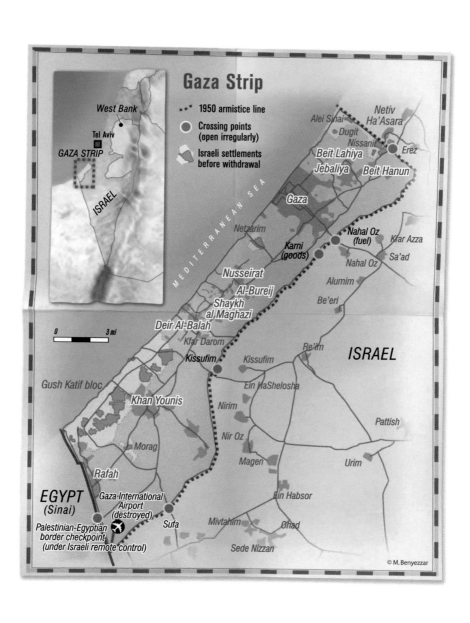

Gaza Strip

- ● ● 1950 armistice line
- ⬤ Crossing points (open irregularly)
- Israeli settlements before withdrawal

West Bank

Tel Aviv

GAZA STRIP

ISRAEL

MEDITERRANEAN SEA

Alei Sinai
Netiv Ha'Asara
Dugit
Nissanit
Erez
Beit Lahiya
Jebaliya
Beit Hanun

Gaza

Netzarim

Nahal Oz (fuel)
Kfar Azza
Karni (goods)
Sa'ad
Nahal Oz

Alumim
Be'eri

Nusseirat
Al-Bureij
Shaykh al Maghazi
Deir Al-Balah
Kfar Darom

Re'im

ISRAEL

Kissufim
Kissufim

Ein HaShelosha

Gush Katif bloc

Khan Younis
Nirim
Nir Oz

Pattish

Morag
Magen
Urim

Rafah
Ein Habsor

EGYPT (Sinai)
Gaza International Airport (destroyed)
Mivtahim
Ohad

Palestinian-Egyptian border checkpoint (under Israeli remote control)
Sufa
Sede Nizzan

0   3 mi

© M. Benyezzar

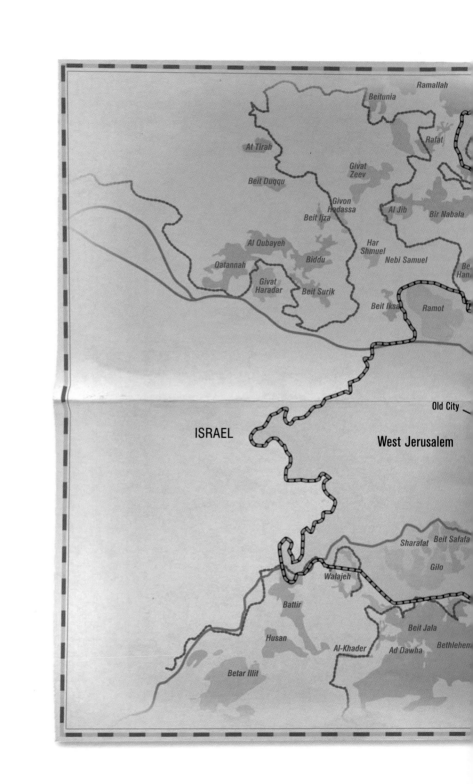

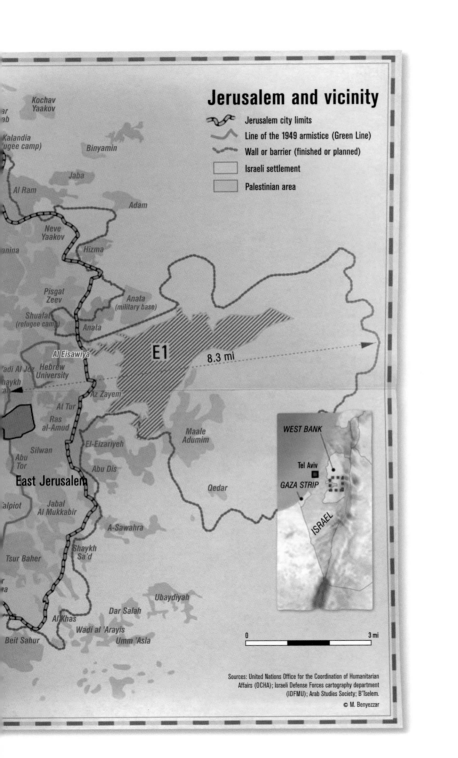

Jerusalem and vicinity

Jerusalem city limits

Line of the 1949 armistice (Green Line)

Wall or barrier (finished or planned)

Israeli settlement

Palestinian area

Kochav
Yaakov

ar
ab

Kalandia
(ugee camp)

Binyamin

Jaba

Al Ram

Adam

Neve
Yaakov

anina

Hizma

Pisgat
Zeev

Anata
(military base)

Shuafat
(refugee camp)

Anata

Al Eisawiya

adi Al Joz
Hebrew
University

haykh
al

Az Zayem

E1

8.3 mi

Al Tur

Ras
al-Amud

Maale
Adumim

Silwan

El-Eizariyeh

Abu
Tor

Abu Dis

East Jerusalem

Qedar

alpiot

Jabal
Al Mukkabir

A-Sawahra

Tsur Baher

Shaykh
Sa'd

Ubaydiyah

Al Khas

Dar Salah

Wadi al 'Arayis

Beit Sahur

Umm 'Asla

WEST BANK

Tel Aviv

GAZA STRIP

ISRAEL

0   3 mi

Sources: United Nations Office for the Coordination of Humanitarian
Affairs (OCHA); Israeli Defense Forces cartography department
(IDFMU); Arab Studies Society; B'Tselem.

© M. Benyezzar

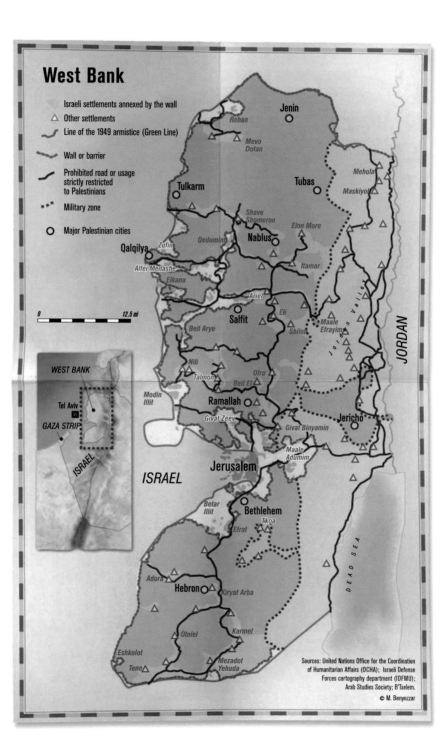

West Bank

Israeli settlements annexed by the wall
△ Other settlements
Line of the 1949 armistice (Green Line)

Wall or barrier

Prohibited road or usage
strictly restricted
to Palestinians

Military zone

○ Major Palestinian cities

0   12.5 ml

WEST BANK

Tel Aviv
GAZA STRIP
ISRAEL

Jenin ○
Rehan
Mevo
Dotan

Mehola

Tulkarm   Tubas ○
△   Maskiyot
Shave
Shomeron   Elon More
Qedumim   Nablus ○
Qalqilya   Zufin   Itamar
Alfei Menashe
Elkana
Ariel
Nili   Eli
Salfit ○   Maale
Beit Arye   Shilo   Efrayim
Modin   Ofra
Illit   Talmon   Beit El
Ramallah ○   Jericho ○
Givat Zeev   Givat Binyamin
Maale
Adumim
Jerusalem

ISRAEL

Betar
Illit   Bethlehem ●
Efrat   Tkoa

Adora
Hebron ○ Kiryat Arba

Otniel   Karmel
Eshkolot
Tene △   Mezadot
Yehuda

Jordan Valley

JORDAN

DEAD SEA

Sources: United Nations Office for the Coordination
of Humanitarian Affairs (OCHA); Israeli Defense
Forces cartography department (IDFMU);
Arab Studies Society; B'Tselem.

© M. Benyezzar

itself is dying. . . . The situation in which [Yasser Arafat] finds himself is largely of his own making. He's missed his opportunities and thereby betrayed the hopes of the people he's supposed to lead. Given his failure, the Israeli government feels it must strike against the terrorist networks that are killing its citizens . . . the occupation must end through withdrawal to secure and recognized boundaries consistent with United Nations Resolutions 242 and 338.

He also announced that he would be sending Colin Powell to the Middle East the following week.

Meanwhile, Anthony Zinni was still in the region. At the Palestinians' request, he was coordinating the humanitarian aid response by pulling strings with his Israeli contacts. Washington also requested more precise information from him about Arafat's situation, and so he went to pay a visit to the PLO leader. Accompanied by his bodyguards, who were clad in helmets and bullet-proof vests, Zinni made his way across the no-man's-land separating the Israeli forces from the Muqata. Alerted of his presence, television crews attempted to follow but were thwarted by Israelis who opened fire in their direction to keep them back.[8] Most of the buildings in the complex had suffered some damage. In one of the buildings that remained standing, more than a hundred people, lacking water and food, and even a telephone, had barricaded themselves. Arafat had holed himself up in a small room, submachine-gun in hand. His advisors were unshaven and completely exhausted. By contrast, the PLO leader seemed to be full of energy. Zinni saw that the old revolutionary was once again in his element. The discussion lasted ninety minutes without tangible results. All Israeli efforts to persuade the Palestinians to surrender were in vain. On a different evening, the European emissary Miguel Moratinos had to manage an emergency:

Arafat called me. On the telephone, I could hear an Israeli army loudspeaker booming: 'Give yourselves up! Come out with your hands in the air. . . . Come out of the headquarters!'

Arafat asked me: 'Please, try to call the Americans to put a stop to that!' I had two telephones, and on the other I called my American colleague, Bill Burns. I asked him to intervene, and we finally managed to put a stop to that.[9]

JENIN

In Jenin, the reservists ordered to take over the refugee camp found themselves caught in an ambush, which resulted in three dead soldiers. The Israeli army sent a bulldozer to systematically destroy homes. Palestinians counted fourteen deaths and confirmed that a massacre was under way in what they called "Jeningrad." When he was interviewed by American news programs, Saeb Erekat spoke of hundreds of deaths. He would later regret it. At this particular moment, the Israeli army was experiencing communications problems. Unable to interview members of the Israeli military on the ground, the international press had to rely on the statements of IDF spokesmen, which were often delivered in faulty English. After the broadcast the previous month of extremely harsh—and censored—images of an operation in Bethlehem, Binyamin Ben-Eliezer, the defense minister, prohibited the embedding of Israeli journalists in combat units. In so doing, Israel abandoned the media battlefield to the Palestinians, with one exception: the army had naturally been obliged to authorize coverage of the siege of the Church of the Nativity in Bethlehem, where nearly 200 Palestinians—some armed—had taken refuge. Any attack on a Christian holy site could have unimaginable consequences. Cranes and a balloon equipped with cameras were deployed on site to allow the military the best possible view.

Sporadic fighting was taking place elsewhere. In Ramallah, emergency services buried twenty-two Palestinians in a makeshift cemetery. In the West Bank village of Tubas, six Hamas officials were killed, including Qais Adwan, accused by Israel of having been one of the organizers of the Passover attack in Netanya.

Meanwhile, in the United States, deliberations over a potential invasion of Iraq were already beginning to play a role in the administration's approach to Israel and Palestine. On April 6, Tony Blair met with George Bush at his Texas ranch to discuss the offensive that the American president intended to launch. Blair explained to Bush that if he wanted to be certain of having the support of other Arab countries in his offensive against Saddam Hussein, he would have to move the peace process forward in Palestine. Accordingly, Bush once again called for Israel's withdrawal from the Palestinian territories "without delay." On CNN, then National Security Advisor, Condoleezza Rice, explained that "without delay" meant "today." To the American demand, a government official in Jerusalem retorted: "We will withdraw our forces without delay when we have finished the job."

On April 8, for the first time since the beginning of the offensive, Ariel Sharon addressed the Knesset. After justifying the length of the operation in the West Bank, he declared:

> Despite the extreme demands included in the resolutions of the conference of Arab leaders in Beirut, I welcome the fact that an important Arab leader such as Abdullah of Saudi Arabia has, for the first time, acknowledged Israel's right to exist within secure and recognized borders.
>
> There is a positive component of the Saudi initiative, but the details must be negotiated between the parties themselves. Peace negotiations cannot be dictated. They must be based on mutual respect and a genuine attempt to reach a compromise. In the absence of open dialogue between the parties, this initiative will remain devoid of any real content. . . . I take this opportunity to reiterate my proposal to meet immediately with moderate and responsible leaders in the Middle East. I am willing to go anywhere, without any preconditions from any party, to discuss peace.
>
> The operation that is underway will continue until the terrorist infrastructure is dismantled. When it has finished its work, the army will withdraw to designated buffer zones. . . . Arafat has created a terrorist regime that supports the training and dispatching of terrorists to kill Israelis.

He also presented documents that he claimed contained proof that the head of the PLO was financing terrorist groups. This "proof" consisted of receipts and requests for financing seized by the military in one the annexes of the Muqata. Dan Meridor, the minister responsible for oversight of the intelligence services, explained to his colleagues that these documents did not prove anything. Indeed, Arafat financed many organizations in the Palestinian territories in the West Bank, and neither Shin Bet nor military intelligence could ever establish a direct connection between Arafat and a terrorist attack. Shimon Peres shared this view. But publicly, Dan Meridor played the game and attributed responsibility for the attacks to Arafat.[10]

The IDF persisted in its operation in the Jenin refugee camp, despite the fact that the Palestinians were still accusing them of having massacred civilians. The army paid the price: on April 9, reservists were trapped in an ambush involving explosives, and thirteen of them were killed.

POWELL TO THE RESCUE

A few hours before the arrival of Secretary of State Powell in Tel Aviv, the army withdrew from twenty-four villages in the West Bank and announced that it had taken full control of the refugee camp in Jenin. Brigadier General Eyal Shlein, the commander of the operation, told several Israeli journalists that his men had not committed a "massacre" in the camp, and that, on the contrary, several leaders of armed Palestinian organizations had been captured.

On April 11, Colin Powell landed in Tel Aviv and readied himself for what would turn out to be some of the worst moments of his career. The following morning, the conversation during his first meeting with Ariel Sharon appeared to be focused on restoring calm. The prime minister was amenable to the possibility of a regional international conference with the stipulation that no preconditions be imposed, and that the Palestinians observe the cease-fire and accept both the Zinni and Mitchell plans. During the press conference that followed the meeting, the American secretary of state refrained from stating that Israel had to withdraw immediately from the autonomous territories, and rather was content to assert that "the parties must talk, the parties must begin negotiations." Sharon reiterated that Israel "is waging a war against the infrastructure of Palestinian terrorism, and Israel hopes to conclude this war very soon." Powell, who was due to take a tour of northern Israel, took leave of his host. Meanwhile, Sharon met with a CBS news team, and knowing perfectly well that Powell intended to meet with Arafat in Ramallah the next day, he nevertheless asserted that "it is necessary to find a replacement for Arafat. As long as all the world's leaders meet with him, it will be difficult to find someone who will agree to take his place as the head of the PLO."

At the same moment that Powell was getting into the helicopter scheduled to take him to Galilee, a muffled explosion shook Jerusalem. A twenty-year-old Palestinian woman had blown herself up near the Mahane Yehuda marketplace, killing six and wounding 104. Al-Manar, Hezbollah's television station, broadcast the demands of the al-Aqsa Martyrs Brigades. Binyamin Ben-Eliezer immediately issued the air force an order to fly Powell's helicopter over the site of the attack so that he could observe "Israeli reality" and be present for the arrival of the emergency services.[11] Then when he arrived at the Israeli-Lebanese border, the secretary of state observed that Hezbollah was shooting at IDF positions. The United States subsequently intervened with the Syrian and Lebanese governments and requested that they put a stop to the attacks of the Shiite militia.

Powell canceled his meeting with Arafat, which was supposed to occur the next day, and postponed it for another twenty-four hours. Saeb Erekat was responsible for organizing the meeting. He said:

> I was the only person authorized to go see Arafat. I literally had to hold my nose . . . like this! There were over 400 people in the headquarters who didn't have running water, not even for flushing toilets. Some of these people had not taken a shower for days. I told the Americans: 'Your secretary of state will not even be able to go to the bathroom!' One hour later, the Israelis turned on the water.

Contrary to Sharon's wishes, Powell went to the Muqata, which was still surrounded by the IDF. Once inside, Powell told Arafat: "Many people in Washington did not want me to come see you. This could be your last chance!"[12] Arafat in turn asked for the implementation of the United Nations Security Council resolution demanding Israeli withdrawal from autonomous zones, without which, he said, "we will not be able to discuss a cease-fire." They had reached an impasse.

THE WALL

Upon his return to Jerusalem, Powell learned that the Israeli government had made a major decision. It decided to establish a buffer zone between the West Bank and Israel, and such a zone would stretch from Mount Gilboa in the north to the Judean desert in the south. They allotted 518 million shekels ($120 million) for the project, 199 of which were to be used for the construction of physical obstacles. Electronic barriers would be constructed in three sectors: near Umm el-Fahem, an Israeli-Arab city; near Tulkarm, in the West Bank; and in the vicinity of Jerusalem. Although the official purpose of the project was to make it impossible for Palestinians to enter Israeli territory, Sharon was actually giving in to the pressure of public opinion by envisioning a unilateral separation from the Palestinians. Until this point he had resisted the construction of a barrier along the pre-1967 line of demarcation, believing that in doing so Israel would renounce specific territories west of the Jordan. General Uzi Dayan, who directed the national security council, recalled that during a working meeting in Jerusalem, Ariel Sharon asked me:

> 'I've been told that you are very interested in demography. How is that related to national security?' I answered: 'In order for the country to be a democratic Jewish state, it needs a solid Jewish majority! Isn't that so?' He agreed. He liked the word 'solid.' I said: 'You cannot continue to ignore that point, and it requires a decision on your part. A historic, solemn decision.' He asked: 'And why?' I answered: 'Because there are

currently, between the Jordan and the Mediterranean, how
many? 10.5 million inhabitants! And because in 2020, there
will be 15 million, and, among them, only 45 percent will be
Jewish. The conclusion is that the demographic clock is tick-
ing. . . . The bottom line is that we must draw our boundaries alone . . . even if we don't have a partner.' I remember
this conversation. It was the beginning of our initiative to
separate [from the Palestinians].[13]

Secretary of State Powell was invited to dine with Sharon, and yet
another surprise was awaiting him. The government had asked the police to gather photographs of the bloodiest attacks—those of torn and
mutilated bodies—into an album that was duly presented to Powell.
Completely shocked, he could not eat a bite.[14] Anthony Zinni, meanwhile, had left for the United States in order to attend the wedding of
one of his daughters. He would not return again.

Meanwhile in Washington, the tone had shifted due to pressure exercised by the Jewish community, supported by evangelical Christians
(who constituted the core of Bush's electoral base and had reacted negatively to Powell's visit to Arafat the "terrorist"). A pro-Israeli demonstration, with participants numbering in the tens of thousands, took place
in Washington D.C. on April 16, and drew such prominent figures as
Benjamin Netanyahu, the former prime minister, Nathan Shcharansky,
Rudy Giuliani, and Elie Wiesel, the winner of the Nobel Peace Prize. The
message of the demonstration was clear: "No pressure on Israel. No negotiations with Arafat." The White House dispatched Paul Wolfowitz,
the deputy secretary of defense, to the scene to take the podium. The
crowd knew that, contrary to his neoconservative colleagues, he was
opposed to Israeli settlements in the West Bank and supported the creation of a Palestinian state. He was booed when he spoke of the need for
a cease-fire and of the humanitarian crisis that the Palestinians were
enduring. At the same moment, the president was dealing with a family
issue: his brother Jeb was seeking reelection as governor of Florida, where
the Jewish community was particularly influential.

Around the same time, there was another demonstration against anti-Semitism taking place in Paris, organized by SOS Racism, CRIF,[15] the League Against Racism and Anti-Semitism, the Union of French Jewish Students, and "Ni putes ni soumises."[16] French politicians from both the Right and the Left led the procession. During the month of April, CRIF reported eighty-nine anti-Semitic acts; twenty-two synagogues had been the target of Molotov cocktails and various acts of vandalism.

That evening, after another round of negotiations with Powell and a telephone conversation with Bush, Sharon announced on Israeli television that the regional international conference could take place in June in the United States. The prime minister repeated to CNN that the Israeli army would remain in Ramallah and would not end the siege of Arafat's headquarters. The secretary of state's entourage spoke of progress that could lead to a joint Israeli-Palestinian declaration concerning "the end of hostilities." But there was no more discussion of a cease-fire.

POWELL FAILS

In Ramallah, Shin Bet finally managed to locate Marwan Barghouti, the secretary general of Fatah in the West Bank, who had gone underground at the beginning of the operation by hiding in the home of a friend, Ziad abu Ain. An elite unit surrounded the house, and Barghouti surrendered without resistance. His arrest would only add to his popularity in the Palestinian territories.

The following day, Powell was able to present Arafat with the outcome of his discussions with the Israelis. He warned: "You must do what you are being asked to do!"[17] The conversation ended in total disagreement. Arafat, under siege and lacking adequate means of communication, was no longer capable of controlling various armed groups or of responding to Israeli demands, and had not been for a long time. His advisors deemed the meeting with the American diplomat "catastrophic." According to Saeb Erekat,

> the Israelis wanted everything to occur in its proper order . . .
> depending on Arafat's ability to wave his magic wand and give

orders to the Palestinians. . . . Imagine. . . . Giving orders to guys on the run . . . to Hamas, to Jihad, to the PFLP, to the DFLP, to factions, to popular groups, to all those people who have been there for more than three years. . . . They wanted Arafat. They believed that Arafat had the power to put a stop to everything, and that the real problem was Arafat. But we all knew that wasn't the case. In several sectors, there was no possibility for exercising control. In several sectors, the Palestinians believed their commander in chief was dead. Dead! He was under siege. Why should they have listened to him? Mr. Powell said: 'I may be the last American official who will come to meet with you, Mr. Chairman. I came here against the wishes of many people in Washington.' And Arafat answered: 'I appreciate that, I respect you, from general to general!' Arafat was a proud man. He could not say the words: 'I cannot do it!'[18]

Before leaving the region, Powell still had to announce the time and place of the international summit. He was ready to give his speech when he received an urgent phone call from Washington. Karl Rove, the White House chief of staff and Bush's top political strategist, asked him to cancel the summit. The demonstration the day before and the pressure exerted by Jewish and evangelical Christian groups had been effective. Rove's explanation to Powell was a big hit among American diplomats who were there: "We need Israel more than Israel needs us!"[19] Richard Armitage, the deputy secretary of state, called his boss and described the situation in Washington: "People are really dragging your sh** through the street!"[20] Larry Wilkerson, Powell's chief of staff, summed up the situation: "Sharon knew that he had the support of the White House. He knew who the support was, and that the secretary of state was not necessarily in contact with those who supported him. Sharon . . . and most importantly, Powell recognized that no one really had any interest in seeing him succeed."[21]

On April 18, when Powell returned to Washington, George Bush gave an assessment of his mission during a meeting with the press in the Oval Office:

He carried that message of hope and peace, that our nation is—will work hard to achieve a peace. He also carried the message that people must—must be focused and must work hard to achieve a peace. People in the region have got certain responsibilities. The short-term responsibilities are these: The Palestinian Authority must act on its condemnation of terror. The Israelis are withdrawing from Jenin and Nablus, and they must continue their withdrawals.

In response to a reporter's question, the president gave his personal assessment of the Israeli prime minister's personality: "I do believe Ariel Sharon is a man of peace. I think he wants—I'm confident he wants Israel to be able to exist at peace with its neighbor—with its neighbors. I mean, he's told that to us here in the Oval Office. He has embraced the notion of two states living side by side."

The Israeli army, having evacuated the Jenin refugee camp, confirmed that only 10 percent of its structures had been destroyed and formally denied charges that a "massacre" had taken place: only twenty-five bodies had been found. But the Palestinians continued to insist that hundreds of corpses were buried beneath the rubble. Ultimately, international pressure succeeded in making an impact. White House spokesman Ari Fleischer announced that "the president has called for the United Nations and the Red Cross to be permitted to have unfettered access to Jenin. The president believes what's important is transparency so all the facts can be developed." The United Nations Security Council unanimously adopted Resolution 1405 stipulating the formation of an international fact-finding team to investigate the events in Jenin. Believing they had nothing to hide, the Israelis agreed. However, they changed their minds when the International Committee of the Red Cross accused the IDF of having breached international law and the Geneva Conventions by attacking civilians and destroying private property. In the end, the final body count for the assault against the refugee camp was raised to fifty-two.

On April 25, Arafat finally made some concessions. A sham trial held in the Muqata for the four PFLP militants who had assassinated Rehavam Zeevi resulted in prison terms ranging from one to four years. Sharon called this step "bizarre" and once again demanded that the four men be turned over to the Israelis, along with the two who were responsible for financing the *Karine A.* The Israelis continued the siege of the Muqata. They maintained that Arafat could leave the building whenever he chose, but he knew very well that the Israeli army would storm the building as soon as he left. The British decided to intervene by sending Alistair Crooke, the security advisor to the European emissary to the Middle East, Miguel Moratinos. Crooke proposed that the six men be confined in a prison in Jericho under the supervision of British and American security agents.

On April 27, two Palestinians disguised as Israeli soldiers infiltrated the Israeli settlement of Adora, near Hebron, and killed four people, among them a child. Forty-eight hours later, the IDF made an incursion into Hebron, during which nine Palestinians were killed, among whom, according to the army, was one of the Adora terrorists. They arrested 200 people.

END OF THE CRISIS

On May 1, American and British security agents transferred the six Palestinians sought by Israel to a prison in Jericho. The following day, tanks withdrew from the perimeter of the Muqata, marking the end of the thirty-four-day siege. Journalists rushed to Arafat's office and found the PLO leader agitated, accusing the Israelis of "Nazi crimes." He would wait twenty-four hours before visiting the wounded in the Ramallah hospital and saying a prayer at the gravesites of the twenty-one Palestinians killed during the preceding weeks. Nevertheless, he declared to the press that Sharon remained an interlocutor for peace. When his black limousine drove by, very few passersby stopped to applaud. Exhausted from weeks of fighting and curfews, the city's inhabitants were only interested in resuming a normal life.

ETHICS

In the end, operation "Shield" resulted in 265 victims on the Palestinian side (including both combatants and civilians) and twenty-nine on the Israeli side (all soldiers). During this period, thirty-three Israelis were killed in suicide attacks, and 7,000 Palestinians were arrested, of whom 5,600 were subsequently freed. It is also necessary to mention the ethical conduct of the Israeli army relative to the Palestinian victims. Different groups—including NGOs, Palestinians and Israelis, and journalists—observed numerous human rights violations. The report by B'Tselem constituted a veritable indictment. Palestinians—including children—had been killed for violating the cease-fire. Some army units demanded that civilians serve as human shields. In Ramallah, most institutions, including a bank and a supermarket, had been wrecked and computers were destroyed or seized.[22] While some units conducted themselves properly, others did not. As journalists Amos Harel and Avi Issacharoff report in their book *Hamilhama Ha Shviit*:

> While breaking into Palestinian houses to take up positions or to arrest suspects, soldiers had numerous opportunities for looting. On various occasions, VCR's, televisions, cameras, cellular phones, and money was stolen. A brigade commander who participated in operation "Shield" said that many soldiers who came from needy families considered looting to be an opportunity to earn 'additional pay.' In some companies, on Fridays, during kit inspection, warrant officers distributed money stolen from the Palestinians to needy soldiers.[23]

Ariel Sharon was in Washington on May 6, 2002, and presented Colin Powell with a dossier on Arafat. It was a dense file that was intended to establish a connection between the head of the PLO and terrorism. The dossier contained papers confiscated at the Muqata, essentially the same letters concerning the transfer of funds that he had already presented in the Knesset. American intelligence specialists who had the opportunity to inspect the documents were not convinced. The prime minister repeated to the secretary of state that an international conference on the Middle East could not serve as a substitute for direct negotiations between the Israelis and the Palestinians. But, he added: "The participation of Arafat in talks is out of the question." Sharon launched a series of reproaches at Saudi Arabia in front of journalists: "It is unacceptable that this country supports the families of Palestinian suicide bombers. The Saudis have never condemned Palestinian terrorism." The controversial subject of the settlements was never raised during the conversation, despite the fact that the previous day Secretary of State Powell emphasized the United States's opposition to the Israeli settlements in the Palestinian territories. Sharon declared to Secretary of Defense Donald Rumsfeld that Israel would never agree to the creation of a Palestinian state as long as Arafat was the leader of the PLO and of the Autonomous Authority.

NO NEGOTIATIONS WITH THE PALESTINIANS

The following day, just as Sharon was sitting down at the White House to meet with President Bush, his aide-de-camp, General Moshe Kaplinsky, informed him that another attack had occurred in Israel. A Hamas terrorist blew himself up in a pool hall in Rishon Letzion, a suburb near Tel Aviv, killing fifteen. Bush expressed his sorrow, and the two men then proceeded to agree upon the need for significant reform of the Palestinian Authority's institutions. Bush declared: "The Palestinians need to develop a constitution, rule of law, transparency. They've got to have a treasury that is able to battle corruption, so that not only does the—do the Israeli people have confidence in the Authority, but so do the Palestinian people have confidence in the Authority." The question would have to be discussed during the international summit on the Middle East, which at that time was anticipated to take place in Turkey. George Tenet, the CIA chief, was called upon to return to the region in order to help pave the way for Palestinian reforms. Sharon drove the point home, insisting that if reforms did not take place, the resumption of negotiations was out of the question. During the press conference following the meeting, a reporter asked Bush whether he agreed with Sharon about Arafat. Bush answered:

I'm never going to tell my friend, the prime minister, what to do or how to handle his business. That's his choice to make. He's a democratically elected official. And I'll reiterate: I have been disappointed in Chairman Arafat. I think he's let the Palestinian people down. I think he's had an opportunity to lead to peace and he hasn't done so.

The Israeli prime minister left for Tel Aviv and told journalists accompanying him on the flight that he and the American president agreed on this point: "There will be no negotiations until the Autonomous Authority has been completely reformed." The news generated consternation as soon as it reached Washington. The Saudis were furious. The statement implied that any negotiations with the Palestinians would be put off indefinitely, just at the moment when the Bush administration was seeking allies in the Arab world.

OUTPOSTS

On May 9, 2002, European negotiators managed to conclude an agreement with Israel to end the siege of the Church of the Nativity in Bethlehem. Accused of being dangerous terrorists, thirteen Palestinians left for Cyprus, while twenty-six others were transported to Gaza where they were given their freedom. The 123 people who had hidden within the holy Christian site and who were not sought by Israel were given their liberty without incident. That evening, in a speech broadcast by radio and television, Arafat condemned the attack in Rishon Letzion and ordered all of the Palestinian security services to direct their efforts toward preventing anti-Israel attacks, a practically impossible mission. In the West Bank, prisons, headquarters of the security forces, and police stations had been destroyed or badly damaged. Moreover, the IDF had reduced the operational capabilities of the Palestinian police to a minimum. This was one measure opposed by Brigadier General Ilan Paz, who commanded the sector in Ramallah: "Law and order will not reign [in the Palestinian territories] if we do not authorize these fundamental things: the deployment of forces, training, etc."[24]

The entire West Bank was once again under the control of the IDF, to the great satisfaction of the settlement movement. Since Sharon's arrival to power, twenty-five new settlements known as "outposts" had been discreetly constructed without the authorization of the Israeli government, and had been reinforced during the previous few months. They had been connected to the electrical grid, had access to running water, and were protected by the Israeli army.[25] Several NGOs, including Peace Now and B'Tselem, alerted the American administration: in the West Bank, the territory reserved for settlements, which had only been 6.8 percent, had been enlarged and represented 35.1 percent of the total area. Developed zones in the settlements represented 1.7 percent of the West Bank.[26]

A PROMISE FROM ARAFAT

With Ariel Sharon's agreement, King Abdullah II of Jordan put a military helicopter at Arafat's disposal to allow him to move about without having to pass through military checkpoints. On May 13, he landed in Jenin, and proceeded to the city hall where he greeted officials and praised the inhabitants of the city, which he called "Jeningrad." However, the crowd did not come out into the streets to welcome him, but rather waited for Arafat's arrival in the ruined refugee camp. Fearing hostile demonstrations from the large crowd that had gathered, Arafat decided not to enter the camp. He was content with circling overhead in his helicopter. In the camp, thousands of Palestinians were furious, demonstrating their anger by tearing posters of Arafat from the walls.

The Palestinian chairman next toured Bethlehem, where he visited the Church of the Nativity, and then returned to the Muqata after the one-day excursion outside Ramallah, a city he would leave only once more before his death.

Under the pressure of the international community represented by what would become the Quartet, Arafat no longer had a choice. He was obliged to engage in the complete reform of Palestinian institutions and thereby satisfy the initial Israeli-American demand for a total overhaul of his security services and of the Palestinian police. Mohammed Dahlan favored this development, as did Jibril Rajoub. On May 15, in a speech given before the Palestinian parliament, Arafat even seemed to broach an apology: "Our interior situation demands complete reform. . . . If mistakes have been made, I am responsible and I will be the one who will correct them." In addition, he pledged the separation of judicial, legislative, and executive powers, and, as proof of his word, he had signed a decree concerning the independence of the courts the previous day. He also announced new elections "for which preparations had to begin immediately." And, once again, he condemned attacks against Israeli civilians: "Arab and Palestinian public opinion has reached the point where [attacks are] not believed to serve either our interests or our objectives." Representatives from the opposition party greeted these statements with suspicion: could Arafat the autocrat actually change? Was it possible to hold an election when Palestinian institutions had been partially destroyed?

On May 17, the Israeli army made a new incursion into the Jenin refugee camp seeking a Hamas militant accused of terrorism. The soldiers did not find him, but destroyed his house. The PFLP claimed responsibility for an attack that occurred two days later in Netanya, when a human bomb exploded at the market, resulting in three deaths and dozens of wounded. On May 22, a suicide attack on a pedestrian street in Rishon Letzion caused two deaths and wounded forty. In Balata, the Nablus refugee camp, four Palestinians were killed during an army operation. Mahmoud Titi, who had organized two attacks, was among those killed. Then on May 27, a suicide attack orchestrated by the al-Aqsa Martyrs Brigades took place in a shopping center in Petah Tikva, a town near Tel Aviv. There were two deaths, including a fourteen-month-old girl. The following day, this same group, which had connections to Fatah, committed two attacks with automatic weapons, one against an Israeli vehicle near Ramallah, and another in a settlement near Nablus. Taken together, these attacks resulted in three deaths.

On May 31, Arafat signed a series of decrees concerning the reform of Palestinian institutions.

On June 3, in a surprising display of their independence, Palestinian magistrates at the high court in Gaza heard the appeal of Ahmed

Saadat, the secretary general of the PFLP who had been accused by the Israelis of the assassination of Rehavam Zeevi and who was imprisoned in Jericho. The judges held that the Autonomous Authority had no evidence against the Palestinian leader, and ordered his release. The Israelis were furious. Binyamin Ben-Eliezer threatened that "if the Palestinians violate the agreement, we will reassert our freedom of action and act according to our interests!" The Palestinian government rushed to issue a statement: "Ahmed Saadat will remain in prison for his own safety.... A spokesman for Ariel Sharon threatened to kill him, and the Israeli army has surrounded Jericho!"[27]

TENET AND ISLAMIC JIHAD

Surprisingly, with Sharon's approval, George Tenet returned to the region charged with the mission of negotiating the overhaul of the Palestinian security services with Arafat. The twelve different services were to be merged into three organizations placed under the responsibility of a minister of the interior, a position that could not be held by Arafat himself. The Israelis, who believed that he practically had no chance for success, added a supplementary condition: the dismissal of General Tawfiq al-Tirawi, the head of Palestinian intelligence, and of Rashid Abu Shbak, Mohammed Dahlan's deputy in Gaza, accused of having encouraged anti-Israeli attacks. The CIA chief presented his new plan to the Palestinian chairman the next day at the Muqata. Arafat accepted the reforms in principle, but named a seventy-three-year-old close colleague, General Hazek al-Yyeyiah, as head of the future ministry of the interior, and refused to dismiss al-Tirawi and Abu Shbak. Hosni Mubarak's personal emissary, General Omar Suleiman, the Egyptian intelligence chief, came to tell Arafat that he had no other option but to accept the reforms.

This was precisely why Islamic Jihad decided to act. On June 5, in northern Israel, a terrorist exploded a car bomb alongside a bus packed with soldiers and civilians, killing seventeen and wounding forty. The Palestinian, from Jenin, was only sixteen years old. Arafat's condemnation of the attack had no impact. The following evening, around twenty tanks and bulldozers took up position in front of the Muqata and began the systematic destruction of the buildings surrounding Arafat's office. The chairman's bedroom was hit by a mortar shell, but he wasn't inside.

In Gaza, Sheik Abdullah Shami, one of the leaders of Islamic Jihad, gave interviews: "The Autonomous Authority is broken. Its institutions are destroyed. How can it assure the security of Israelis if it can't even protect its own people?" He was arrested by the Palestinian police.

DICK CHENEY VS. POWELL AND ARAFAT

After a few phone calls from the White House, the Israeli army pulled back. Meanwhile, the American administration was putting finishing touches on a new Middle East initiative. Every sentence in George Bush's speech announcing the plan was subject to careful scrutiny. A veritable arm wrestling match was taking place between Colin Powell and his team and the neoconservatives led by Vice President Dick Cheney. The secretary of state was advising Bush against including language in the text demanding the departure of Arafat from the Palestinian leadership. The vice president's entourage thus contacted the prime minister's office in Jerusalem and asked for evidence establishing the connection between Arafat and terrorism. They judged the dossier presented a few weeks earlier in Washington by Ariel Sharon to be insufficient. In Tel Aviv, the intelligence services got to work and ultimately found a recording caught by wiretaps near the Muqata in which Ahmed Barghouti, the younger cousin of the Fatah secretary general, was caught on tape bragging to a militant that his leader [Arafat] had paid him $20,000 to commit an anti-Israeli attack. Dan Meridor, the minister charged with intelligence oversight, didn't take this "proof" very seriously. First, he said, the payments made by Arafat to various organizations were usually smaller, and in addition, even more importantly, the evidence was circumstantial.[28] Lacking anything better, the recording was sent to Cheney who presented it as irrefutable proof.

When Bush welcomed Hosni Mubarak to Camp David on June 8, the Egyptian president pressed for the creation of a Palestinian state early in 2003, and tried to persuade Bush to give Arafat a chance. Bush responded: "That's an interesting point of view. I also happen to believe that there is plenty of talent amongst the Palestinians! . . . We're not ready to lay down a specific calendar, except for the fact we need to get started quickly, soon, so that we can seize the moment." On June 9, in Ramallah, Yasser Arafat formed a new government. The White House observed with satisfaction the appointment of Salam Fayad as finance minister. He was a former high official in the International Monetary Fund with a doctorate in economics from the University of Texas. His job was to clean up the Palestinian finances and eliminate corruption.

Two days later, while the Israeli army was once again busy in Ramallah, placing the city under curfew and surrounding the Muqata, Sharon arrived in Washington. He had read an interview with Powell in the London Arab daily *al-Hayat* in which the secretary of state revealed that the Bush administration envisaged creating a Palestinian state within provisional borders. The prime minister's entourage rejoiced: the administration's position was identical to Israel's.

From Sharon's point of view, the meeting with Bush could not have gone better. During a joint press conference, Bush, referring to the operation that was taking place in Ramallah at that moment, declared only that "Israel has a right to defend herself." To a reporter's question he added:

> You're talking about the proposed summit this summer, a ministerial summit of people that come together to work toward the conditions necessary to establish a peace. See, the conditions aren't even there yet—that's because no one has confidence in the emerging Palestinian government. And so, first things first, and that is, what institutions are necessary to give the Palestinian people hope, and to give the Israelis confidence that the emerging government will be someone with whom they can deal?

The issue of the construction of settlements was never raised.

On June 17, Binyamin Ben-Eliezer summoned the press to a small ceremony at the Givat Oz kibbutz, north of Jenin, to declare the inauguration of the construction site for the first section of the future security fence. The Israeli defense minister explained that the structure would be "around" 350 kilometers (218 miles) long, the same length as the former line of demarcation separating Israel from the West Bank.[29] Meanwhile, Condoleezza Rice signed the death warrant for Colin Powell's latest initiative for a Middle East summit: "The conditions are not yet ready for a regional peace conference. In the current circumstances, it is not possible to negotiate towards a final status. . . . The Palestinian Authority, which is corrupt and cavorts with terror, is not the basis for a Palestinian state moving forward."[30]

THE HAMAS STRATEGY

The following day, a suicide bomber sent by Hamas set off an explosion that tore through a bus that runs from Gilo to the center of Jerusalem, via the Palestinian village of Beit Safafa. Among the nineteen people killed were numerous Jewish and Arab students; seventy-four were also wounded. For the first time since becoming prime minister, Sharon visited the site of a bombing, bowing before the bodies of the victims. The Palestinian Authority condemned the attack and vowed to pursue the perpetrators. Then, on June 19, yet another attack occurred in Jerusalem, this one claimed by the al-Aqsa Martyrs Brigades, which killed seven and wounded fifty. After inspecting work on the security fence in the vicinity of the Alfei Menashe settlement, Sharon decided that it would be built to the east of the settlement, more than 4 kilometers inside the borders of the West Bank. Qalqilya, the neighboring Palestinian city, would thus be surrounded by the structure, a single road connecting it to the rest of the Palestinian territory. Arafat called again for a halt to anti-Israeli attacks, explaining that "the Sharon government uses them as a pretext for occupying our land." A statement published by fifty-five Palestinian intellectuals and politicians, led by Sari Nusseibeh, the president of Al Quds University in East Jerusalem, expressed agreement with Arafat:

> We call upon the parties behind military operations targeting civilians in Israel to reconsider their policies and stop

driving our young men to carry out these operations. . . . [These operations] strengthen the enemies of peace on the Israeli side and give Israel's aggressive government under Sharon the excuse to continue its harsh war against our people. This war targets our children, elderly, villages, cities.

For their part, several of Arafat's advisors demanded action against Hamas, even if it entailed bloody inter-Palestinian confrontations. Mohammed Dahlan was among those who took this position:

I insisted that the strategy of Hamas was clear. By attacking Israel, the Islamists show the Palestinian public that they are resisting the occupation and, in addition, by retaliating against the Autonomous Authority, the Israelis weaken it. Hamas thereby attains two of its objectives. By attacking and taking measures against innocent civilians, by destroying the Palestinian Authority, the Israelis pushed the entirety of Palestinian society into a confrontation with Israel. I have repeated this over and over, not only to the chairman [Arafat], but also to the Americans and the Israelis.[31]

Arafat was hesitant. Since the beginning of the intifada, he feared the outbreak of civil war in Gaza while Israel continued to launch attacks against his security services.

On June 20, two PFLP militants attacked Itamar, a settlement near Nablus, killing five people, including a mother and her three children. The assailants were killed by soldiers, but settlers conducted a reprisal raid in the neighboring town, where they killed one Palestinian. The following day, the IDF made an incursion into Jenin, causing four deaths, including that of three children.

The daily *Haaretz* published a breakdown of the casualties since the beginning of the intifada at the end of September 2000: 1,403 Palestinians, including many noncombatants, and 530 Israelis, half of whom were civilians, had been killed. The violence had achieved a steady rhythm: attacks, reprisals, targeted killings of Palestinian militants.

PERES AGAINST THE WALL

On June 23, the Sharon government approved the construction of a new stretch of the security fence: 115 kilometers, at 1 million dollars per kilometer. But when Shimon Peres looked at the plan in question on a map entitled "Israel map of interest," he nearly leapt out of his chair. Israel was getting ready to annex the Jordan Valley, which represented about 22 percent of the West Bank! The following are excerpts from the ensuing debate:

> **Peres:** "I cannot remain a member of a government that approves such a map!"
> **Sharon:** "We have no intention of giving up on any minister, certainly not you. This map does not present a border, but rather obstacles."
> **Peres suggested another option:** "End the occupation!"
> **David Levy, a Likud minister:** "What are you saying? That is precisely the demand of Arafat, and you too support it?"
> **Peres:** "All the troubles began because the Likud would not implement the Oslo Accords."
> **Danny Neveh:** "More than a thousand Israelis have been murdered since you brought Arafat here and signed the Oslo agreements."
> **Peres:** "There were terror attacks and murders even before that!"[32]

Finally, the government provisionally approved a plan for a barrier in principle, but not the actual map. The ministers had one month to present proposals to modify the plan, and Sharon and his security cabinet would make the final decision. In the West Bank, the Israeli army imposed a curfew in six cities; 600,000 Palestinians could no longer leave their homes, except for a few hours, more or less regularly, when they were permitted to buy food.

BUSH FOR A PALESTINE WITHOUT ARAFAT

On June 24, in Washington, George Bush approved the twenty-seventh version of his keynote speech on the Israeli-Palestinian conflict. Revisions of the text had been made up to the very last minute. Forty-eight hours earlier, Dick Cheney had met Nathan Shcharansky during a conference at the American Enterprise Institute, the main neoconservative think tank. The former Soviet dissident turned Israeli minister was one of the stars of the American Right. He had told Cheney: "The mere mention of a Palestinian state rewards Arafat for terrorism!" Benjamin Netanyahu, the finance minister, was also networking in the capitol. And on June 24, the press was invited to the White House Rose Garden where George Bush presented the new United States policy:

> For too long, the citizens of the Middle East have lived in the midst of death and fear. The hatred of a few holds the hopes of many hostage. The forces of extremism and terror are attempting to kill progress and peace by killing the innocent. . . . For the sake of all humanity, things must change in the Middle East. It is untenable for Israeli citizens to live in terror. It is untenable for Palestinians to live in squalor and occupation. And the current situation offers no prospect that life will improve. Israeli citizens will continue to be victimized by terrorists, and so Israel will continue to defend herself. In [this] situation the Palestinian people will grow more and more miserable.
>
> My vision is two states, living side by side in peace and security. There is simply no way to achieve that peace until all parties fight terror. Yet, at this critical moment, if all parties will break with the past and set out on a new path, we can overcome the darkness with the light of hope. Peace requires a new and different Palestinian leadership, so that a Palestinian state can be born.
>
> I call on the Palestinian people to elect new leaders, leaders not compromised by terror. I call upon them to build a

practicing democracy, based on tolerance and liberty. If the Palestinian people actively pursue these goals, America and the world will actively support their efforts. If the Palestinian people meet these goals, they will be able to teach agreement with Israel and Egypt and Jordan on security and other arrangements for independence. . . .

Today, the Palestinian authorities are encouraging, not opposing, terrorism. This is unacceptable. And the United States will not support the establishment of a Palestinian state until its leaders engage in a sustained fight against the terrorists and dismantle their infrastructure. This will require an externally supervised effort to rebuild and reform the Palestinian security services. . . . Israel also has a large stake in the success of a democratic Palestine. Permanent occupation threatens Israel's identity and democracy. A stable, peaceful Palestinian state is necessary to achieve the security that Israel longs for. So, I challenge Israel to take concrete steps to support the emergence of a viable, credible Palestinian state.

As we make progress towards security, Israeli forces need to withdraw fully to positions they held prior to September 28, 2000. And consistent with the recommendations of the Mitchell Committee, Israeli settlement activity in the occupied territories must stop.

The Palestinian economy must be allowed to develop. As violence subsides, freedom of movement should be restored, permitting innocent Palestinians to resume work and normal life. Palestinian legislators and officials, humanitarian and international workers, must be allowed to go about the business of building a better future. And Israel should release frozen Palestinian revenues into honest, accountable hands. . . .

I can understand the deep anger and anguish of the Israeli people. You've lived too long with fear and funerals, having to avoid markets and public transportation, and forced to put armed guards in kindergarten classrooms. The Palestinian Authority has rejected your offer at hand, and trafficked with terrorists. You have a right to a normal life; you have a right to security; and I deeply believe that you need a reformed, responsible Palestinian partner to achieve that security.

I can understand the deep anger and despair of the Palestinian people. For decades you've been treated as pawns in the Middle East conflict. Your interests have been held hostage to a comprehensive peace agreement that never seems to come, as your lives get worse year by year. You deserve democracy and the rule of law. You deserve an open society and a thriving economy. You deserve a life of hope for your children. An end to occupation and a peaceful democratic Palestinian state may seem distant, but America and our partners throughout the world stand ready to help, help you make them possible as soon as possible.

Ariel Sharon had won. Yasser Arafat, his old foe, had been sent to the bench. The Oslo Accords now only existed on paper. It was also a victory for the American neoconservatives who, in 1996, had sent Benjamin Netanyahu, prime minister at the time, a letter suggesting that Israel "change the nature of its relations, including upholding the *right of hot pursuit* for self defense into all Palestinian areas and nurturing alternatives to Arafat's exclusive grip on Palestinian society."[33]

It was also a victory for all those who, in the leadership of the Israeli army, had worked to "arafatize" the conflict. According to sociologist David Retner, military leaders who were faced with the need to clearly define the source of the conflict had relentlessly depicted the head of the PLO and Palestinian chairman as the main actor in the violence. They gave the following reasons:

The intifada created a chaotic situation of crisis in which it was sometimes difficult to distinguish good from evil, true from false, 'here' from 'there,' between war and dialogue, between the military and the political. The creation of the 'myth' of Arafat allowed these difficult dilemmas to be confronted. . . . This raises the question of whether in focusing their discourse on Arafat, [the military leaders] contributed to efforts to reach an end to the hostilities or, on the contrary, made them fail.[34]

David Retner published this analysis in 2004, in a work that the Israeli defense minister consecrated to the study of low-intensity warfare.

CHAPTER 6

THE FAILURE OF ABBAS

On July 9, 2002, Moshe Yaalon succeeded Shaul Mofaz as chief of staff of the Israeli army. His mother was a Holocaust survivor; his father was a Ukrainian who immigrated to Palestine in 1925. At the age of fifty-two, he was the first chief of staff of the army who had been born in Israel. During his first meeting with the military staff, "Boogie," his nickname since childhood, read the generals a poem by Nathan Alterman, the apologist for the Israeli Right, published after the Six-Day War and the occupation of the territories:

"The Besieged"
Then the devil said:
This besieged one—
How shall I defeat him?
He has courage and skill to act
He has weapons and wisdom on his side.
And he said: I will not take away his strength
Neither bridle nor bit will I put on him
Nor will I make him fainthearted

Nor will I weaken his hand in days of old.
Only this shall I do:
I shall dull his mind,
And he will forget that his cause is just.
Thus said the devil,
And the heavens paled with fear
As they watched him rise
To carry out his plan.

In the following weeks, Yaalon clarified his thinking: "The Palestin-ian threat contains cancerous elements that it is necessary to root out completely. We must win in such a way that the Palestinians understand they will gain nothing through terrorism."[1] The IDF was directed to confront this "cancer" without compunction, while being careful not to get innocent civilians involved. Next, the general recited another one of Alterman's poems to the military staff, this one written in 1948 after the death of innocent Palestinian civilians during the taking of the city of Lod:

"For This"
He crossed the conquered city in a jeep—a brave, armed boy—a
   lion's whelp.
And in the desolated street an old man and a woman pressed back
   against the wall.
The boy smiled with milk teeth: "I'll try the machine gun" . . . and
   did.
The old man just hid his face in his hands . . . and his blood covered
   the wall.
. . . For those who bear arms and we alongside, whether in action or
   with pats on the back, are pushed, muttering "no choice" and
   "revenge". . . .[2]

The same day, the police and Shin Bet searched the offices of Sari Nusseibeh, president of Al Quds University in Jerusalem, seizing docu-ments and lists of personnel and students. The White House and the State

Department immediately called Ariel Sharon's entourage. Nusseibeh, who was extremely moderate and was protected by Washington, would not be bothered again.

On July 16, 2002, there was another attack: a bomb exploded next to a bus near the Emmanuel settlement. Hamas terrorists disguised as Israeli soldiers opened fire. In all, nine were killed and twenty wounded.

A ONE-TON BOMB

On the afternoon of July 21, Miguel Moratinos's entourage called to tell me that the leaders of Tanzim, the armed organizations of Fatah, were preparing to publish a unilateral call for a cease-fire in both the Palestinian press and in the *Washington Post*. Sheik Ahmed Yassin, the founder of Hamas, had given his approval. Later that afternoon, I received a copy of the document:

> We, the representatives of the Tanzim and of Fatah, in the name of our comrades and our organizations in all the cities and towns of the West Bank and Gaza, declare that, starting at this moment, we will stop all attacks against innocent non-combatants, men, women, and children. We appeal to all organizations and Palestinian political movements to immediately put a stop to these kinds of attacks, without hesitation or preconditions. For our part, we will stop these attacks and will work with other Palestinian political organizations in order to gain their support. We will supervise these organizations in order to insure that none of these actions are planned or executed, and we will participate in a national dialogue aiming to persuade our people of the necessity of taking this just direction.
>
> Our revolution begins based on new principles. We will pursue our fight and defend our people: we will oppose all aggression against our cities and our families, against the confiscation of our lands, against the occupation of the West Bank by the Israeli army.

This statement was the product of a long round of negotiations led by the team of Alistair Crooke, the British security advisor to Miguel Moratinos. During the twenty-four hours leading up to the announcement, the leaders of the Tanzim, who had gathered in Jenin, finally gave their approval.

But, later that evening, local correspondents in Gaza made emergency calls to their bureau chiefs posted in Jerusalem and Tel Aviv: "Israeli combat planes have bombed buildings in Gaza. Numerous people have been killed or wounded." The IDF had assassinated Salah Shehada, the founder of the commando unit Ezzedin al-Qassam, the armed wing of Hamas. The bomb was extremely powerful: the four-story house had been destroyed, and the neighboring houses were damaged. A preliminary count totaled fourteen deaths, including Shehada, his wife, their three sons, and four other children, and around twenty wounded.

Abroad, the attack was unanimously condemned: the images of the corpses being pulled from the wreckage were particularly shocking. The next day, Ariel Sharon declared that "it is one of our greatest successes in the fight against terrorism!" In a statement, the air force expressed regret for the loss of innocent lives. Military correspondents soon learned that the bomb used had weighed a ton . . .

Fatah reacted by announcing that its cease-fire initiative was rendered null and void by this attack, and Abdel Aziz Rantisi of Hamas announced that no future peace initiatives were planned: "We are going to pursue the Zionists in their homes, in their apartments, the same way that they destroyed our houses and our apartments."

An internal investigation revealed that the intelligence to which the IDF had access was faulty: military officials had believed that the neighboring house was uninhabited. The use of "targeted killings" as a tactic once again became controversial. Since Ariel Sharon's rise to power on February 6, 2001, sixty-seven Palestinian militants had been assassinated, along with twenty-four civilians—men, women, and children—as "collateral damage." The Israeli peace group Gush Shalom threatened to give the name of the pilot to the International Criminal Court at the Hague so that he would be tried for war crimes. In the streets, insults were painted on some cars belonging to pilots. General Dan Halutz, the air force commander, responded a month later in an interview with the daily *Haaretz*, in which he implied that the "leftists" who were criticizing him were traitors. In response to a question, he said: "If you really want to know what I feel when I drop a bomb, I'll tell you: I feel a slight bump in the plane after dropping a bomb; a second later, it's over, and that's it!" Several leftist organizations filed an appeal at the high court against the nomination of Halutz to the post of deputy chief of staff, arguing that in the name of ethics he was not up to the job. The judges demanded that he respond in writing, and Halutz seized the opportunity to lament the loss of innocent human lives. The appeal was rejected.

HAMAS AGAINST ARAFAT

Two more attacks took place on July 30: the al-Aqsa Martyrs Brigades of Fatah killed two Israelis in the Itamar settlement, close to Nablus, and a Hamas suicide bomber attacked in Jerusalem, wounding five. The next day, Hamas committed another suicide attack in a cafeteria at Hebrew University, killing nine and wounding eighty-five.

On August 1, King Abdullah of Jordan, welcomed to the White House by George Bush, persuaded the president to consider a new international initiative to create a Palestinian state and to set a timetable based on the latest peace plans. Bush agreed, and Colin Powell, who attended the meeting, took note. He asked Undersecretary of State William Burns to work with the other members of the Quartet to prepare a document.

The next day, when the IDF made an incursion into the casbah in Nablus, four Palestinians were killed during the fighting. On August 4, 2002, Hamas claimed responsibility for a suicide attack on a bus in the north of Israel that killed nine Israelis. In retaliation, the Israeli army destroyed the houses of nine perpetrators of suicide attacks, and Hamas announced that it would stop publishing the names of its martyrs. Israel prohibited the movement of Palestinians between the towns and cities of the West Bank. On August 20, the army withdrew from Bethlehem and put an end to more than two months of occupation. But it kept the city sealed off: its inhabitants were only permitted to go to Jerusalem with the authorization of the military administration.

Speaking before the legislative council in Ramallah on September 9, Arafat condemned acts of terrorism targeting Israeli civilians, but did not call for an end to suicide attacks. Two days later, his government lost the parliamentary majority and resigned. Legislators criticized his autocratic control of Palestinian institutions and his lack of transparency in managing public finances. Taking advantage of international pressure, these legislators, in turn, demanded the reform of the Autonomous Authority.

On the evening of September 19, immediately following a Hamas suicide attack on a Tel Aviv bus that resulted in six deaths and fifty wounded, Sharon's cabinet unanimously decided to isolate Arafat in his headquarters. They also demanded the surrender of thirty other Palestinians, namely, those responsible for the *Karine A* affair and security agents that Israel accused of terrorism. Less than an hour after the vote, tanks and bulldozers began to systematically destroy the Muqata, with the exception of the building containing Arafat's office.

On September 21, soldiers planted the Israeli flag on its roof and destroyed water pipes. Meanwhile, a bulldozer tore through the kitchen on the ground floor, and barbed wire was wrapped around the rest of the building. Several demonstrations of support took place in Gaza and the West Bank. That evening, water, electricity, and telephone lines were cut. Learning the news by radio, Binyamin Ben-Eliezer gave the order to restore water and electricity. Miguel Moratinos told the Israelis that he wanted to visit Arafat, and the Israeli foreign minister refused. The State Department and the White House anxiously followed the latest developments. Arafat's death could throw the region into turmoil, just at the moment when the United States was at war in Afghanistan and was preparing for another offensive in Iraq. Under American pressure, the siege was lifted eleven days later, though the IDF left three observation posts within the vicinity of the Muqata. Chairman Arafat had been warned: the army would intervene if he left the building. He would not leave again until he succumbed to a fatal illness.

Jewish organizations abroad began to intensify their campaigns against press outlets deemed to be pro-Palestinian. In France, on numerous occasions, following the initiative of the Jewish Defense League and Lawyers without Frontiers, a disinformation prize was given to several journalists, as well as to Agence France-Presse. During a protest in front of the headquarters of France 2 in Paris, this dubious honor, originally called the Goebbels prize, was given to the author of a broadcast report relating the death of young Mohammed al-Durreh in the Gaza Strip city of Netzarim, at the start of the intifada on September 30, 2000. (I had asserted that the child had been the target of bullets coming from an Israeli position.) In November 2000, Yom Tov Samia, the Israeli general commanding forces in the West Bank, had personally organized a reconstruction of the incident before concluding in his report that "a comprehensive investigation conducted in the last weeks casts serious doubts that the boy was hit by the Israel Defense Forces' fire. . . . It is quite plausible that the boy was hit by Palestinian bullets."[3] Parisian demonstrators brandished protest signs saying "Enderlin Liar," demanding the broadcast of a German documentary that adopted General Samia's conclusions. This marked the beginning of a long defamation campaign, pursued in France and the United States, namely through the intermediary of internet sites claiming that the child's death had been staged in order to provoke the intifada. France 2 never received a complaint or a formal demand from the Israeli authorities on this matter.

TOWARD EARLY ELECTIONS

In Israel, Ariel Sharon's Labor allies rebelled. This was not surprising. During his tenure as prime minster, Shimon Peres had been regularly marginalized by the leadership of his party. Specifically, in the present case, Labor members rejected the government's policy toward the Palestinians. They demanded a reduction of the budget allotted to settlements and refused any supplemental taxation of the middle classes and the underprivileged. On October 27, Sharon put his foot down and demanded that all of his partners approve his finance law. He threatened the Labor Party by proposing to name Shaul Mofaz—who was no longer in uniform—as defense minister in the event that the Labor Party resigned from the government. On October 30, 2002, the Knesset voted on the government budget. The Labor Party ignored Sharon's threats and resigned from the government anyway. Polls showed that more than 61 percent of Israelis disapproved of the dissolution of the national unity government.

On November 5, Ariel Sharon summoned the press to announce that elections would be held early. The parties launched their campaigns. Benjamin Netanyahu returned to run in the primary elections of the Likud Party, which were to be held on November 28. Sharon won, carrying 55.8 percent of the vote as opposed to Netanyahu's 40 percent.

On November 19, 2002, Amram Mitzna, the mayor of Haifa and a general of the reserve, was elected leader of the Labor Party. His proposal for a unilateral withdrawal from Gaza and the opening of negotiations with the Palestinians elicited bitter criticism from his right-wing opponents.

On November 21, another suicide attack on a Jerusalem bus killed eleven and wounded fifty. One week later, Palestinian members of Fatah broke into the headquarters of the Likud Party in Beit Shean, a northern Israeli town, and opened fire. They killed six people and wounded dozens more.

In London, Tony Blair was furious. He wanted to convene a mini-summit on the Middle East in order to discuss reform of the Palestinian Authority and to restart the peace process. But Sharon prohibited Palestinian leaders from making the trip. Netanyahu, who had replaced Peres as the foreign minister, had a tumultuous argument with Jack Straw, his British counterpart. Finally on January 15, 2003, Saeb Erekat participated in the meeting via webcam from Ramallah.

On January 5, 2003, Hamas committed a double suicide attack in Tel Aviv that resulted in the deaths of twenty-three and the wounding of around a hundred—mostly foreign workers. On January 7, *Haaretz* revealed that a government prosecutor had opened an investigation into Ariel Sharon's campaign finances during the Likud primaries in December 2000. The Sharon family allegedly received an illegal loan of $1.5 million from Cyril Kern, a South African businessman. Investigators suspected the Sharon family—the prime minister and his sons, Omri and Gilad—of electoral fraud and of giving false testimony. The affair would exert little influence on the elections that were held on January 28, 2003. The voter turnout of 68 percent was one of the weakest in the history of the country. The Labor Party suffered a stinging defeat, and gained only nineteen seats, as opposed to the thirty-eight that went to Likud. The Right and the extreme Right counted sixty-six ministers, and easily won a majority by forming the new parliamentary coalition. Amram Mitzna would leave political life behind only a few months later.

On March 3, eight Palestinians were killed in an Israeli raid on the Bureij refugee camp in the Gaza Strip. Two days later, Hamas claimed responsibility for a suicide attack on a Haifa bus in which seventeen were killed and fifty-three wounded. Meanwhile, Arafat was under constant pressure exerted by Terje Larsen and Miguel Moratinos. Hosni Mubarak and King Abdullah of Jordan also insisted that he agree to the reform of the institutions of the Autonomous Authority. Yasser Abed Rabbo, in addition to other close advisors to Arafat, also pressured him. Finally, Arafat agreed, in principle, to the creation of the post of prime minister.

WAR IN IRAQ

The Middle East waited with bated breath. The Americans and the British were putting the finishing touches on their preparations for the offensive that they were planning to launch in Iraq. This was a war Israeli officials viewed with intense satisfaction. Extremely favorable scenarios were making the rounds in the corridors of power in Jerusalem. Raanan Gissin, a spokesman for Ariel Sharon, declared to anyone willing to listen: "Everything is going to change in the region! The defeat of Saddam Hussein will set a domino effect in motion. After the fall of the Iraqi dictator, all of the other enemies of Israel will be in trouble, and Arafat comes first." General Amos Gilaad announced on Israeli television that "American forces will make important discoveries" in Iraq. Analysts for the ministry of foreign affairs observed another favorable aspect of the political fallout: the anti-American attitude of France and Germany—both opposed to war in Iraq—would distance them from the Israeli-Palestinian problem and would leave the field open to America, Israel's main ally.

Following the army's advice, the government decided to put the country on a heightened state of alert. Israelis were asked to check their anti-gas kits since, according to military intelligence, Saddam Hussein was still in possession of around twenty ground-to-ground Scud missiles capable of reaching Israel. The French intelligence services, which were exchanging information with their Israeli counterparts, disagreed. Paris believed the Iraqis were in possession of, at most, a single Scud missile! The Americans, meanwhile, were claiming the existence of a terrifying arsenal of unconventional weapons hidden in Iraq. Whatever the case, the Israeli generals were anticipating the war with glee. The eastern front, which for decades had been one of the main threats to the Jewish state, was on the verge of being eradicated. The American army was going to destroy an Arab regime with huge petroleum resources, a regime whose dictator offered generous financial compensation to the families of Palestinian suicide bombers. From an Israeli perspective, war in Iraq was an excellent development.

In Washington, George Bush planned to announce that he would accept the roadmap designed by the Quartet in order to appease the Arab world. The problem was that Sharon was not satisfied with the latest version of the plan. The absolute rejection of violence and terrorism, as well as the rejection of Arafat, were not spelled out in black and white. The prime minister sent the head of his cabinet, the lawyer Dov Weisglass, and the head of the national security council, Ephraim Halevy, to Washington to convince the American administration. Condoleezza Rice was persuaded: the roadmap would not be altered, but the president would also announce that Israel would be permitted to propose amendments. During a press conference on March 14, George Bush announced that

> the Palestinian Authority has created the new position of prime minister. . . . To be a credible and responsible partner, the new Palestinian prime minister must hold a position of real authority. We expect that such a Palestinian prime min-

ister will be confirmed soon. Immediately upon confirmation, the road map for peace will be given to the Palestinians and the Israelis. This road map will set forth a sequence of steps toward the goals I set out on June 24, 2002, goals shared by all the parties. . . . Once this road map is delivered, we will expect and welcome contributions from Israel and the Palestinians to this document.

On March 17, seven Palestinians were killed during an incursion by the Israeli army into the Nusseirat refugee camp in Gaza. In Ramallah, Yasser Arafat, after weeks of hesitation, finally gave in to pressure exerted by the Quartet and the Palestinian legislative council. He signed the decree transferring a portion of his power to a prime minister—the position that had just been created. But, to the great displeasure of the members of the Quartet, Chairman Arafat was to retain control of the security services. Mahmoud Abbas, the second-in-command of the PLO, opposed to the intifada and to armed struggle, was supposed to be named prime minister. The Israeli army removed a document from its Internet site that described him as a revisionist of the Holocaust. In his doctoral thesis, published in Moscow in 1984, the man who was an architect of the Oslo Accords had expressed some doubts concerning the number of Jewish victims of the Holocaust.

The offensive in Iraq was launched the next day. Batteries of anti-missile Patriot missiles were deployed in Tel Aviv and Haifa. Although the passive defense recommended that Israelis move and bring their anti-chemical kits along with them, very few complied. The great majority of the public demonstrated a clearer vision of the situation than the military officials.

The Israeli press followed the war, day in and day out. Caroline Glick from the *Jerusalem Post* was embedded with the 2-7 Mechanized Infantry Battalion from the U.S. Army's 3rd infantry division's first brigade. She published an interview with its operations officer, Major Rod Coffey, in which she described him as an avid follower of the work of Brigadier General (ret.) Shimon Naveh from OTRI, the Israeli think tank. She wrote:

He believes that what the US military accomplished in its offensive has shown that as Naveh argues, the German all-out combined arms operations from World War II is not necessarily the key to winning in modern warfare.

'What we did here on an operational level has never been done before,' Coffey explains. 'We showed that if your objective is to destroy a regime, you do not have to engage at every location. We made very clear to the regular Iraqi army before we invaded that it was not our target. We also signaled very clearly to the Special Republican Guard that it was our target. We rightly assumed that the Iraqi people themselves would not fight for Saddam's regime.

'All of these actions and presumptions informed our military planning and operations. We did not get bogged down. We moved straight to our objective. Our messages were received by the proper Iraqis and they behaved accordingly.'[4]

Did the new Israeli doctrines of warfare influence the American strategy in Iraq?

On March 30, meanwhile, violence erupted on the Mediterranean coast, in a suicide attack near Netanya wounding fifty-three. On April 3, the Israeli army made a series of incursions into the West Bank and Gaza, causing the deaths of six Palestinians. On April 8, missiles were fired on the car of a Hamas leader in Gaza, killing him, his bodyguard, and five bystanders, one of whom was a child. On April 19, the IDF made another incursion—this time into Rafah, killing four and wounding forty-eight.

ARAFAT GIVES UP
In Ramallah, Arafat was delaying the confirmation of Mahmoud Abbas, obliging the Quartet to step in. Miguel Moratinos recalled:

You have to understand the situation. Arafat was in a difficult position. He was the leader, the chairman of the Authority, and he was saying to himself, 'Why do I need a prime minister? I don't need one. I'm the one who makes the decisions!' Arafat and Abbas did not trust each other, and did not respect each other. We had to beg both of them, 'Please, speak to each other!'[5]

Terje Larsen was even more direct:

> We consulted the other members of the Quartet and we went to see Yasser Arafat to let him know, without placating him, that there was no other possible way. His response was negative. I reiterated that this was his last chance, and that if he didn't comply. . . . I showed him the door, saying: One day, it will open and it will be a soldier who walks through it, wearing the uniform of the Israeli army. That will be the end for you. Your only option is to renounce your power and create the post of prime minister.[6]

With great reluctance, Arafat officially granted Mahmoud Abbas the responsibility of creating a new government. Arafat, however, did not approve the composition of the cabinet until April 23. He refused the nomination of Mohammed Dahlan to the post of interior minister. But finally, the former head of preventative security in Gaza was appointed secretary of state of the new cabinet, and assumed responsibility for some security matters. Just reaching this point required the intervention of both Omar Suleiman (Hosni Mubarak's special envoy) and Andrei Vdovin (the Russian emissary to the Middle East), who frequently shuttled back and forth between the Muqata and the new prime minister's office.

THE ROAD MAP IN THE HANDS OF SHARON AND ARAFAT

On April 30, a Briton of Pakistani origin committed a suicide attack on a seaside bar in Tel Aviv, causing three deaths. His accomplice, also a British citizen, would be found later on a beach, drowned.

In Ramallah, several hours after the swearing in of the new Palestinian government, Miguel Moratinos, Terje Larsen, and Andrei Vdovin officially presented Arafat with the road map. Meanwhile, Sharon received it from the hands of the U.S. Ambassador Dan Kurtzer, who later recounted that Sharon did not expect to receive the text. He was clearly hoping that his allies in Washington would manage to delay this moment for as long as possible.[7]

The road map outlined an initial phase that would last until the beginning of June 2003, during which the Palestinians would be required to unconditionally and definitively put an end to violence. The Israeli army would, in turn, be called upon to withdraw to the positions that it had occupied before the beginning of the intifada. Israel would also be required to halt construction of settlements in the West Bank, as well as to improve the humanitarian situation in the Palestinian territories. The second phase, lasting until the end of 2003, would lead to the establishment of a Palestinian state within provisional borders. Negotiations on the final status would begin at the end of this phase.

The Israeli government scrutinized the document for five days, culminating in government ministers demanding no less than fourteen amendments, of which the main one, proposed by Sharon, was the following: "Calm must be established immediately, following the stages established by the road map. The Palestinians will disarm existing security services, and then will proceed to carry out security reform by establishing new security services that will fight against terrorism, violence, and the incitation to violence (the incitation to violence must stop immediately, and the Palestinian Authority must encourage peace through education). The new security services must launch real preventative operations: arrests, investigations into terrorism and violence. . . . The Palestinians must have accomplished the disarmament of terrorist organizations (Hamas, Islamic Jihad, the Popular Front, the Democratic Front, and others) before passing to the next step of the road map. . . ." Condoleezza Rice replied to Sharon's statement that same evening: "The objections of the parties will be taken into account, but no change will be made to the text of the road map."[8]

POWELL RETURNS

On May 1, an Israeli incursion into the Gaza Strip resulted in twelve deaths. Since the situation was again deteriorating, George Bush decided to send Colin Powell back to the Middle East in order to encourage the Israelis and the Palestinians to implement the road map. Powell arrived in Jerusalem on the evening of May 10, just as Israel was beginning to open checkpoints and unseal Palestinian territories. According to the *New York Times*, Bush administration officials had been criticizing Israel for not making any gestures of good will toward the Palestinians (the West Bank and Gaza would be sealed again two days later, after Powell's departure). During a four-hour meeting on May 11, Sharon explained to Powell that Israel would not accept a cease-fire that could allow terrorist movements to reorganize. But, he continued, Israel was nevertheless prepared to negotiate with Mahmoud Abbas within the next few days. During a meeting with the press that followed, Sharon enumerated, before Powell, the reasons it was necessary for construction to continue in the settlements: "And demographic growth? If a young man completes his military service and wants to get married, to raise a family, what are we going to do? Force his wife to get an abortion?"

Powell's discussion with Mahmoud Abbas in Jericho failed to produce any significant results. The new Palestinian prime minister did not have the ability to respond to the Israeli demands that Powell relayed, notably those concerning the rapid disarmament of terrorist organizations. On May 17, a Hamas suicide bomber struck in Hebron, killing two Israelis, including a pregnant woman. Sharon was in a bad mood when he received Abbas, Mohammed Dahlan, and Nabil Shaath, the foreign minister, at his office in Jerusalem. The atmosphere during the meeting was glacial, and it ended without any agreements being reached.

On May 23, the Bush administration promised to address the fourteen amendments proposed by Israel, but without changing the text of the road map.[9] Sharon had gained the upper hand, and was thus able to agree to the text. It was nevertheless unlikely that the Palestinians would manage to reorganize all of their security services and disarm terrorist organizations within the time allotted. Forty-eight hours later, the Israeli government unanimously approved the Quartet's peace plan. On May 26, Sharon faced the Likud members of Parliament and was interrogated by those on the extreme right of the party. Ehud Yatom, a former member of Shin Bet, demanded: "Where is the reciprocity? We recognize the formation of a Palestinian state, and they don't recognize a Jewish state for the Jewish people? They need to at least recognize that!" David Levy, a former minister under Menachem Begin, accused: "The government has, in effect, decided to create a Palestinian state! At that price, the left would have already achieved peace a long time ago! Mr. Prime Minister, I believe you when you say that you are in favor of a compromise . . . but for the love of God, this road map is going to lead us straight to something that you do not want! To give up everything! Everything!" Sharon's response was a page out of history: "How can you imagine or believe that it is possible to remain under occupation. . . . Under occupation! For it's an occupation! You may not like the word, but that's what this is about! How can you imagine keeping three and a half million Palestinians under occupation? From my point of view, it's a bad solution, and cannot last forever. Do you really want to stay in Jenin, in Nablus, in Ramallah, in Bethlehem, forever? Forever? I do not think that that is just!" The whole scene unfolded before television cameras that had been authorized to film the meeting. This was the first time that Ariel Sharon, godfather of the settlement movement, had uttered the word "occupation."

This new language made Elyakim Rubinstein, the legal advisor to the government, very anxious. He called and then wrote to the prime minister in order to ask him to publish a denial and to use the term "disputed territories" instead of "occupied territories." The following day, in front of the parliamentary commission on foreign affairs and the defense, Sharon stated that that he had been misunderstood. After having listened to his explanations of the road map, the right-wing ministers left the meeting reassured. According to Shaul Yahalom, a legislator from the

National Religious Party, "it would take a miracle for Mahmoud Abbas and Dahlan to eradicate terrorism! This is nothing other than a political maneuver on the part of the prime minister!"

Unofficially, several European negotiators of the Quartet admitted that their peace plan was dead on arrival, but, they said: "It's that or nothing. At least we have a document that can serve as a foundation for starting work."[10]

SUMMITS AT SHARM EL-SHEIK AND AQABA

While GIs were attacking pockets of resistance in Iraq, the Bush administration presented the Arab world with a road map, proof that it was working to create a Palestinian state! George Bush asked Hosni Mubarak to organize a meeting for him with the leaders of the other Arab states. The mini-summit convened on June 3 at Sharm el-Sheik. It brought together Crown Prince Abdullah of Saudi Arabia, Mahmoud Abbas, King Abdullah of Jordan, and King Hamad bin Isa Khalifa of Bahrain, who presided over the Arab League. These five Arab leaders agreed to lend their support to the road map and condemned terrorism, but they refused to consider Yasser Arafat "out of play" as Bush wanted.

A second summit occurred the next day at the Red Sea port of Aqaba in Jordan. Sharon met with Abbas under the aegis of George Bush and King Abdullah. A camera captured a conversation between Shaul Mofaz, the Israeli defense minister, and Mohammed Dahlan:

> **Mofaz:** "We've weakened Arafat, but he continues to cause you problems."
> **Dahlan:** "I'm taking care of it. Only three years ago, he would have never admitted that I was at the side of Mahmoud Abbas. That makes all the difference."
> **Mofaz:** "He's manipulating you. . . . He pushes you around."
> **Dahlan:** "Maybe, but today he calls me ten times a day."[11]

The official ceremony began, and King Abdullah greeted his guests and gave Mahmoud Abbas the podium:

Our goal is two states, Israel and Palestine, living side by side, in peace and security. The process is one of direct negotiations to end the Israeli-Palestinian conflict, and to resolve all the permanent status issues [of Palestinian refugees], and end the occupation that began in 1967, under which Palestinians have suffered so much. At the same time, we do not ignore the suffering of the Jews throughout history. It is time to bring all this suffering to an end. Just as Israel must meet its responsibilities, we, the Palestinians, will fulfill our obligations in order for this endeavor to succeed. We are ready to do our part.

Let me be very clear: There will be no military solution to this conflict, so we repeat our renunciation, a renunciation of terror against the Israelis wherever they might be. Such methods are inconsistent with our religious and moral traditions and are dangerous obstacles to the achievement of an independent, sovereign state we seek. These methods also conflict with the kind of state we wish to build, based on human rights and the rule of law. We will exert all of our efforts, using all our resources to end the militarization of the intifada, and we will succeed! The armed intifada must end, and we must use and resort to peaceful means in our quest to end the occupation and the suffering of Palestinians and Israelis. . . .

Ariel Sharon responded:

My paramount responsibility is the security of the people of Israel and of the state of Israel. There can be no compromise with terror. And Israel, together with all free nations, will continue fighting terrorism until its final defeat. Ultimately, permanent security requires peace, and permanent peace can only be obtained through security. And there is now hope of a new opportunity for peace between Israelis and Palestinians. Israel, like others, has lent its strong support for President Bush's vision expressed on June 24, 2002, of two states,

Israel and a Palestinian state, living side by side in peace and security. The government and people of Israel welcome the opportunity to renew direct negotiations according to the steps of the road map as adopted by the Israeli government.[12]

It is in Israel's interest not to govern the Palestinians, but for the Palestinians to govern themselves in their own state. A democratic Palestinian state, fully at peace with Israel, will promote the long-term security and well-being of Israel as a Jewish state.

There can be no peace, however, without the abandonment and elimination of terrorism, violence and incitement. We will work alongside Palestinians and other states to fight terrorism, violence and incitement of all kinds. As all parties perform their obligations, we will seek to restore normal Palestinian life, improve the humanitarian situation, rebuild trust and promote progress, follow the president's vision. We will act in a manner that respects the dignity, as well as the human rights of all people. We can also reassure our Palestinian partners that we understand the importance of territorial contiguity in the West Bank for a viable Palestinian state. Israeli policy in the territories that are subject to direct negotiations with the Palestinians will reflect this fact. We accept the principle that no unilateral actions by any party can prejudge the outcome of our negotiations. In regard to the unauthorized outposts, I want to reiterate that Israel is a society governed by the rule of law. Thus, we will immediately begin to remove unauthorized outposts.

Next it was George Bush's turn to take the podium:

I'm pleased to be here with Prime Minister Sharon. The friendship between our countries began at the time of Israel's creation. Today, America is strongly committed, and I am strongly committed, to Israel's security as a vibrant Jewish state. I'm also pleased to be with Prime Minister Abbas. He represents the cause of freedom and statehood for the Palestinian people. I strongly support that cause, as well. Each of us is here because we understand that all people have the right to live in peace.

Great and hopeful change is coming to the Middle East. In Iraq, a dictator who funded terror and sowed conflict has been removed, and a more just and democratic society is emerging. Prime Minister Abbas now leads the Palestinian Cabinet. By his strong leadership, by building the institutions of Palestinian democracy and by rejecting terror, he is serving the deepest hopes of his people. All here today now share a goal: the Holy Land must be shared between the state of Palestine and the state of Israel, living in peace with one another and with every nation of the Middle East.

I welcome Prime Minister Sharon's pledge to improve the humanitarian situation in the Palestinian areas and to begin removing unauthorized outposts immediately. I appreciate his gestures of reconciliation on behalf of prisoners and their families, and his frank statements about the need for the territorial contiguity.[13]

ARAFAT AND HAMAS ACCUSE ABBAS

In Ramallah, Chairman Arafat was following events minute by minute. Yasser Abed Rabbo described the scene: "During the Aqaba summit, we all knew that Arafat was not going to appreciate the images on television. While he's imprisoned, here's another Palestinian leader standing next to King Abdullah of Jordan, Bush, and the others, discussing peace and shaking the hand of Sharon, his jailer. But we did not expect Arafat to launch a campaign against us. He spoke of treason, high treason, and, without mentioning Mahmoud Abbas by name, said that we don't need another Karzai here [in Palestine]."[14]

Islamists organized demonstrations against Abbas. In Gaza, Abdel Aziz Rantisi, of Hamas, declaimed: "Now the suffering of the Jews has become important? From being the victims, we have now turned into the aggressors! Arafat would have mentioned the Haram al-Sharif [the esplanade of the mosques in Jerusalem] at least three times! He would have talked about martyrs, about prisoners!" On June 10, this Hamas leader narrowly escaped an attempted "targeted killing" that resulted in the deaths of three Palestinians. The following day, Hamas responded by sending a young Palestinian from Hebron, disguised as an ultra-orthodox Jew, to set off his explosive belt on a Jerusalem street, resulting in seventeen deaths and one hundred wounded. An hour later in Gaza, a helicopter launched a missile at a car, killing two Hamas militants and four bystanders. Another raid took place the following evening. Two members of the armed branch of Hamas died. Mahmoud Abbas blamed the attack on the Israelis and issued another call for a cessation of violence. The peace process was on the verge of falling apart. Condoleezza Rice called Dov Weisglass, the head of Ariel Sharon's cabinet, and asked him: "Why did you launch this operation against Rantisi?" His answer is not known.

Colin Powell announced that he would return on June 20. The day before, the IDF evacuation of an "outpost" was caught on camera, and scenes of confrontation between soldiers and settlers opened television news broadcasts. Sharon insisted to the secretary of state: "No peace while there is terrorism!" In Jericho, Mahmoud Abbas told the prime minister that he still did not have the means to control Hamas, and that he needed to be able to offer the possibility of a political solution to the Palestinians. A security meeting between General Amos Gilaad and Mohammed Dahlan, overseen by John Wolf, the new American emissary, ended in failure. But given the pressure from the Bush administration, the discussions nevertheless continued.

AYALON AND NUSSEIBEH PROPOSE PEACE

On June 25, Ami Ayalon, the former head of Shin Bet, surprised everyone. During a press conference in Tel Aviv, he launched a new peace initiative with Sari Nusseibeh, the moderate Palestinian intellectual. The two men asked the people of Israel and Palestine to sign onto a plan to settle the conflict. They had negotiated the text during the previous few months:

1. Two states for two peoples: Both sides will declare that Palestine is the only state of the Palestinian people and Israel is the only state of the Jewish people.

2. Borders: Permanent borders between the two states will be agreed upon on the basis of the June 4, 1967 lines, UN resolutions, and the Arab peace initiative (known as the Saudi initiative).
   • Border modifications will be based on an equitable and agreed-upon territorial exchange (1:1) in accordance with the vital needs of both sides, including security, territorial contiguity, and demographic considerations.
   • The Palestinian state will have a connection between its two geographic areas, the West Bank and the Gaza Strip.
   • After establishment of the agreed borders, no settlers will remain in the Palestinian state.

3. Jerusalem: Jerusalem will be an open city, the capital of two states. Freedom of religion and full access to holy sites will be guaranteed to all.
   • Arab neighborhoods in Jerusalem will come under Palestinian sovereignty, Jewish neighborhoods under Israeli sovereignty.
   • Neither side will exercise sovereignty over the holy places. The state of Palestine will be designated guardian of al-Haram al-Sharif for the benefit of Muslims. Israel will be the Guardian of the Western Wall for the benefit of the Jewish people. The status quo on Christian holy sites will be maintained. No excavation will take place in or underneath the holy sites without mutual consent.

4. Right of return: Recognizing the suffering and the plight of the Palestinian refugees, the international community, Israel, and the Palestinian state will initiate and contribute to an international fund to compensate them.

• Palestinian refugees will return only to the state of Palestine; Jews will return only to the state of Israel.[15]

Ami Ayalon confirmed that the majority of the Israeli public was in support of the effort. He hoped to collect 200,000 Israeli signatures and 100,000 from the Palestinians. Sari Nusseibeh stated that the campaign was aimed at generating support for the leaders of both sides during their negotiations. This statement led to an opening of checkpoints in the Palestinian territories. But Nusseibeh was accused of behaving like a traitor for surrendering the right of return of refugees.

Yossi Beilin, the former Israeli justice minister, and Yasser Abed Rabbo were also negotiating. During regular, discreet meetings at the Norwegian consulate, in hotels, and sometimes abroad, they had been preparing nothing less than a document containing a definitive agreement between Israel and Palestine. Numerous well-known Israeli and Palestinian moderates had also lent a hand.

THE ISRAELI ARMY REDUCED TO A MINIMUM

As a result of the intifada, Israel was suffering its gravest economic crisis of the past twenty years. Fearing terrorist attacks, tourists and investors were no longer visiting. As part of the austerity program that Benjamin Netanyahu, the finance minister, had gotten approved by the government, all ministries had to cut their budgets by 10 percent. The defense ministry, which had obtained a supplement of two billion shekels ($500 million) the previous year, was particularly hard hit.[16] It was going to have to repay 500 million due to a reduction of 2.8 million for the current year, and a million each year for the two following years. IDF leaders were thus forced to revisit their priorities. Moshe Yaalon and most of the members of the military believed that the strategic environment had changed completely. The threat of an eastern front against Israel had completely disappeared with the invasion of Iraq by the American army —Syria's armaments were obsolete. This left the Palestinian conflict, which was not costly, and Iran, which was attempting to acquire nuclear weapons. The decision was thus made to prioritize the air force, which was to acquire 102 American F16I bombers with long-range weapon capability. The number of armored tank units was to be reduced by 20 percent, and the training of reservists was to be canceled. Aviation and remaining land forces would have to suffice for the confrontation with the Palestinians.

This decision was not welcomed by General Yiftah Ron-Tal, the commander of ground forces. On June 25, in a long report addressed to Moshe Yaalon, the chief of staff, he recalled that in the Middle East the air force alone is not capable of translating decisions into military terms. And he warned that in the case of a conflict beyond the border, the reduction of the mechanized forces would reduce the capacity of the IDF to achieve victory the only way possible, that is, on the ground. And Ron-Tal also criticized the abandonment of the absolute principle (which was espoused, he said, by all armies in the world) of the combined terrestrial maneuver as a fundamental tactic.

His efforts failed, and he was depicted as a troublemaker going around in circles. Following a bizarre affair involving undeclared rent, the general found that his promotion was blocked. Moshe Yaalon and Dan Halutz decided to give budgetary preference to the airborne forces. Tank units and large reserve units would be reduced to the bare minimum. During the offensive against Hezbollah in 2006, over a hundred soldiers would pay with their lives for this policy.[17]

On June 27, Mohammed Dahlan and Israeli military officials agreed in principle to place Gaza under the responsibility of Palestinian security. Lacking the necessary military means to confront Hamas, Mahmoud Abbas negotiated a truce with the Islamic movement. This cease-fire agreement was called the *hudna*, from the name of the treaty concluded by the prophet Muhammad with the Quraysh tribe. According to Islamic jurisprudence, such a truce with non-Muslims must be limited to ten years. Hamas and Islamic Jihad agreed to halt attacks against Israel for three months, on condition that the Israeli army, for its part, put a stop to "targeted killings," the destruction of Palestinian property, and arrests. Fatah, for its part, announced that its truce would last six months.

THE "WALL"

Henceforth baptized the "security fence," the construction of the barrier designed to separate Israel and the West Bank continued. In certain spots, the structure was equipped with electronic detection systems, consisted of ditches, a patrol walkway, wire mesh, and barbed-wire fencing, and reached 50 to 70 meters (164 to 230 feet) in width. It did not exactly follow the green line, but rather encroached upon the territory of the West Bank. In so doing, it separated Palestinian farmers from their land, destroyed their plantations, and cut off roads. The plan aimed to encompass Israeli settlements on the Israeli side. The town of Qalqilya was surrounded by an 8-meter high concrete wall that allowed for only one exit to the east, which was under the army's control. An identical wall was under construction in Tulkarm. Protests became more and more numerous. Palestinians accused Israel of implementing a fait accompli policy, of determining the future borders by annexing a large part of their territory. Mahmoud Abbas sounded the alarm to the American administration. Palestinian public opinion was growing increasingly angry, and was accusing him of not acting against the "wall." Even worse, in everyone's eyes, he was beginning to look like an impotent leader. Colin Powell reacted:

> All of us put fences up when we feel a need for a fence on our property, and we try to do it in a way that does not prejudice anyone else's property or anyone else's rights. In the case of this fence, Israel felt there was a need to put up such a fence for security purposes, and the president has said that we understand that.
>
> It is when the fence begins to intrude on land that is not on the Israeli side of the green line, or starts to intrude in a way that makes it more difficult for us to make the case for a viable Palestinian state, or starts to cut off certain towns and villages or in other ways interferes with Palestinian activity in Palestinian towns and villages, then it is appropriate for us to say to our Israeli friends, 'Look, we have a problem

here,' and particularly as they are getting ready for the next stages of this fence construction project.[18]

Condoleezza Rice traveled to the Middle East on June 28 to put the peace process back on track and demand modifications to the barrier blueprint. Sharon responded that "Israel will make no concessions on its security. The barrier is a necessity for security, even if the United States doesn't agree!" Benjamin Netanyahu reminded Rice: "250 perpetrators of suicide attacks have come to Israel from the West Bank! Not one came from Gaza, which is surrounded by a security barrier!" Rice responded by asking Israel to demonstrate its understanding of the Palestinians. The meeting with Mahmoud Abbas took place in Jericho, and Rice promised him supplementary financial assistance.

ABBAS ON SHARON'S TURF

On July 1, Mahmoud Abbas and his most important ministers made an official visit to Jerusalem. Ariel Sharon greeted his Palestinian counterpart:

> "Good afternoon. How are you?"
> **Abbas:** "I'm tired, horribly tired!"
> **Sharon:** "It's tough being prime minister."
> **Abbas:** "Yes, it's hard."
> **Sharon:** "I finally learned!"
> **Abbas:** "What if you and I left, if we made a visit to your ranch. That would be better for us!"
> **Sharon:** "While it's hard, there are a lot of people who want the prime minister's job."
> **Abbas:** "Let them have it!"[19]

Next, the two men exchanged niceties for the press.

> **Sharon:** "I give a warm welcome to Prime Minister Abbas and the members of his cabinet who are with us today. I have no doubt that the message sent from here today to the people

of Israel, to the Palestinian people, and to the whole world, is one of hope and optimism. . . . I will do everything I can to achieve a political solution that will lead to calm and—with the help of God—to peace. That is the mission that I have always aimed for. . . . Even if the price is high, and painful compromises are necessary to achieve peace, I am ready to make them. But there will be no negotiating with terrorism."

Abbas: "We have no interest in continuing the conflict with Israel. . . . We must take a new path in which mutual respect and a vision for the future surpass doubts and past memories. Peace is the fundamental objective towards which we aspire and devote all of our efforts. We have passed through important stages leading to this aim, notably by restoring calm thanks to our agreement and to the Israeli withdrawal from Gaza. Later, there will be a total withdrawal from all the other cities, towns, and Palestinian refugee camps."

The Palestinian prime minister presented three demands to Sharon: to liberate prisoners, to open military checkpoints in the West Bank, and, most importantly, to restore the freedom of movement of Yasser Arafat, who had been under house arrest at the Muqata since December 2001. Sharon promised to examine the first two, and categorically refused the third.

ABBAS AND SHARON IN WASHINGTON

On July 25, Mahmoud Abbas arrived in Washington, marking the first time that George Bush ever received a Palestinian leader at the White House. The purpose of the visit was thus primarily symbolic. The American administration wanted to send a message to the Arab world and to Israel, namely that the Palestinian prime minister was an ally of the United States. Abbas received a check for $20 million, and Bush announced the creation of an American-Palestinian economic development group. During a joint press conference, Abbas announced:

The outcome [of negotiations] must correspond with your vision, Mr. President, achieving a peace that will end the occupation that started in 1967. The establishment of a sovereign, independent Palestinian state, with East Jerusalem as its capital. . . . This vision cannot be realized if Israel continues to grab Palestinian land. If the settlement activities in Palestinian land and construction of the so-called separation wall on confiscated Palestinian land continue, we might soon find ourselves at a situation where the foundation of peace, a free Palestinian state . . . is a factual impossibility. . . . For the sake of peace, and for the sake of future Palestinian and Israeli generations, all settlement activities must be stopped now, and the wall must come down.

Bush admitted that that was indeed a problem: "It is very difficult to develop confidence between the Palestinians and Israel with a wall snaking through the West Bank."

Relative calm reigned in the region as a result either of the *hudna* decreed by the Palestinian organizations, or, according to the IDF, of military operations in the West Bank and Gaza and the construction of the security fence. On July 29, Ariel Sharon made his eighth visit to the White House, and promised his interlocutors that he would make an effort to ensure that the plan for the security fence infringe as little as possible on the everyday lives of the Palestinian people. He repeated this phrase a number of times at the president's side during the traditional press conference. President Bush responded:

I fully understand that the most effective campaign to enhance the security of Israel, as well as the security of peace-loving people in the Palestinian territories, is to get after organizations such as Hamas, the terrorist organizations that create the conditions where peace won't exist. And therefore, I would hope in the long-term a fence would be irrelevant. But, look, the fence is a sensitive issue.

The Americans asked Ariel Sharon to help Mahmoud Abbas stabilize his power because he was falling under extreme criticism on the streets of the West Bank and Gaza, while in the Muqata, Yasser Arafat did not lose any opportunity to criticize his prime minister. Sharon began to try to release Palestinian prisoners, but met resistance from those in his government who refused freedom to any detainee "with blood on his hands." In other words, no prisoner of any importance would be freed, especially not Marwan Barghouti. Abbas rejected the first list of "free-able" prisoners drawn up by the army and Shin Bet, and let his disappointment be known by canceling a meeting with Sharon planned for August 5. Two days later, Israel planned to release 400 detainees. In solidarity with his comrades who were not given this opportunity, one prisoner decided to remain in his prison cell. Only 399 prisoners were thus freed. Palestinian officials were profoundly angry and disappointed. Among these prisoners, ninety-nine were to be freed anyway in eight days; 159 would see their prison term expire before the end of the year, among whom thirty-one would see it expire before the end of the month; 183 had been imprisoned for breaches of security; 157 were administrative detainees, imprisoned without being charged or given a trial; fifty were considered common criminals; and forty-nine had been arrested for illegally residing in Israel. In Tel Aviv, the defense minister reacted to the criticisms by issuing a statement asserting that "264 prisoners had already been released since June 29, which brings the total number of Palestinians freed to 603, or, 10 percent of the total number."

On August 7, after seven months of relative calm, tensions increased once again along the northern border. Hezbollah launched new attacks against the Israeli position at Shebaa Farms, and the Israeli army responded with combat helicopters and artillery targeting Shiite militia in Lebanon. Two days later, a mortar shell exploded near the Israeli border community of Shlomi, killing a teenager and once again spurring airborne reprisal raids by the Israelis against Hezbollah positions.

On August 8, the IDF made an incursion into Nablus. They acted on the basis of intelligence concluding that two Hamas militants were fabricating explosive belts in a clandestine laboratory there. Both were killed during a skirmish, along with one Israeli soldier. Hamas promised to avenge the two men and three days later, two suicide bombers launched separate attacks in Rosh Haayin, an Israeli town, and in the settlement of Ariel, killing two civilians.

On August 13 in Hebron, when soldiers attempted to apprehend Mohammed Sidr, an official from the armed wing of Islamic Jihad, he resisted and opened fire. The IDF summoned a bulldozer to the site and destroyed his house, crushing the militant beneath the rubble. Islamic Jihad vowed revenge.

In spite of these clashes, the *hudna* appeared to hold. Mohammed Dahlan pursued the negotiations that had been broached with the Israelis in July. The IDF was supposed to withdraw from several Palestinian cities, but was permitted to leave military checkpoints in place at their entrances. According to the press, the possibility still existed that an agreement could be reached within the next forty-eight hours, when some of the 170 checkpoints scattered throughout the West Bank would be opened.

HAMAS AGAINST THE TRUCE

Once again Hamas decided to strike in order to torpedo the political process. On the evening of August 19, in Jerusalem, near the neighborhood of Shmuel Hanavi, the imam of a Hebron mosque got into a bus packed with ultra-orthodox families and set off his explosives, killing twenty-three people and wounding 130. There were numerous children among the victims. The televised images were appalling. *Haaretz,* the most moderate Israeli press outlet, published an editorial that was particularly critical of the Palestinian government:

> Palestinian Prime Minister Mahmoud Abbas recognized that truth when he denounced the terror attack in Jerusalem as an evil act that also harmed the national interests of his own people. But during the last two months of the fragile ceasefire, despite U.S. support and encouragement, Abbas did not prove that he is determined enough to translate that recognition in principle into the language of practice. No significant steps have been taken against Hamas and Islamic Jihad

activists in Gaza, where the security forces are subordinate to Abbas and his security minister, Mohammed Dahlan. The terrorists train without interference. In the West Bank, as well, even though security responsibility has not been transferred in most of the cities to the Palestinian Authority, there has been no sign from the PA that it is preparing or intends to prepare to deal with terror organizations.

Hamas broadcast a video recorded by the terrorist before his departure for Jerusalem. He confessed that he was seeking vengeance for militants from Hamas as well as for Mohammed Sidr of Islamic Jihad, killed by Israel. Hebron, the city from which the terrorist hailed, was sealed and partially occupied by the IDF.

ABBAS RESIGNS

Forty-eight hours later, another "targeted killing" took place in Gaza. A helicopter launched a missile into a vehicle carrying three men, among whom was Ismail Abu Shanab, a Hamas political official. On September 1, another raid on Gaza resulted in the killing of one Hamas militant and the wounding of twenty-five bystanders. Again, on September 5, the Israeli army made an incursion into Nablus, killing a Hamas official.

Mahmoud Abbas drew up the balance sheet: the *hudna*—the cease-fire —was over. The violence had recommenced. His popularity was waning. The endless confrontation with Yasser Arafat was preventing him from governing. He made his decision. The following day, Yasser Abed Rabbo delivered Abbas's resignation letter to Arafat.

Arafat, all smiles, with a greedy expression on his face, asked: "What are you bringing me? A letter?" Abed Rabbo replied, "You know perfectly well what this is about." Arafat opened the envelope and, in an ironic tone, read its contents out loud:

> I did everything in my power, and even beyond that, to help further interior and political progress, and I informed the

legislative council of that. Apparently, the problem does not concern the progress in question, but the desire to cause the failure of this government by all means possible, legitimate and illegitimate, including through bloodshed and accusations of treason. Brother Abu Amar, you are the sole person who can end the mandate of this government. Your intention was clear: to leave it in place in order to blame it for all failures, to make it the target of the hatred that fills all hearts. Our government had been weakened to the point that it is quite easy to shoot poisoned arrows without thinking of what it would have been able to achieve for the good of the nation. More serious is the method used by some to twist the truth. ... Since you are convinced that I am the Karzai of Palestine, that I betrayed the trust with which I had been invested, I return my mandate.[20]

Within the hour, Abbas gave his resignation speech before the legislative council. It was his chance to settle accounts with Yasser Arafat, the Israelis, and the Americans:

Every country in the world has a retirement system. How long are we going to keep the grandfather, the father, and the grandson, in the same government while our country has 18,000 educated young people who are unemployed? It is also time to rule on the taxes withheld from the salaries of the employed, which in some cases is as high as 15 percent. Speaking for myself, I have no idea where this money goes. Why do we need monopolies for fuel, tobacco, and other companies? Whose interests does that serve? When we liquidated the fuel monopoly, we noticed a tremendous difference in the returns between July and August, due to the elimination of the commission on sales: six million dollars per month, or seventy-two million dollars per year, had thus been stolen.

Abbas then explained that he had wanted to appoint a new high commissioner to the civil service in order to unify the Palestinian administration, but that Arafat had sent armed men to guard the Gaza building which holds that seat. He continued:

> The real problem is that Israel rejected even the most basic requests that we have presented and with which the Americans agreed. Even those concerning Palestinian prisoners. If [the Israelis] had freed more, if they had stopped construction on the barrier around our land and lifted the siege. . . . But they offered nothing, although, regularly, [the Israelis] insisted that they wanted to support the government of Abu Mazen. I am not an employee working for them or anyone else. If they want this government to remain in place, then they should help it. That has not been the case, and that is precisely the proof that they do not want it. . . . The Americans talk day and night of offering us assistance . . . but nothing comes [from the United States].

The following day, Arafat invested Ahmed Qureia, the president of the Parliament, with the responsibility of forming a new government. But, before accepting, Qureia demanded guarantees from the United States and Europe. He had learned a lesson from Abbas.

On September 9, 2003, Hamas committed a suicide attack at a bus stop near a military base and close to a hospital near Tel Aviv. In all, nine soldiers were killed and thirty wounded. That same afternoon, a suicide bomber struck at Café Hillel in Jerusalem, killing seven and wounding fifty. On September 10, warplanes bombed the home of Mahmoud Zahar, a Hamas leader, killing two, including his son. Zahar and his wife were only wounded.

Twenty-four hours later, after a meeting of the Israeli security cabinet, the prime minister's office announced that Sharon

has instructed the security forces to act relentlessly, continu-
ously, and determinedly, to eliminate the terrorist organizations and take all appropriate measures against their leaders,
commanders, and operatives until their criminal activity is
halted. . . . Events of the recent days have reiterated and proven
again that Yasser Arafat is a complete obstacle to any process of reconciliation between Israel and the Palestinians. Israel will work to remove this obstacle in a manner, and at a
time, of its choosing.

Israeli sources explained that the idea was to expel Arafat by force and
deport him to an Arab country. Immediately after the broadcast of this
announcement, thousands of Fatah supporters flooded the Muqata compound in Ramallah. Greeting them, Arafat proclaimed, "They can kill
me with their bombs but nobody will force me to leave."

On September 14, Ehud Olmert, the vice-prime minister, told Kol
Israel (Israel's public radio) that "Arafat can no longer be a factor in what
happens here. The question is: how are we going to do it? Expulsion is
certainly one of the options, and killing is also one of the options."

The situation in the Palestinian territories was catastrophic. It was,
according to the World Bank and most charitable organizations, the
gravest humanitarian crisis in the region since the 1950s. According to
the United Nations Relief and Works Agency (UNRWA), 70 percent of
the Palestinians in Gaza, and 55 percent of those in the West Bank, were
living below the poverty line, established at $2 a day per person. The per
capita income had decreased by 41 percent since December 2001, while
30 percent of Palestinian children were suffering from chronic malnutrition, and 18 percent from serious malnutrition. The unemployment
rate had reached 67 percent in Gaza, and 48 percent in the West Bank.
When the curfew was in effect in the West Bank, unemployment had
reached 63 percent.

CHAPTER 7

WITHDRAWAL FROM GAZA

In September 2003, a controversy erupted within the Israeli air force. In a letter addressed to General Halutz, a group of pilots, both on active duty and in the reserve, spoke out against the policy of "targeted killings." They wrote to express their refusal to participate in future missions in Gaza and the West Bank that put the lives of civilians at risk. Two colonels, five lieutenant-colonels, nine commanders, six captains, and, notably, General (res.) Yiftah Spector, who had led the attack on the Osirak nuclear reactor in Iraq in 1981, signed the letter:

> We air force pilots who were raised on the values of Zionism, sacrifice, and contributing to the state of Israel, have always served on the front lines, willing to carry out any mission . . . , to defend and strengthen the state of Israel. We, veteran and active pilots alike, who served and still serve the state of Israel for long weeks every year, are opposed to carrying out attack orders that are illegal and immoral of the type the state of Israel has been conducting in the territories. We, who were raised to love the state of Israel and contribute

to the Zionist enterprise, refuse to take part in air force attacks on civilian population centers. We, for whom the Israeli Defense Forces and the Air Force are an inalienable part of ourselves, refuse to continue to harm innocent civilians. These actions are illegal and immoral, and are a direct result of the ongoing occupation which is corrupting all of Israeli society.

Approximately one hundred pilots were contacted, and twenty-seven signed the letter, including instructors who, by order of General Halutz, were immediately dismissed. Nine of the other signatories on active duty were forbidden to fly and were expelled from the air force. Politicians almost universally condemned the pilots' gesture. A Likud minister accused the signers of "mutiny and ideological crime." Several politicians on the Left expressed the view that the pilots should not have moved the debate to the political level. Only Yossi Sarid, the minister from the Meretz Party, defended their action. He explained that their position was not ideological but rather reflected their refusal to attack innocent civilians. One of the signatories, a colonel, expressed regret and rejoined the ranks.

On October 1, the Sharon government approved the plan for a new section of the security fence from Elkana, on the western side of the West Bank, to the Negev desert. According to the plan approved earlier in 2003, the structure was to be 430 kilometers long and was estimated to cost a billion dollars.[1] The largest settlements—Ariel, Gush Etzion, and those south of Hebron—would be located west of the barrier; 80 percent of settlers would be located on the "Israeli" side, but 60,000 Palestinian inhabitants of neighboring towns would be there as well. In order to avoid conflict with the White House, the wall would not be extended to the outskirts of Ariel and Kadumim, in the central West Bank. The Bush administration disapproved of the plan for some segments, and threatened to deduct the cost from the total aid given to Israel. In London, the Blair government condemned the plan outright, stating that "breaking up the West Bank with the fence and settlements like Ariel are an ob-

stacle to the two-state solution and harm Israel's long-term security."
The next day, Israel announced the construction of 604 residential units
in two settlements. United Nations Secretary-General Kofi Annan expressed concern stemming from the "government of Israel's decisions
to proceed with the construction of the separation wall deep in the West
Bank and to build 600 new housing units in the West Bank settlements.
. . . These are serious obstacles to the achievement of a two-state solution. Moreover, the wall continues to cause great hardship to thousands
of Palestinian families." Javier Solana, the foreign policy chief for the
European Union, also condemned the new plan for the barrier.

On October 4, a Palestinian woman detonated her explosive belt in
Maxim, a restaurant in Haifa jointly owned by a Jewish and an Arab family. She killed twenty-one and wounded sixty. A former admiral, his wife,
his son, and his two grandchildren, along with another entire family, were
among the casualties. The terrorist, a lawyer from Jenin, was also an Islamic Jihad militant. Israel responded with an aerial raid on a training
camp for the Palestinian organization in Syria, north of Damas.

THE GENEVA INITIATIVE

On October 9, 2003, after two years of negotiations, Yossi Beilin and
Yasser Abed Rabbo reached the final stage of their project. They brought
together moderate figures from both sides at the Movenpick Hotel on
the Jordanian coast of the Dead Sea. The Israeli delegation included
ministers Haim Oron, Avraham Burg, Amram Mitzna, Nehama Ronen,
former Chief of Staff Amnon Lipkin-Shahak, General (res.) Shlomo Brun,
former head of the police Alik Ron, and the writer Amos Oz. Participants
from the Palestinian side included Nabil Kassis and Hisham Abdel-Razek,
deputies Mohammed Hurani and Kadoura Fares, two young Fatah officials. On the same day that these discussions concerning a future peace
agreement got underway in Jordan, a contingent of armored cars, tanks,
and bulldozers plowed into the refugee camp in Rafah, in the Gaza Strip,
in order to search for tunnels used for smuggling contraband. Approximately a hundred houses were destroyed and 1,500 Palestinians were left
homeless.

Days later, at nine o'clock on the morning of October 12, 2003, the document was finally completed. The very detailed agreement envisioned a global resolution to the conflict. Israel would evacuate 98 percent of the West Bank and most settlements, and the entirety of the Gaza Strip. A protected passage would be built between the West Bank and Gaza. Jerusalem would be the capital of both states, with all Arab neighborhoods as well as the esplanade of the mosques under Palestinian sovereignty, and the Western Wall and the Jewish quarter of the Old City remaining under Israeli sovereignty. The Palestinian refugees of 1948 would be compensated, and the right of return to Israeli territory would be placed under the control of Israel.

Each participant made some remarks during the closing session. Hisham Abdel-Razek, the Palestinian minister of prisoners, chose to give his speech in Hebrew:

> I have mixed feelings. This Palestinian-Israeli group succeeded in launching a political initiative that will be presented to two peoples, to two governments, and to the whole world, so that everyone knows that there is an alternative to the current conflict, that there is hope. We are using a political tool, but it is now necessary for serious people to defend it in order to convince public opinion on both sides, as well as for them to encourage their leaders to implement it. I hope that we will bring hope to our children by proving to the entire region that another solution, that peace, is possible, so that we will all be victorious and no one will be vanquished.

Amos Oz took his turn at the podium:

> I was born in Jerusalem in 1939, 1,200 meters from the Italian hospital in the Old City where Nabil Kassis was born a few years after me. I was born to a couple of poor Jewish refugees who came to Jerusalem for two reasons. No one else wanted them in the entire world, and they believed that the

Jewish people, like all other peoples, had the right to be a majority on a small piece of land. I committed my first militant act when I was 7 years old. In the streets of Jerusalem, I threw stones at British patrols yelling the only English words I knew: *British go home!* I therefore have longer experience in the business of intifada than my Palestinian friends who join me here today. . . . The Palestinian people suffered a terrible tragedy in 1948. It suffered another in 1967, and it concerns me, even if I am not responsible for it. It concerns me because I am not at peace. My children will not live in safety, my grandchildren will not lead normal lives, as long as the Palestinian people endure this tragedy. . . . I was surrounded by people who had been brainwashed by dint of having absorbed the three slogans that destroy us today: 'They do not want us here! They will never recognize our right to exist as a people and as a nation! We cannot trust them!' Through my personal contacts, I know that the Palestinian people have also been brainwashed: 'These Jews will never treat us as equal human beings because they do not think that we are their equals. These *Yahud* will never put an end to the occupation because they are content to merely change its name and form.' Today, we have begun to eradicate these stereotypes.

Kadoura Fares, of Fatah, added: "We should all be proud of the group gathered here. Each of us has fought and is proud of it. You wanted victory; like us. But what we have accomplished here must, even more than victory, fill us with pride."

Avraham Burg, former president of the Knesset, spoke next:

My mother was born in Hebron and half of her family had been massacred (by Palestinians) in 1929. My mother and the other half of my family had been saved by their landlord, an Arab of Hebron. Since then, my family has been divided in two between those who will never believe you no matter what you do, and those who will always seek out the Arab with whom to build a new future. During the past thirty years, the first half of my family tried to shape my future and yours by promoting vengeance and sending false messianic messages. A few minutes ago, I called my mother and told her, 'Mom, I found the Palestinian on the other side, he who is ready to build a new future with our half of the family!' . . . . This moment is particularly symbolic in my view. Today, four of my children are doing their military service. My dear daughter, Avital, joined the army this morning. For eighteen years, I promised what we have all promised our children: 'When you reach the age to enter the army, there will no longer be an intifada, a military service; there will no longer be a conflict!' But I failed because I was not able to offer my daughter a better future. . . . In spite of everything, today, I have the sense that I can return home and say to Noam, my youngest: 'When you enter the army—and he will go as your children will go serve your nation—it will be to serve peace rather than to make war.'

The plan for the agreement was named the "Geneva Initiative" as a gesture of thanks for the support offered by the Swiss government. The official presentation was to take place on the shores of Lake Geneva.

The reaction to the document was immediate. Ariel Sharon insisted that the agreement was dangerous for Israel: "It is the most serious historic error made since Oslo." The prime minister's office in Jerusalem called Beilin and Abed Rabbo's effort an "irresponsible act that will endanger Israel. In a time of war, Labor Party leaders are rushing to conclude an agreement on the basis of all the errors of the past, and that at a time when a democratically elected government is fighting terrorism. It is the same naïve vision of the Middle East situation to be found in the Oslo and Camp David accords."

Ehud Barak, the former prime minister, also condemned the Geneva Initiative. It is, he said, a "maneuver sponsored by Arafat. I do not understand how serious people like Beilin and Mitzna allowed themselves to be taken in." Shimon Peres, the president of the Labor Party, who had not been consulted, believed that more successful solutions existed and rejected the document. According to a poll published by *Yedihot Aharonot* on October 15, 2003, 39 percent of Israelis were in favor of the accord, and 70 percent believed that the Left should not negotiate without the green light of the government.

Within the inner circle of the Palestinian Authority, close advisors to Arafat reasoned that it was only a virtual agreement, and that real negotiations had yet to take place. However, Arafat had been informed of the Movenpick negotiations minute by minute. Hamas and Islamic Jihad distributed pamphlets condemning the "traitors who deal with the enemy in a time of war and are therefore excluded from the legitimate national consensus."

Reactions elsewhere in the world were positive on the whole. As expected, the Bush administration did not consider itself to be involved in this private initiative. Nevertheless, off camera, American officials congratulated Yossi Beilin and Yasser Abed Rabbo. Colin Powell ignored the objections of Jewish American organizations railing against the Geneva Initiative, and announced that he would receive Yossi Beilin and Yasser Abed Rabbo in Washington: "I'll meet with whomever I want!" he shot back at his critics, in so many words.

THE NEOCONSERVATIVE SUMMIT

Was it just a coincidence? Receiving slim attention in the press, a neoconservative summit opened at the King David Hotel in Jerusalem on October 12. Several of Colin Powell's adversaries were in attendance: Richard Perle, the former president of the Defense Policy Board, where he still held a position; Daniel Pipes, who hounded pro-Arab Middle East experts on American campuses and participated in the Special Task Force on

Terrorism and Technology at the Pentagon; Morton Klein, the president of the Zionist Organization of America; Malcolm Hedding, the director of the International Christian Embassy, the outpost for the evangelist movement in Jerusalem; and a Republican senator from Kansas. The Israeli Right and extreme Right were also well represented, notably by ministers Yuri Stern and Benny Elon of the National Union Party, which favors the relocation of Arab populations. Elon was the main contact for evangelists in Israel. Benjamin Netanyahu, the finance minister, was also present to greet his allies and scholars known for their opposition to the Oslo process.

After three days of debate, the summit, financed by Michael Cherney, proclaimed the "Declaration of Jerusalem"[2]:

> We have commenced this conference because we realize our civilization has reached a turning point. While its basic security and fundamental humanistic values are challenged by a new form of totalitarianism called Radical Islam, our resolve to fight it is simultaneously undermined by the false philosophy of Moral Relativism. . . . Our opponents have hijacked issues like human rights and national self-determination and use them to falsely mask the ideology of Jihad. Existing international organizations provide virtually no effective moral compass. We must find a new basis for uniting the nations and use it to develop an effective moral, military and political strategy for defending our civilization.

The neoconservatives, the evangelists, and the Israeli extreme Right proposed to create a "Council of Civilizations" in place of the United Nations, which "has betrayed its democratic principles, turning into a tribalized confederation hijacked by Third World dictatorships, eager to aid and abet radical Islam in any way possible."

The document continued as follows:

> Israel [is] the key to the harmony of civilizations. Billions of people believe that Jerusalem's spiritual and historical im-

portance endows it with a special authority to become a center of the world's unity. Israel's unique geographic and historic position at the crossroads of civilizations enables it to reconcile their conflicts. Israel's unique spiritual experience enables it to find a golden mean between the fault lines dividing civilizations: between tradition and modernity, religion and science, authority and democracy. We call upon all nations to choose Jerusalem, the eternal and indivisible capital of Israel, as a center for this evolving new unity. We believe that one of the objectives of Israel's divinely inspired rebirth is to make it the center of the new unity of the nations, which will lead to an era of peace and prosperity, foretold by the Prophets. . . . For the sake of the entire world and therein, the land of Israel must belong to the people of Israel. . . . Supporting the creation of a PLO state in Judea and Samaria is a historical injustice of colossal proportion. . . . We call on the government of Israel to provide moral leadership to the world in the struggle against terror. Cease negotiating with terrorists and proffering mass releases of captured murderers. Eliminate the terror-sponsoring capabilities of the Palestinian Authority!

Conferences of this kind would continue to be held in ensuing years, in South Africa, in Singapore, in the Philippines, in South Korea . . .

On October 15, a roadside bomb exploded alongside a diplomatic American convoy in Gaza, killing three. Members of the United States embassy in Tel Aviv were on their way to interview Palestinian academics applying for Fulbright scholarships. George Bush condemned the attack and accused Yasser Arafat of blocking the reform of security services and the Palestinian administration. Over the next few years, no American diplomats would go into Gaza. No one took responsibility for the attack. Palestinian security services arrested suspects, PFLP militants, but they were released due to lack of evidence.

CONDEMNATION OF THE WALL

On October 22, the UN General Assembly took up the problem of the wall. A resolution presented by the Arab nations was put to a vote:

> The General Assembly. . . . Reaffirming the principle of the inadmissibility of the acquisition of territory by force. . . . Condemning all acts of violence, terrorism, and destruction. . . . Deploring the extrajudicial killings and their recent intensification, in particular the attack on October 20, 2003 in Gaza. . . . Demands that Israel stop and reverse the construction of the wall in the Occupied Palestinian Territory, including in and around East Jerusalem.

There were 144 delegations in favor of the resolution, four against, and twelve abstentions. In Israel, Ehud Olmert, the vice-prime minister and minister of commerce and industry, defied the resolution, insisting that "the fence will continue to be built, and we will go on taking care of the security of Israel's citizens." One week later, Ami Ayalon and Sari Nusseibeh were received by the UN secretary-general in New York. They presented the document of their initiative bearing the signatures of 100,000 Israelis and 60,000 Palestinians.

On October 24, three Palestinians infiltrated a military post within the settlement of Netzarim and succeeded in killing three soldiers before they themselves fell victim to gunfire. Hamas and the al-Aqsa Martyrs Brigades, two groups that frequently cooperated in Gaza and in some West Bank cities, jointly claimed responsibility for the attack. According to a decree issued by the IDF, Palestinians aged twelve and over living within the immediate vicinity of the security barrier were henceforth required to possess a residence permit, even to live in their own homes. On October 28, Ahmed Qureia assumed the responsibility of forming a new Palestinian government by stepping into the role of prime minister.

Moshe Yaalon, the chief of staff, believed that political leaders were not heeding his advice. On October 29, he told the major Israeli newspapers that the Sharon government had contributed to the failure of Mahmoud Abbas by not making significant enough concessions to reinforce the authority of the Palestinian leadership. And, he added, "the curfews and checkpoints prevent the Palestinians from harvesting the olives, from farming their lands. . . . In our tactical decisions, we are operating contrary to our strategic interests."[3] Ariel Sharon and Shaul Mofaz were furious and recalled him to reserve duty.

SHIN BET'S WARNING

On November 14, 2003, four former heads of Shin Bet intervened in the public debate and issued a solemn appeal to Israeli public opinion and the government. In a long interview with the newspaper *Yedihot Aharonot*, they criticized Israeli policy on the Palestinian territories. Avraham Shalom, who served from 1980 to 1986, declared that

> the security barrier as it has been constructed creates a political and security reality that will become a problem because it creates hatred, expropriates land, and annexes hundreds of thousands of Palestinians to the state of Israel. The result is that the fence achieves the exact opposite of what was intended. . . . As long as we fail to understand that we went into the Arab world and that it was not the Arabs who came into ours, nothing new will happen here. We are heading straight for an abyss, for our policies are contrary to a desire for peace.

Yaakov Perry, the head of Shin Bet from 1988 to 1995, reiterated that

> we are heading straight for an abyss. If something doesn't happen here, we will continue to live by the sword, we will continue to wallow in the mud, and we will continue to destroy ourselves. The biggest mistake of the Israeli political leader-

ship is the controversy surrounding the following question: do we have, or do we not, a Palestinian partner? The destruction of the security services of the Palestinian Authority was also a mistake.

Carmi Gillon, head of Shin Bet from 1995 to 1996, added that "the problem, as of today, is that the political agenda has become solely a security agenda. It only deals with the question of how to prevent the next terror attack, not the question of how it is at all possible to pull ourselves out of the mess that we are in today."

Ami Ayalon, who succeeded Gillon until 2000, further stated that "we are taking sure and measured steps to a point where the state of Israel will no longer be a democracy and a home for the Jewish people. What we are doing today in the West Bank and Gaza is not moral in any case."

On November 16, the orthodox movement Habbad asked its followers to not read the text of the Geneva Initiative which had been distributed in all mailboxes. In the city of Kiryat Malakhi, rabbis organized an auto-da-fé of the documents. On November 30, 250 rabbis issued a religious opinion: "The Israelis who signed the Geneva Initiative are traitors."

TESTING THE WATERS

Meanwhile, Ariel Sharon was making more and more trips abroad. Within a few weeks he traveled to Russia and India. On November 17 he went to spend two days in Italy, far from the leaden atmosphere that prevailed in Israel. Prime Minister Silvio Berlusconi was a faithful supporter of Israel, and the visit unfolded without a hitch. Sharon did not request an audience with John Paul II, who condemned the separation wall as an "obstacle on the path towards peaceful cohabitation." In the great synagogue in Rome, Sharon issued an appeal to Italian Jews to immigrate to Israel: "It is the surest way to escape the great wave of anti-Semitism that is shaking Europe." Two days earlier, in Istanbul, attacks against two synagogues caused the deaths of twenty-three and the wounding of 260.

But the Israeli prime minister also had another more discreet meeting. It was with Elliott Abrams, the official responsible for the Middle East dossier for the White House National Security Council, and who had made the trip to Rome specifically to meet with Sharon. To journalists in Washington who made inquiries concerning the purpose of the meeting, officials responded that "Mr. Abrams expressed to the prime minister the concern of the Bush administration over his settlement policy." In fact, Sharon had revealed to his American interlocutor that he intended to change his policy. He told journalist Uri Dan, his confidant, that

> [Elliott Abrams] came to have a discussion with me concerning the situation in the Middle East and Syria, which seemed ready to begin peace negotiations with Israel—at least, the propaganda campaign launched in Damascus suggested as much. I stated that I was willing to pursue this if the Syrians broke their ties to terrorism, which was not the case. . . . I nevertheless emphasized that it was preferable to concentrate above all on a single problem, that of the Palestinians, and to not impose an additional burden on Israel. Following this meeting, Washington never again put the question of negotiations with Damascus on the table.[4]

The withdrawal from Gaza permitted possible negotiations with Syria to be deferred indefinitely. National security advisor Giora Eiland was privy to the secret, and was assigned the mission of preparing for a withdrawal from the Gaza Strip:

> Ariel Sharon made the decision after the resignation of Mahmoud Abbas. In his view, that was proof that as long as Arafat was in place, there was no chance of reaching an agreement or of generating enough momentum on the Palestinian side to make progress towards an agreement. That helped him to make his decision. If it was impossible [with the Palestinians], we wanted to see what we could do alone.[5]

The events of the preceding weeks had convinced Sharon that it was time to act. The letter from the pilots and the statements made by his chief of staff made him fear increasing unrest within the army as well as recall bad memories of the war in Lebanon in 1982, when entire units threatened mutiny. The campaign led by Ami Ayalon and Sari Nusseibeh, who were collecting an increasing number of signatures, seemed finally to rouse the Israeli Left. The Geneva Initiative, which had been praised by numerous governments, was gaining credibility abroad. The Israeli press had widely reported the strong statements by the former heads of Shin Bet. This confluence of events encouraged Sharon to muddle the issue. Was he also, as several Israeli journalists speculated, seeking to camouflage the police investigation into the electoral fraud that involved him and his family? There was no evidence to confirm it.

The first phase of his plan, to prepare the politicians and the public for what was to come, was set in motion on November 20. During a speech in Tel Aviv, Sharon let slip a phrase that confused his listeners: "We are still engaged in implementing the road map as it has been adopted by the government and defined according to our agreements with the Americans, but, beyond that, I am not excluding taking unilateral measures." He said nothing more. Those close to him revealed that he had been preparing to launch a new policy initiative, but renounced it in order not to distract attention from events following the Istanbul attacks. Three days later, he added a new piece to the puzzle during a meeting with Likud ministers, who had heard rumors concerning his intentions. He said: "If I am convinced that it is useless to continue to wait and wait for advances from the Palestinian government, I do not exclude the possibility of taking unilateral measures, not to make concessions, but to defend our interests; in short, unilateral measures in our favor."

On November 26, the American administration rescinded $289.5 million from the $3 billion loan guarantee package accorded Israel for the current year. In fact, these guarantees permitted Israel to float loans at favorable rates on the international markets, and the total loss would only be $4 million per year. But Washington thereby signaled to the Arab world its discontentment with the settlement policy in the West Bank and with the plans for the security wall in Palestinian territory.

GENEVA

The official ceremony to present the agreement concluded on the coast of the Dead Sea was held in Geneva on December 1. There were 700 prominent figures, including fifty-eight top-ranking politicians, who arrived from all over the world to express their support for a peace plan that required an Israeli withdrawal from 98 percent of the West Bank and East Jerusalem—with the exception of the Jewish quarter in the Old City and the Western Wall. This, in reality, implied the Palestinians' abandonment of the right of return of refugees. The American actor Richard Dreyfuss and former President Jimmy Carter were there, along with Mikhail Gorbachev and Frederick Willem de Klerk of South Africa. Nelson Mandela participated with the help of a video hookup. Palestinian cabinet ministers Hisham Abdel-Razek and Kadoura Fares, who had in the meantime become a minister without portfolio within Qureia's government, were also present. The latter stated that Yasser Arafat expressly asked him to make the trip. Egypt was represented by one of Mubarak's advisors, and Jordan by its ambassador in Switzerland. A number of left-wing legislators came from Israel, including Yuli Tamir, Roman Bronfman, and Amram Mitzna. Yossi Beilin and Yasser Abed Rabbo issued a communal appeal: "What counts is civil society! Don't count on governments!" In Israel, the right wing was fulminating. Nathan Shcharansky stated that the Geneva Initiative would put Israel under pressure. "It is," he said, "a return to the path of unilateral concessions." In the West Bank and Gaza, Hamas, Islamic Jihad, and some Fatah groups demonstrated against the "treachery of Geneva."

The next day, while waiting in a departure line at Cornavin Airport in Geneva, Yasser Abed Rabbo was jostled by an unknown person. He turned around but did not see the person who had bumped into him, and discovered a few seconds later that his bag had been stolen. It contained more than a thousand pages of a private journal that he had been keeping for three years. A document which, he would later say, would make very interesting reading for Shin Bet.

On December 5, Yossi Beilin and Yasser Abed Rabbo were received at the State Department by Colin Powell, who warmly congratulated them. This warmth, however, was not reflected in the statement released following their meeting. Therein, Powell reiterated that the road map was the only appropriate means for achieving peace.

OLMERT SWERVES TO THE LEFT?

December 5, 2003 marked the anniversary of the death of David Ben-Gurion, and an official ceremony was held in Sde Boker, in the Negev, in front of the tomb of the founder of the state of Israel. Ariel Sharon was ill, and so his stand-in, Ehud Olmert, read the speech written by the prime minister: "Ben-Gurion's greatness was ... his capacity to limit himself to what was possible within the era. He [Ben-Gurion] declared: Let's suppose that militarily we are capable of conquering the entirety of the land of western Israel[6]—and I am certain that it is possible—what will happen next? We will form a single state that must be democratic. ... At the time of the first elections, we will be the minority. Thus, when the question is asked, we chose a Jewish state without the totality of the Land [of Israel]." The leaders of the Labor Party couldn't believe it. Shimon Peres, who had clashed with Ehud Barak for years, turned to him and whispered, "You saw it! A new partisan of Ben-Gurion!" In 1975, Ehud Olmert had praised the founding of one of the first settlements in the West Bank, proclaiming that "Zionism is not a hollow slogan, it is necessary to give it life! It is necessary to say yes to the settlement in Samaria!" He had, three years later, voted against the Camp David accords concluded by Menachem Begin and Anwar Sadat. And now, the prince of the Israeli Right was making a 180 degree ideological turn ...

The following weekend, Olmert pursued the communications mission begun by Ariel Sharon. In a long interview with the newspaper *Yedihot Aharonot*, he clarified his thinking, stating that "the current situation is leading Israel, as a Jewish state, to its ruin. We are approaching the day when the Palestinians will be the majority and will renounce their state in order to claim the right to vote in Israel. ... I am a partisan of a state that consists of 80 percent Jews and 20 percent Arabs, the borders of which will not be those of the land of Israel as I had been hoping until this moment."

THE SETTLEMENTS WILL BE EVACUATED

On December 9, Ariel Sharon appeared before the parliamentary commission of foreign affairs and of the defense. Ehud Yatom, of Likud, asked him if the unilateral measures he was planning entailed the relocation of settlements. Sharon responded that "at this stage, there might be displacements of settlements, including inhabited settlements." The Right reacted that same day. Uzi Landau, the interior security minister, asserted that "these declarations relating to unilateral measures endanger Israel and the fight against terrorism. Once again, the Palestinians receive concessions without fulfilling obligations provided for in the road map and without fighting terrorism." The council on settlements called for Sharon's resignation: "The transfer of Jews that he proposes is illegal and immoral. To uproot Jews from their homes in the land of Israel is contrary to Zionism; it will ultimately give a gift to Palestinian terrorism." The National Religious Party threatened to quit the government coalition. For the nationalist Right and the messianic movement, this development was no less than an ideological earthquake. Sharon had turned the page to the Zionism of Zeev Jabotinsky and Menachem Begin. In their eyes the Israeli government under Sharon's leadership had already damaged the ideal of a Great Israel that stretches from the Jordan to the Mediterranean coast, especially when he adopted the principle of the institution of a Palestinian state as defined in the road map. Likud hawks, all the while vehemently protesting it, were convinced that the peace plan proposed by the Quartet would remain a dead letter. But the most experienced in the party saw their fears confirmed, namely, that Sharon had never been a supporter of Jabotinsky's ideas. He was seen as a man of the land who had come of age within the hard-line wing of the Labor Party and had never relinquished its ideological commitments.

Aligning himself with Labor Party figures such as David Ben-Gurion and Yigal Allon, Sharon intended to define the borders of the Jewish state by seeking a geographical solution that was primarily concerned with security, not ideology. As a minister in 1977, he presented a plan to the Begin government that involved the creation of a Jewish development zone around the Arab neighborhoods of Jerusalem in order to ensure that it remain under Israeli sovereignty, as well as the construction of settlements on the West Bank watershed in order to ensure the defense of the coastal strip where most of the population and industry of Israel were located. To turn his great plan into reality, Sharon found "under officers": militants of the nationalist messianic movement Gush Emunim, the Bloc of the Faithful. "Without the sudden flow of pioneering nationalism this movement represented, the need to achieve a Jewish presence in Samaria and Judea might well have remained unfulfilled," he wrote in his autobiography, published in 1989.[7] The godfather was thus capable of separating himself from his godchild: the settlement movement. For Sharon, the land of Israel had never been sacred in the religious sense of the term.

December 10 was a bad day for the Sharon family. The Supreme Court unanimously ordered Sharon's son, Gilad, to hand over all documents concerning Cyril Kern's infamous loan to a Tel Aviv court. Apparently, of the $3 million borrowed, half had been used to repay donations illegally made to Sharon during the Likud primaries in 1999. This development was the lead story of all the televised news programs and newspapers.

On December 11, an Israeli operation in Rafah caused six deaths. On December 16, the IDF occupied Nablus and carried out searches for clandestine laboratories used for fabricating explosives. On December 18, Sharon took another step forward in a much-awaited speech given before the prestigious fourth economic conference in Herzliya: "Taking into consideration the challenges we are facing—if the Palestinians are not making a comparable effort to resolve the conflict—Israel will take the initiative of a unilateral security measure of 'disengagement' vis-à-vis the Palestinians. Israel will not remain in all the places where we are found today." Likud hawks, as well as three ministers and five legislators, demanded of Sharon that any decision to withdraw be submitted to a vote of the Likud central committee.

On December 22, 2003, yet another letter was sent from soldiers refusing to serve in the territories. This time, thirteen reservists from the elite commando unit Sayeret Matkal were writing to Sharon: "We say to you today, we will no longer give our hands to the oppressive reign in the territories and the denial of human rights to millions of Palestinians, and we will no longer serve as a defensive shield for the settlement enterprise." Among the signatories were three officers who were dismissed from service.

On December 23, an Israeli incursion into the refugee camp in Jebaliya, in the northern Gaza Strip, resulted in nine deaths. On December 25, missiles launched at a car in Rafah killed seven. A suicide bomber set off his explosives at a bus station near Tel Aviv, killing four. The attack was claimed by the PFLP.

In Cairo, negotiations to reestablish the *hudna*, led by Ahmed Qureia with representatives in Hamas, failed. In Israel, those opposed to the evacuation of the settlements began to organize.

Between September 29, 2000 and December 31, 2003, 2,316 Palestinians and 879 Israelis had been killed. On January 9, 2004, the IDF withdrew from Nablus in a three-week operation resulting in the deaths of nineteen Palestinians, including eleven noncombatants. The settlement movement went to war against the plan for unilateral withdrawal and organized at Rabin Square in Tel Aviv on January 11, the largest demonstration that had been seen in Israel in many years. There, 120,000 people listened to speeches given by four members of the government as well as fifteen legislators belonging to the parliamentary coalition. They also booed Sharon. Benny Elon, the tourism minister and leader of the extreme right National Union Party issued an appeal to the prime minister: "We will not allow your old age to hamper our youth. Don't permit yourself to believe that the people are tired. This nation will not disengage from the Torah, from its history, from its land!" A video of Sharon was projected on a giant screen, taken at the time when, as leader of the opposition, he criticized Ehud Barak's Labor government by proclaiming, "It's not the people who are tired, it's the leaders!"

On January 14, a Palestinian woman, in possession of authorization to receive medical treatment in Israel, set off explosives at the Erez checkpoint, killing four soldiers and security agents. On January 20, Hezbollah committed another attack in northern Israel near Zarit, which killed one soldier and wounded three others. The air force responded by bombing Shiite military targets in south Lebanon. On January 28, an Israeli incursion into the Zeitun neighborhood in Gaza resulted in the deaths of eight Palestinians.

ISRAEL-HEZBOLLAH

January 2004 marked the end of three years of difficult negotiations mediated by the German secret service. It resulted in an exchange of prisoners between Israel and Hezbollah. The head of the Shiite militia, Sheik Nasrallah, secured the liberation of sixteen Arabs of diverse nationalities, of 400 Palestinians detained in Israel, and of fourteen Lebanese, including two militia leaders abducted by the IDF in Lebanon: Sheik Obeid, a Hezbollah leader, abducted in 1989, and Mustafa Dirani, of the Shiite movement Amal, abducted in 1994. In exchange, the bodies of three soldiers abducted by Hezbollah in October 2000 were returned to Israel, along with Elhanan Tannenbaum, a colonel kidnapped in Qatar by the Shiite militia in 2000. On January 28, a German military aircraft from Beirut landed at a Bundeswehr air base outside Cologne, with Elhanan Tannenbaum and coffins of the three soldiers on board. At the same moment, an Israeli aircraft transporting the Lebanese prisoners landed, and in Israel, the 400 Palestinians to be freed were transported by bus within the proximity of military checkpoints in the West Bank and Gaza, while in Rosh Hanikra, on the Lebanese-Israeli border, fifty-nine militants from Hezbollah and other Arab countries were turned over to the International Red Cross. In Cologne, experts on Israeli judicial identity confirmed that the three bodies were indeed those of the soldiers. There was a positive response and the exchange was made.

Hezbollah's popularity was at its peak in the West Bank and Gaza. In part, this was because the release of the 400 Palestinian prisoners was attributed to Hezbollah's abduction of the Israelis, an act that showed how the organization could succeed where the Palestinian Authority only failed.

That same day, the al-Aqsa Martyrs Brigades and Hamas celebrated the event by committing a suicide attack on a bus in Jerusalem, killing eleven and wounding fifty.

According to some military experts, this prisoner exchange gave a false impression of détente on the Israeli-Lebanese border. In reality, incidents there were frequent. On October 6, 2003, after an IDF aerial raid against a Palestinian training camp in Syria, Hezbollah had responded by bombing Israeli territory. For forty-eight hours, an exchange of gunfire wounded many and resulted in two Israeli deaths—a soldier and a teenager. On January 18, 2004, gunfire from the Shiite militia killed one soldier and wounded another. This situation worried the ministers of the commission on foreign affairs and the defense for months. On February 25, Yuval Steinitz, member of the Likud Party and chairman of the foreign affairs and defense committee, along with the two officials of the under-commissions charged with overseeing the army and the ministry of defense, Ephraim Sneh (of Labor) and Omri Sharon (of Likud), sent Sharon and Shaul Mofaz, the minister of defense, a secret letter containing a warning that would only come to light three years later:

> Iran, through the intermediary of Hezbollah and Syria, has deployed a strategic threat. . . . If the ground-to-ground missile system in south Lebanon is activated, a quarter of the Israeli population will be in danger, from a line through Hadera northwards. [In such a case,] the life of the entirety of the country will be disturbed for weeks, and thousands of inhabitants of northern Israel will take refuge in the center. . . . There is a critical lack of necessary intelligence for a [military] operation that would allow for the [destruction] of this missile system. . . . Without an operation on the ground, the launching of rockets on Israel could last for weeks.

This letter received no response. Ariel Sharon and army officials did not believe in the possibility of a Hezbollah offensive. They were mistaken.

Besides, the Israeli prime minister had other things on his mind. On February 2, Sharon chose to reveal the details of his plan to the newspaper *Haaretz*, the Israeli press outlet that was most critical of him. The editorialist Yoel Marcus was offered the scoop. The godfather of the settlement movement proclaimed to Marcus that "this vacuum, for which the Palestinians are to blame, cannot go on forever. So as part of the disengagement plan I ordered an evacuation—sorry, a relocation —of seventeen settlements with their 7,500 residents, from the Gaza Strip to Israeli territory." He said the process would take one to two years.

On February 8, the settlement movement launched an operation to populate the Gaza settlements that entailed moving 500 families there. Thousands of protesters planted 3,000 trees in the Gush Katif settlement bloc. Resistance to Sharon was beginning to get organized. The Palestinians welcomed these developments with intense satisfaction, but with suspicion as well. The editorial pages in all the Ramallah and East Jerusalem newspapers expressed the conviction that Sharon was acting in complicity with the United States and was only willing to let go of Gaza in order to tighten his grip over the West Bank.

ISRAEL-USA

But ironically, that is exactly what Washington sought to avoid. The White House wanted Israel's withdrawal plan to agree with President Bush's vision, which essentially involved a two-state solution to the conflict. Consequently, it was absolutely necessary that the Gaza settlers not be transferred to the West Bank. Authorizing Israel to construct a barrier to the east, between the Jordan Valley and the rest of the West Bank, was also out of the question.

Despite these public declarations by the White House, Sharon's entourage learned through its unofficial contacts within the Bush administration that not only would the Americans approve of the disengagement plan, but also of the plan to create settlement blocs in the West Bank. The notion had already been raised during the Taba negotiations in February 2001. This was negotiated by Dov Weisglass, the head of Sharon's cabinet, and General Giora Eiland, both of whom were in direct contact with Bush's advisors.

On February 19, Steve Hadley, Condoleezza Rice's deputy, Elliott Abrams, a member of the National Security Council, and William Burns, Colin Powell's assistant, arrived in Israel, where they listened to Sharon's plan. The Americans wanted to know whether settlements would also be evacuated from the West Bank, and demanded an explanation concerning the building of settlement blocs there. They also sent a message: Israel had no choice but to change the plan for the separation wall.

On February 22, a suicide attack in a Jerusalem bus, for which the al-Aqsa Martyrs Brigades took responsibility, claimed the lives of eight and wounded sixty, including eleven schoolchildren. The next day, the International Court of Justice, at the request of the United Nations General Assembly, began hearings concerning the legality of the security wall. The Israeli government chose not to appear before the judges to plead its case. They launched a media battle instead. The burnt-out shell of a bus in which eleven Israeli civilians had lost their lives due to a Palestinian suicide attack was placed before the court house where families of the victims also demonstrated in silence. During the month of February, the death toll reached fifty-one on the Palestinian side, and eleven on that of the Israelis.[8]

On March 6, the al-Aqsa Martyrs Brigades and Hamas perpetrated a joint attack on the Erez checkpoint in which four assailants and two Palestinian policemen were killed. The next day, after rockets were launched on Sderot, an Israeli town, the Israeli army made an incursion into the refugee camps in Bureij and Nusseirat, located in the center of the Gaza Strip, causing the deaths of fourteen Palestinians, including three children. Meanwhile, Hamas and the al-Aqsa Martyrs Brigades were planning an attack on oil reserves and chemical products at the port in Ashdod. Such an operation, if successful, would have caused incalculable damage. Two volunteers hid in a double-sized container that passed easily through the Karni checkpoint. Arriving at the port on the evening of March 14, they crawled out of their hiding place, but did not make it all the way to the containers. Only one managed to set off his explosives, while the other was shot down. Ten Israelis died and sixteen were wounded. Ariel Sharon canceled a planned visit with Ahmed Qureia, the Palestinian prime minister.

AHMED YASSIN

The Sharon government viewed Hamas as the main organizer of the attack: in its eyes, the movement had just crossed a line drawn in the sand. Shin Bet once again presented the file on Sheik Ahmed Yassin, the movement's founder. On September 6, 2003, the air force had already made an attempt to assassinate him by bombing a house in which he had gathered together a dozen Hamas officials, notably the leaders of its armed branch. The operation failed. The missile managed to destroy the fourth floor of the building while the meeting was taking place on the ground floor. This time, Shin Bet and the Israeli army had no intention of failing again. Avi Dichter reflected on the situation:

> We had intelligence confirming that Sheik Yassin was behind the attempted attack at Ashdod. . . . His image as a disabled man caused us a lot of problems. After all, he was a paraplegic. He could barely speak. Everything about this man aroused pity. But the degree of evil that he contained within himself was shocking. . . . During the discussion, before the operation, some suggested that it would result in chaos, that it would cause the territories to go up in flames.[9]

Giora Eiland also participated in the debate:

> From the moment we became certain that he was really the one who chose the dates for suicide attacks, he was no longer just a spiritual leader or a political leader, but was in fact directly carrying out a policy of terrorism. That facilitated—I would not say morally—but it justified the operation, even while we feared that it would set off a firestorm [in the Palestinian territories].

On March 22 at five o'clock in the morning, as he was returning from the mosque in the Al Sabra neighborhood in Gaza City, Ahmed Yassin was killed by three missiles fired from a helicopter, along with seven members of his entourage. A few minutes later, the loudspeakers on all the mosques blared "The Sheik is a martyr!" Tens of thousands of people came out into the streets and made their way toward Shifa Hospital, where the body had been transported. Hamas issued the following statement: "Sharon has opened the gates of hell and nothing will stop us from cutting off his head. The Zionists did not execute this operation without the approval of the American terrorist machine, which must bear responsibility for this crime. Hamas will seek revenge in Palestine and abroad." The Autonomous Authority declared three days of mourning. Yasser Arafat broadcast a declaration from the Muqata, where he was still under house arrest: "This act of cowardice against the Sheik will strengthen national union between Palestinian factions." In Lebanon, Sheik Nasrallah appeared live on Hezbollah television and declared: "The Zionists will soon discover that they have committed an act of madness which will add to their other acts of madness."

The next day, 150,000 people attended the funeral of the founder of Hamas. Abdel Aziz Rantisi, who assumed the leadership of the organization, proclaimed, "War has been declared, by any means!" The names of the other members of the Ashura—the supreme council of Hamas—were to remain secret. Israel made it known that Rantisi's days were numbered.

At CIA headquarters in Langley, special agents assigned to the unit tracking Osama bin Laden observed a new phenomenon. Mike Scheuer, a consultant to this unit, noted:

> The death of Sheik Yassin gave us a rare opportunity to demonstrate that the Israeli-Palestinian conflict influenced global jihad. Demonstrations took place in Herat and Jalalabad in Afghanistan. I worked on the Afghan file during the '80s, during the Soviet invasion, and there was not one Afghan in twenty who could say where Israel was located and who had

the least notion of what the Israeli-Palestinian conflict was about. That was not the case after the death of Sheik Yassin. There were anti-Israeli reactions in unexpected places, in Manila in the Philippines and elsewhere. That forced us to appreciate the degree to which bin Laden had sensitized the Muslim world to his message.[10]

Fearing reprisals, Israel put the police and the army on a state of alert. The Palestinian territories were sealed off. Sharon congratulated the IDF for the success of the operation and declared that "the main leader of Palestinian terrorist assassins is no more!" At the United Nations Security Council, the American ambassador blocked a vote on a resolution condemning Israel. During the month of March 2004, eleven Israelis and eighty Palestinians had been killed.

THE AMERICANS APPROVE

On March 31, three American emissaries returned to the region to pursue negotiations on the disengagement plan. An agreement was drawn up that was to be made public during a visit by Ariel Sharon to the White House. Hadley, Abrams, and Burns then met Ahmed Qureia in Jericho, since it was out of the question for them to go to Ramallah, where Arafat was based. The Palestinian prime minister told them, "We support the withdrawal from Gaza, but only as an integral part of a political plan of withdrawal from all the territories." The Americans insisted that "in order to participate in a political process, the Autonomous Authority had to fight terrorism." Saeb Erekat, the main Palestinian negotiator, explained that the Israelis refused any and all discussion with him concerning the withdrawal from Gaza. "When I spoke to Dov Weisglass, he told me that he was not authorized to speak to us about it."[11]

On April 1, UNRWA suspended emergency food aid distributed to 600,000 refugees in the Gaza Strip due to the sealing off of towns and cities and restrictions imposed by Israel upon the transfer of goods following the Ashdod attack. The humanitarian situation deteriorated as confrontations between the Israeli army and Palestinian organizations in Gaza became daily events. Hand-made rockets were launched on neighboring Israeli settlements, while the army responded with military incursions, the destruction of houses, and "targeted killings." Gaza was sinking into anarchy.

On April 12, a visit by Ariel Sharon to Maale Adumim, the city constructed on occupied territory to the east of Jerusalem, received heavy media coverage. Occurring the day before his latest trip to the United States, it provided him with the opportunity to further clarify his conception of the "settlement blocs." He said: "Only an Israeli initiative will permit us to assure the future of large settlement blocs like Maale Adumim, Ariel, Givat Zeev, and the Etzion bloc, which will continue to be reinforced and developed. I should add Hebron and Kyriat Arba."

On April 14, Israeli-American negotiations were brought to a conclusion and Sharon arrived in Washington, but not without a delay of several hours. He had postponed his departure because he was not happy with the text of a new American letter of agreement. The matter was settled after a few corrections had been made. Dov Weisglass had convinced Condoleezza Rice of the necessity that the president of the United States sign such a document. Without it, Likud, and even the Israeli government, might not approve the withdrawal from Gaza, and that would mean a return to square one, with a political crisis in Israel to boot.

It was the Israeli prime minister's tenth visit to the White House since assuming power. After a brief meeting in the Oval Office, the two men made short speeches to the press. George Bush reviewed the terms of the letter transmitted to Sharon, which contained the phrase that the Israelis were waiting for:

> As part of a final peace settlement, Israel must have secure and recognized borders which should emerge from negotiations between the parties, in accordance with U.N. Security Council Resolutions 242 and 338. In light of new realities on the ground, including already existing major Israeli population centers, it is unrealistic to expect that the outcome of final status negotiations will be a full and complete return to the armistice lines of 1949 [between the West Bank and Israel].

And all previous efforts to negotiate a two-state solution have reached the same conclusion. It is realistic to expect that any final status agreement will only be achieved on the basis of mutually agreed changes that reflect these realities.

A new reality was lurking beneath the euphemisms and political jargon: the United States had just officially changed its policy. For the first time since 1967, it accepted the existence of "Israeli population centers"— settlements in the West Bank—and admitted that, within the framework of a peace agreement, Israel could not completely withdraw from the entirety of the occupied territories.

Sharon warmly thanked the president and continued:

> I came to you from a peace-seeking country. Despite the repeated terror attacks against us, the people of Israel continue to wish for the achievement of a viable peace in accordance with our Jewish tradition as outlined by Israel's prophets. . . . I, myself, have been fighting terror for many years, and . . . I have never met a leader as committed as you are, Mr. President, to the struggle for freedom and the need to confront terrorism wherever it exists. I want to express my appreciation to you for your courageous leadership in the war against global terror and your commitment and vision to bring peace to the Middle East. Thank you, Mr. President.

Bush replied: "Thank you, Mr. Prime Minister. *Good job, good job!*" In his response to the president, Sharon revealed that

> having reached the conclusion that for the moment a Palestinian partner does not exist with whom to advance peacefully towards a resolution to the conflict, and since the current impasse does not allow us to achieve our common aims, I decided to begin a gradual process of disengagement in the hopes of reducing friction between Palestinians and Israelis.

... At the end of this plan, the state of Israel will have relocated military installations and all Israeli towns in the Gaza Strip, as well as other military installations and a small number of towns in Samaria.

The Israeli prime minister confirmed that the separation wall was temporary: "Its plan will take into account security needs and its impact on Palestinians not engaged in terrorism." Sharon also promised to make an effort to limit the growth of settlements and to evacuate unauthorized outposts.

Up until the very last minute, two Arab leaders, Abdullah, Crown Prince of Saudi Arabia, and President Hosni Mubarak, who was on an official visit to the United States, tried to prevent this shift in American policy. Salam Fayad, the Palestinian finance minister, otherwise close to the Bush administration, even made three trips to Washington. All of these attempts to intercede at the White House were conducted in vain. Amr Moussa, the secretary general of the Arab League, stated that "the position taken by President Bush is negative and regrettable for it nullifies all existing [legal] frameworks and represents a dangerous development in the Israeli-Arab conflict." The reaction in Europe was not favorable. The Irish minister of foreign affairs defined the position of the Fifteen as follows: "The European Union recalls its established position, restated by the European Council on March 25 and 26 that the Union will not recognize any changes to the pre-1967 borders other than those arrived at by agreement between the parties."

On April 24, during an interview with Israel's Channel Two, Sharon disclosed that he had told President Bush the week before that he would no longer be bound by the pledge he had made three years ago not to physically harm Arafat: "I am released from this commitment. I release myself from this commitment regarding Arafat." A few hours later, sources at the White House and the State Department repeated that they remained opposed to any attempt to assassinate Arafat. "Nothing has changed in the U.S. position," spokesman Richard Boucher told journalists.

CHAPTER 8

OLMERT

The new leader of Hamas was killed on April 17, 2004. A helicopter fired a missile into Abdel Aziz Rantisi's car, once again plunging Gaza into turmoil. Thousands of Hamas partisans gathered in front of the hospital where his body was taken, along with those of the two militants accompanying him. Ismail Haniyeh, who had been Sheik Yassin's assistant, threatened: "His blood will not be wasted. It is our destiny, that of Hamas and of the Palestinians, to die as martyrs. Israel will regret this operation. Vengeance will not wait!" Demonstrations erupted in several cities in the West Bank, and a general strike was proclaimed throughout the Palestinian territories. Ahmed Qureia, the Palestinian prime minister, accused: "The Israeli terrorist offensive is the direct result of the encouragement and partial attitude of the United States towards Israel, which America supports in its usurpation of Palestinian land."

The next day, on several talk shows, Condoleezza Rice justified the targeted killing: "It is important that Israel have the right to defend itself. Everyone must understand that Israel is conducting a war against terrorism. . . . The United States was not informed in advance of this operation." She added that Israel also needs to "take account of the consequences of what they're doing."[1]

On April 21, the Israeli army made an incursion into Beit Lahiya, in the northern Gaza Strip, searching for rocket launchers. The day before the operation took place, there were four deaths, and nine on the actual day of the operation, among whom, according to Palestinian sources, were three noncombatants. UNRWA resumed the distribution of emergency food aid after having reached an agreement with Israeli military authorities.

In April 2004, three Israelis and fifty-three Palestinians were killed.

On May 2, members of the Likud Party were called to vote on the withdrawal plan proposed by the president of their party. Ariel Sharon allowed himself to be persuaded to let the vote proceed because he thought it would silence the opposition. But in the weeks leading up to the vote, the settlement movement launched a campaign among the 193,000 members of Likud, and that same day, an attack confused the issue even more. A few hundred meters from the checkpoint in Kissufim, on the road from the settlements in Gush Katif, two Palestinians broke through security. They approached a car and murdered a pregnant woman and her four children. Responsibility for the attack was claimed by Islamic Jihad and the Committees for Popular Resistance, a new armed organization gathering militants from the main Palestinian movements. They circulated a pamphlet claiming that "this operation is part of Palestinian reprisals for the crimes committed by the occupation army."

The results of the vote were as follows: 59.5 percent voted against the withdrawal from Gaza, and only 39.7 percent voted in favor, with 51.6 percent of the members participating in the referendum. Ariel Sharon was placed in the minority, and his opponents were ecstatic and proposed modifications to his disengagement plan at the Knesset the very next day.

On May 11, during an incursion into the Zeitun neighborhood in Gaza, six Israeli soldiers were killed when their troop transport was hit by an antitank grenade. During the ensuing fight fourteen Palestinians were killed and eighty-eight were wounded. The next day, a mine weighing 100 kilos (220 pounds) blew up another armored vehicle, killing five soldiers—this was the highest number of deaths suffered by the Israelis in individual incidents during the past two years. On May 13, in Rafah, two more Israeli soldiers and thirteen Palestinians were killed. The army proceeded to destroy houses in the refugee camp in order to clear a security zone along the border between Gaza and Egypt.

On May 14, *Yedihot Aharonot* published a poll showing that Israelis overwhelmingly supported a unilateral withdrawal from Gaza: 71 percent supported a withdrawal and 24 percent were against it. The next day the unthinkable happened: the Left demonstrated in favor of Ariel Sharon. At Rabin Square in Tel Aviv, 150,000 people asked Sharon not to abandon his plan to withdraw from Gaza. The Peace Now movement and partisans of the Geneva Initiative marched alongside members of the Meretz Party under the slogan, "60,000 Likud militants will not decide the future of the country." Shimon Peres, the Labor leader and head of the opposition, spoke to the crowd, and rounded up the numbers: "80 percent of Israelis who support withdrawal will not be held hostage to the 1 percent of the population that voted against it during the Likud referendum!"

On May 18, another army incursion into Rafah resulted in the deaths of 20 Palestinians, including children. The operation unfolded during the ensuing days, and on May 19, a missile launched close to a demonstration killed ten people, including five children, and wounded dozens. On May 20, there were another seven deaths, including two children.

In Tel Aviv, the trial of Marwan Barghouti, secretary general of Fatah in the West Bank, came to a close. He was found guilty on five counts, and each carried a sentence of life in prison for murders committed during attacks that he had ordered. The verdict, however, only solidified his popularity among the Palestinian people.

The death toll for the month of May 2004 rose to nineteen on the Israeli side, and 112 on that of the Palestinians. Nothing could put a stop to the day-to-day bloody routine that had become entrenched in Gaza. Armed organizations continued to launch rockets on Israel, not claiming any victims for the most part. The IDF, however, responded with incursions by armed vehicles, aerial bombings, and "targeted killings."

Ariel Sharon decided not to abandon his withdrawal plan and to submit it once again to a government vote, to the great displeasure of the extreme Right, who were grumbling and threatening to leave the national coalition. He dismissed two ministers from the National Union movement, which, in the absence of these opponents, allowed him to rally a majority on June 6: fourteen votes for, and seven against. In order to placate hesitant ministers, the document, entitled "Revised Plan for Disengagement," had been modified and provided for a later vote on the evacuation of the settlements. The government aimed to complete the withdrawal by the end of 2005. For Ehud Olmert, it marked "a historical turning point in the policy of the state of Israel."

Forty-eight hours later, two members of the National Religious Party resigned, thereby aligning themselves with the orders of their spiritual guide, Rabbi Mordechai Eliahu. The rabbi claimed that "God forbids the uprooting of Jewish settlements from the land of Israel and the transfer of the land to foreigners." Sharon did not worry too much since he was not at risk of being consigned to the minority by the Knesset. Since April 15, the Labor Party had been making an effort to prevent the collapse of the government while it continued to promote withdrawal from Gaza. The prime minister was counting on these voices from the Left.

On June 9, an ad hoc government commission published a timetable for withdrawal. In July 2004, the IDF would begin making preparations for the transfer of its installations from Gaza. Settlers who wanted to leave voluntarily could do so, and would receive a subsidy compensating them for their gesture. Negotiations with international organizations concerning the transfer of property to the Palestinians were to be completed by October. In February 2005, the government would vote on the first stage of the evacuation of the settlements, and vote on the last stage in July. Settlers were permitted to leave voluntarily until August 14, 2005, after which the forced evacuation, set for September 1, would begin. On September 30, the withdrawal from Gaza would be complete. Israel would retain control of a narrow security zone along the Egyptian border. On June 15, 2004, Sharon finally received some good news: the government legal council had abandoned its investigation into the illegal loan given to his son, Gilad, by the businessman Cyril Kern. Nevertheless, the investigation into false statements made by Omri Sharon to the state controller was still ongoing.

JUSTICE AND THE WALL

Construction of the security barrier continued. Information on the exact length of the planned structure was often contradictory. Humanitarian organizations traced the government's budgetary decisions and followed construction on the ground as well as requisition orders presented to Palestinian landowners. They concluded that the structure would be more than 600 kilometers (approximately 373 miles) long. The surveys of these NGOs reported that more than 100,000 olive and fruit trees had been uprooted and 37 kilometers (23 miles) of irrigation pipe destroyed in order to allow the barrier to pass through.[2] According to UNRWA, fifteen Palestinian villages inhabited by more than 150,000 Palestinians were directly affected. The city of Qalqilya was deprived of a third of its water resources. Frequent confrontations erupted on various construction sites between the Israeli army and the Palestinians, often supported by movements on the Israeli Left. On June 30, in Jerusalem, the High Court of Justice ruled on an appeal filed by the inhabitants of Al Ram, a Palestinian village to the northwest of Jerusalem, against the construction of the separation barrier running through their lands. Several Israeli organizations helped them present their case, notably B'Tselem and reserve officers of the Council for Peace and Security. The judgment handed down on June 30 ordered the defense minister to reroute the barrier 30 to 40 kilometers (approximately 19 to 25 miles). The judges ruled that constructing a barrier for the purposes of security was legal, but that the state of Israel was obliged to take the needs of local residents into account.

During the month of June 2004, five Israelis and forty Palestinians were killed.

On July 10, the International Court in the Hague handed down its decision. It first set out to clarify the terminology applied to the structure: "[T]he 'wall' in question is a complex construction, so that that term cannot be understood in a limited physical sense. However, the other terms used, either by Israel ('fence') or by the secretary-general ('barrier'), are no more accurate if understood in the physical sense. In this Opinion, the court has therefore chosen to use the terminology employed by the General Assembly [that is to say, 'wall'].'' The judges cited the latest statistics provided by Kofi Annan's services: 975 square kilometers (16.6 percent of the West Bank) were situated between the Green Line (the demarcation line that separated Israel and the West Bank prior to June 1967) and the wall, where 160,000 Palestinians were living. If the planned route was completed, 320,000 Israeli settlers—among them 178,000 in East Jerusalem—would be living between the Green Line and the wall:

> The Court considers that the construction of the wall and its associated régime create a 'fait accompli' on the ground that could well become permanent, in which case, and notwithstanding the formal characterization of the wall by Israel, it would be tantamount to *de facto* annexation. . . . [T]he construction of the wall and its associated régime impede the liberty of movement of the inhabitants of the Occupied Palestinian Territory (with the exception of Israeli citizens and those assimilated thereto). . . . The Court having concluded that, by the construction of the wall in the Occupied Palestinian Territory, including in and around East Jerusalem, and by adopting its associated régime, Israel has violated various international obligations incumbent upon it. . . . As regards the legal consequences for Israel, it was contended that Israel has, first, a legal obligation to bring the illegal situation to an end by ceasing forthwith the construction of the wall in the Occupied Palestinian Territory, and to give appropriate assurances and guarantees of non-repetition. . . . [A]ll States are under an obligation not to recognize the illegal situation arising from the construction of the wall, not to render aid or assistance in maintaining that situation and to co-operate with a view to putting an end to the alleged violations and to ensuring that reparation will be made therefore.

The next morning, an explosion in a Tel Aviv bus killed one and wounded thirty, and provoked Ariel Sharon to respond in such a way to reveal his displeasure with the court's decision: "The act of terrorism that took place this morning occurred under the auspices of the opinion handed down by the International Court of Justice at The Hague. The sacred right to fight terrorism was given a slap in the face by these judges who are demanding the dismantling of the enclosure wall for the prevention of terrorism."

On July 21, unknown gunmen broke into the home of Nabil Amr in Ramallah. A former information minister at the Palestinian parliament, he was one of the main critics of Yasser Arafat and his policies. The assailants wounded him seriously in the leg, which had to be amputated.

On July 25, tens of thousands of settlers and their supporters held a demonstration, forming a human chain between the Nissanit settlement, in Gaza, and the Western Wall, in Jerusalem.

In July 2004, three Israelis and 57 Palestinians were killed.

ATTACKS AND REPRISALS

On August 1, the Sharon government initiated the construction of 600 supplementary residential units in Maale Adumim, east of Jerusalem. In Gaza and the West Bank, tension was mounting between supporters and opponents of Yasser Arafat. In Nablus, armed men broke into a room where seventy ministers and Fatah officials were gathered to discuss reforms. They fired shots in the air, spurring the participants to flee. In an interview with a Kuwaiti newspaper, Mohammed Dahlan, the former security official in Gaza, accused the PLO leader of "lamenting over the bodies and the destruction while Palestinians are in desperate need of a new breath. The Autonomous Authority received 5 billion dollars,[3] and we don't know where it's gone. If the chairman does not make the necessary reforms, 30,000 protesters will flood the streets of Gaza."[4]

Yasser Arafat was not the only one facing difficulties from within his home base. Since the departure of the ministers on the extreme Right, Ariel Sharon no longer possessed a stable parliamentary majority. He wanted to draw the Labor Party back into his coalition since the party was still presided over by his old friend Shimon Peres, a strong supporter of the withdrawal from Gaza. But, in order to accomplish this, Sharon needed to secure the agreement of the central committee of Likud, and the hawks were wary. Uzi Landau, the minister of interior security and a fierce opponent to withdrawals from the settlements, was lying in wait. He proposed a motion prohibiting any agreement with Labor. And, for the second time, Ariel Sharon was rebuffed by his own party. Delegates approved the Landau motion by a vote of 843 for and 612 against. The prime minister would have to settle for the Left's support in the parliament, without it being officially included in the coalition. The Meretz-Yachad Party, led by Yossi Beilin, also pledged to help prevent the collapse of the government.

On August 31, closely timed twin suicide bombings detonated in two buses in Beersheba, killing sixteen and wounding more than a hundred. In a statement, Hamas and Ezzedin al-Qassam, the Hamas military wing, claimed responsibility for the attack, asserting that "this is but one of a series of responses the Ezzedin al-Qassam brigades have vowed to carry out in response to the martyrdom of the leaders of our movement, Sheik Ahmed Yassin and Abdel Aziz Rantisi." The two terrorists came from Hebron. The Palestinian Authority criticized the attacks, condemning "all attacks on civilians, Palestinians or Israelis." A week later, helicopters fired five missiles on a Hamas training center in Gaza, killing fourteen Palestinians and wounding thirty. According to the Palestinians, at least eleven victims had been affiliated with the Islamic movement. Fifty thousand people attended their funerals and clamored for vengeance.

In August 2004, seventeen Israelis and thirty-nine Palestinians were killed.

On September 15, an Israeli raid on Nablus resulted in six deaths, including four members of the al-Aqsa Martyrs Brigades and one from the DFLP, as well as an eleven-year-old child. On September 21, a poll conducted by Bir Zeit University revealed a clear advantage for Yasser Arafat in the election scheduled for the spring. Of the Palestinians polled, 46 percent said they would vote for him, whereas only 11 percent said they would choose Marwan Barghouti if he ran for office. On September 22, a female suicide bomber sent by the al-Aqsa Martyrs Brigades set off her explosives in Jerusalem. She killed two Israelis and wounded seventeen. The next day, three Palestinians attacked a military outpost in Morag, a settlement in Gaza, killing three soldiers before they themselves were killed in firefights.

On September 26, Shin Bet published statistics pertaining to the conflict. Since the beginning of the intifada, in September 2000, 1,017 Israelis had been killed; 70 percent of the victims were civilians, and the rest were members of security services. The Palestinians had committed 13,730 attacks with automatic weapons, and 138 suicide attacks. Among the 5,600 Israeli wounded, 82 percent were civilians. Since the beginning of 2004, ninety-seven Israelis had been killed, and 441 wounded, significantly lower than in 2002, when 452 Israelis had been killed, and 2,308 wounded.[5]

On September 29, Hamas launched a Qassam rocket on Sderot, killing two Israeli children, two and four years old respectively, and wounding sixteen. The next day, the Israeli army launched a major operation called "Days of Reckoning" in the large refugee camp in Jebaliya, in Gaza. By the next day, twenty-nine Palestinians had been killed and approximately a hundred wounded, along with a soldier and an Israeli woman.[6] The fighting continued for several days.

In concert with its military efforts, the IDF was launching a media battle against UNRWA, which was regularly issuing troubling reports concerning the humanitarian situation in Gaza. Soldiers believed that they had discovered proof of a connection between the UN organization and Palestinian militants. The army press services broadcast images filmed by a drone in which it was possible to discern a man taking a long object out of a UNRWA ambulance. "It's a missile!" the army claimed. A timely investigation established that it was in fact a stretcher. Embarrassed, the army ultimately admitted its error, and the image was removed from official Israeli internet sites.

On October 5, the army was once again in the hot seat. A thirteen-year-old schoolgirl had been killed by soldiers on her way to school near the Rafah front line. Iman el-Hams was shot twenty times in the body and five times in the head, despite the fact that no incidents had been reported in the sector. This tragic story was widely circulated by the international press. The army's initial explanation claimed that soldiers feared that the girl, who should not have been walking in what was considered to be a dangerous area, was carrying a bomb in her schoolbag. An officer was brought before a military tribunal, but he was ultimately acquitted.

On October 7, al-Qaeda attacked three tourist centers on the Egyptian coast of the Red Sea. Car bombs exploded next to the Hilton hotel in Taba and on two beaches killing thirty-two, including twelve Israelis. Within a few hours, tens of thousands of Israeli tourists who had come to spend their vacations in the Sinai turned around and recrossed the border at Taba.

In Gaza, the Israeli operation continued, killing eighty-four Palestinians, including at least twenty under the age of sixteen.

PALESTINE AND FINLAND

On October 8, 2004, Dov Weisglass, Sharon's cabinet leader, explained the benefits of the disengagement plan to Israelis and to settlers in particular in the newspaper *Haaretz*. He began by listing the reasons that led the prime minister to make this decision. In contrast with the West Bank, Gaza was not, in his view, an area of national interest. He next evoked the context of the fall of 2003: the situation had been stuck as much on the international level as inside the country. The economy was stagnating, and the Geneva Initiative was gaining increasing support. Even the armed forces were expressing their deep disapproval, as letters from pilots and reservists from the military staff commando unit have confirmed. Confronted with this stagnation, Sharon reached the point of making a genuine about-face:

> There is an American commitment such as never existed before, with regard to 190,000 settlers. . . . The significance is the freezing of the political process. And when you freeze that process you prevent the establishment of a Palestinian state

and you prevent a discussion about the refugees, the borders, and Jerusalem. Effectively, this whole package that is called the Palestinian state, with all that it entails, has been removed from our agenda indefinitely. And all this with authority and permission. All with a presidential blessing and the ratification of both houses of Congress. What more could have been anticipated? What more could have been given to the settlers?

And we educated the world to understand that there is no one to talk to. And we received a no-one-to-talk-to certificate. That certificate says: 1) There is no one to talk to. 2) As long as there is no one to talk to, the geographic status quo remains intact. 3) The certificate will be revoked only when this-and-this happens—when Palestine becomes Finland. 4) See you then, and shalom.

The interview provoked a general outcry, and Mr. Weisglass subsequently backed off from his statements.

Buoyed by the support of the parties on the Left, Sharon did not give in to the threats of four Likud ministers being pressured by Benjamin Netanyahu, who demanded a national referendum. He submitted his withdrawal plan to a vote in the Knesset. Thousands of settlers demonstrated in front of the parliament in vain. The Right was beaten, having received forty-five votes against sixty-seven for the Left. Half of the Likud deputies and half from ultraorthodox groups voted with the opposition. That same day, the IDF made an incursion supported by aerial raids into Khan Younis, killing fourteen and wounding sixty-three.

On October 12, after eating dinner, Yasser Arafat became nauseous, vomiting and experiencing severe abdominal pain. A doctor diagnosed him with an intestinal flu and recommended rest.

ARAFAT

At the Muqata, Arafat's condition did not improve. He had lost 10 kilos (22 pounds) and appeared to be very weak. His entourage was worried. Ashraf Kurdi, his personal physician, arrived from Jordan, and specialists from Tunisia and Egypt were called to his bedside as well. Medical tests were conducted at a hospital in Ramallah, and doctors decided to transfer the PLO leader to a modern medical facility. France offered its services and on October 29, Arafat was transported in his Jordanian helicopter to Amman, where he departed for Clamart, southwest of Paris, in order to receive treatment at the Percy military hospital that was known for its discretion. He would not agree to leave until he received a formal guarantee from the Israeli government that he would be permitted to return as soon as he was well. Mahmoud Abbas returned to service and took control in the interim.

In October 2004, four Israelis and 140 Palestinians were killed.

On November 1, a sixteen-year-old suicide bomber sent by the Popular Front for the Liberation of Palestine struck at a Tel Aviv market, killing three Israelis. The next day, the Israeli army destroyed his house as well as those of two leaders of the cell that sent him to die in Tel Aviv. Demonstrations supporting Arafat took place in several cities in the West Bank, and rumors began to circulate that his health was deteriorating. Some even said that he was in a coma. Palestinian leaders who rushed to the hospital discovered that they did not have permission to see their chairman because according to French law, only family members are authorized to see a patient. That being the case, Arafat's wife, Soha, assumed control of the situation, and barely any information trickled out of the hospital. Arafat was suffering from a serious blood ailment, the cause of which had still not been determined. In Gaza, the five main Palestinian organizations agreed to a call from the Palestinian Authority requesting them to maintain calm while their leader remained ill.

On November 2, George Bush was reelected president with sixty-two million votes to John Kerry's fifty-nine million. Colin Powell had already announced he would not return to the position of secretary of state. The other members of the team that had directed American policy during the previous four years would remain. Vice President Dick Cheney and Secretary of Defense Donald Rumsfeld stayed on as head of the neoconservative camp, and made certain that their camp remained behind Israel.

On November 11, at 3:30 a.m., the father of Palestinian nationalism, the founder of Fatah, the leader of the PLO and of the Autonomous Authority, the signer of the Oslo Accords with Israel, passed away. Yasser Arafat died at the age of seventy-five. A mourning period of forty days was declared in the Palestinian territories. His body was to be transported to Cairo, where the Arab world would bid its farewell before the funeral in Ramallah. The Israeli government refused permission to bury his body in the Esplanade of the Mosques in Jerusalem, a wish that Arafat had expressed in his will. The army and police remained on a state of alert in order to prevent any clandestine attempts to transport his body to Jerusalem.

THE FUNERAL

France organized a ceremony fit for a head of state by having the Republican guard honor the departure of the coffin in the presence of Jacques Chirac and his prime minister, Jean-Pierre Raffarin, at the Villacoublay aerodrome. The next morning, in the center of the Heliopolis military club in Cairo, the PLO leader was received with honors accorded only the most important men of the Arab world. A dozen heads of state were present, and all Arab and Muslim countries were represented. All European foreign affairs ministers made the trip. The United States sent William Burns, the deputy secretary of state responsible for the Middle East. Far from crowds, the ceremony was short, following Egyptian military protocol. The coffin was then transported by plane to El Arish, in the Sinai, where it was placed aboard an Egyptian army helicopter. Yasser Abed Rabbo and Saeb Erekat chose to accompany their leader on his final journey. Mahmoud Abbas and other Palestinian dignitaries took their places in a second helicopter. In Ramallah, at the esplanade of the Muqata, in adjoining streets and on rooftops, an enormous crowd waited for their leader, whom they called by his nom de guerre, Abu Amar. Saeb Erekat recalled that "when the helicopter appeared above the square, the Egyptian pilot told me that he couldn't land. There was an ocean of people who were jumping, yelling, running, and shooting in the air . . . enough so that it would only take one bullet to turn the helicopter into a ball of fire."

Yasser Abed Rabbo added that "the helicopter finally landed, but the crowd swarmed around it and blocked our exit. The shooting did not stop, and the Egyptian pilot began to pray. We opened the door slightly, begging, yelling to the crowd to stop shooting and to give us space."

Saeb Erekat: "I began to yell like a madman: 'We have the body of the fighter for Palestine, he is your commander in chief!'"[7]

Yasser Abed Rabbo: "After a half an hour, we were able to get the coffin out of the helicopter. A kind of wave swept through the crowd, and I saw the coffin disappear. Those were my last moments with Arafat."

The casket, covered with the Palestinian flag, was carried through the crowd to the grave, accompanied by the lament taken up by thousands of Palestinians: "With our soul, with our blood, we support you, Abu Amar!" In the great hall of the Muqata, foreign representatives who had come to pay their last respects were waiting. No one had told them that the funeral was over. A little after seven in the evening, the square was suddenly empty, and the streets were deserted. It was soon the hour of *iftar*, the meal marking the end of the fast of Ramadan. Life was assuming its usual rhythms once again.

The mystery of Arafat's death persisted. French doctors had been unable to determine the origin of the blood infection that caused his death: a dispersed intravascular coagulation. Laboratory tests eliminated the theory that he had been poisoned by a known substance. There was no trace of cancer or leukemia, and no infectious agent had been found. The *New York Times*, along with Israeli journalists who had access to the medical file at Percy Hospital, observed that the AIDS test was not mentioned, a detail that fed rumors despite the fact that the symptoms and all other medical tests contradicted this possibility.[8] Arafat's personal physician, Ashraf Kurdi, and several other prominent Palestinian figures, nevertheless remained convinced that Arafat had been poisoned. Some accused Israel, which issued a formal denial.

In December 2006, new information reopened the debate over Arafat's death. In his book of interviews with the Israeli prime minister, Uri Dan recalled that during Sharon's visit to the White House on April 14, 2004,

George Bush had advised him to leave Arafat's fate in the hands of divine providence. Sharon answered, half-jokingly, half-seriously, that sometimes providence has a helping hand. President Bush remained impassive, "without giving Sharon approval to assassinate Arafat and, without looking to impose new promises upon him either." In this same book, Dan states that after a particularly bloody attack, he demanded of Sharon, "What are we doing? We're not killing Arafat, we're not getting rid of him. So, he has absolute immunity?" Sharon responded, "Let me handle things in my own way!" Sharon's confidant proceeded to observe that "Sharon had barely regained his freedom to act following the April 14 meeting with President Bush when Arafat's health deteriorated."[9]

In November 2004, three Israelis and forty Palestinians were killed.

Forty-eight hours after Arafat's funeral, the Palestinian authorities decided to hold an election on January 14, 2005.

On December 2, a new political crisis shook Jerusalem. In the Knesset, the deputies and ministers of the secular Shinui Party voted against Sharon's proposed 2005 budget. Sharon dismissed them and thereby lost the parliamentary majority. Early elections were inevitable if he did not manage to forge a new coalition, and thus once again he requested that the Likud central committee authorize negotiations with the Labor Party and the ultraorthodox parties. The vote was held on December 9, and this time it favored Sharon: 62 percent of the delegates of the central committee voted for, and 38 percent against.

On December 12, Hamas and Fatah conducted a joint operation against the border post in Rafah, situated between Gaza and Egypt. A powerful bomb placed in a tunnel destroyed the Israeli military checkpoint guarding its entrance, and two Palestinians infiltrated the post and opened fire. They were killed in the ensuing firefight, along with five soldiers. The border was closed and thousands of Palestinians would remain locked in for several weeks. On December 18, Ariel Sharon finalized his agreement with the Labor Party. Shimon Peres returned to service and became the vice-prime minister.

PALESTINIAN ELECTIONS

On December 26, 560 prominent Palestinian political and intellectual figures published a call in the West Bank press to end armed attacks: "We affirm our legitimate right to fight the occupation, but we demand the reestablishment of the popular character of our intifada and the halting of actions that reduce the support for our cause and damage the credibility of our fight."

In December 2004, nine Israelis and sixty Palestinians were killed as a result of skirmishes, targeted killings, and IDF incursions.

On January 2, 2005, the IDF withdrew from the Khan Younis sector, where for three days infantry and armed tank units had been searching for rockets and mortars. Eleven Palestinians had been killed and a dozen houses destroyed. During an electoral meeting in Jebaliya, Mahmoud Abbas issued a call to halt the launching of rockets on Israel: "Do not give [the Israelis] a pretext to fight us, this is not the time!" Six Palestinian organizations, including Hamas, responded the next day in a joint statement: "The missiles of the resistance will continue to be the nightmare of the Zionist colonies."

On January 4, a mortar fired by a tank exploded in a strawberry field near Beit Lahiya, in the northern Gaza Strip. Seven Palestinians were killed, including three brothers aged nine to thirteen, their three cousins aged 10, twelve, and twenty-two, as well as a neighbor, who was twenty. The IDF claimed that the targets were rocket launchers located in the field. But, according to the Palestinians, the militants had left the field long before the explosion. In Khan Younis, where he was campaigning, Mahmoud Abbas declared that "we come to you praying for the martyrs killed today by the mortar of the Zionist enemy!" Neither Jerusalem nor Washington was pleased with this statement—Ehud Olmert judged it to be "intolerable and unacceptable"—while a state department spokesman said that the kind of language Abbas was using "has no place in a process of resuming dialogue."

The Palestinians voted on January 9, 2005, and Mahmoud Abbas was triumphantly elected with 62 percent of the vote, becoming the new chairman of the Palestinian Authority. That very evening, even before the election results were made public, Ariel Sharon called Abbas to congratulate him. A team of international observers led by Senators Joseph Biden and John Sununu confirmed that the Palestinian election took place without interference, transparently and honestly. Colin Powell, who had completed his term as secretary of state, called Abbas, as did numerous foreign leaders. The international community hailed the Palestinian leader who demanded the cessation of the intifada.

On January 13th, Hamas, the al-Aqsa Martyrs Brigades, and the Popular Committees attacked the checkpoint at Karni, through which all cargo in and out of Gaza was transported. This was one of the last remaining symbols of cooperation between Israel and the Palestinians. A truck bomb exploded and penetrated the wall on the Palestinian side. Three assailants passed through the breach and opened fire on the Israelis. They were killed in the ensuing firefight, along with six Israeli civilians. The checkpoint was closed until further notice. Nothing more would pass through there. Gaza was thereby completely sealed off.

The Rafah border post still had not been reopened. On the Egyptian side, 10,000 Palestinians were waiting to return to their homes. In Israel, the defense minister suffered another defeat at the High Court of Justice. The judges ruled in favor of the inhabitants of the town of Beit Surik, northwest of Jerusalem, who demanded modifications in the path of the wall. Work on this section of the barrier came to a halt.

THE SUMMIT OF HOPE

On January 15, Mahmoud Abbas was sworn in at the legislative council in Ramallah. In his inaugural speech, he called for the resumption of the negotiations with Israel: "I say to the Israeli people and its leaders: we are two peoples destined to live side by side and to share this land. The pursuit of the occupation and the conflict is the only alternative to peace." The new chairman gave his security services instructions to prevent the launching of rockets from Gaza onto Israeli territory, and 3,000 police were deployed all along the front line. The measure was above all a symbolic one. After five years of conflict and the destruction of a part of its means, the Palestinian police did not have the power to enforce a cease-fire among armed organizations, especially Hamas. Mahmoud Abbas thus wanted to negotiate a truce. Talks with the Islamists and groups linked to Fatah began on January 18 in Gaza, and an agreement that established a truce was concluded four days later. With the exception of Islamic Jihad, all of the movements pledged to temporarily suspend their attacks against Israel, on the condition that the IDF halt its operations in Gaza as well as its "targeted killings." Moshe Yaalon, the chief of staff, gave instructions to the army in accordance with this agreement.

For Hamas, armed struggle assumed secondary importance as the Islamic organization began to focus its strategy and efforts on the acquisition of political power. On December 24, during the municipal elections that took place in twenty-six localities throughout the West Bank, its candidates won 109 municipal council seats, as opposed to the 136 that went to Fatah. Thanks to its alliances with other movements, Hamas managed to take control of the majority of the councils in question. And, as a sign of the times, a few Palestinian women were elected to the position of mayor for the first time in history.

On January 27, the Hamas victory was even clearer in Gaza. The Islamists were the majority in seven out of the ten localities where a municipal election was held. Fatah was crushed, carrying only thirty-nine seats of the 118 that had been vacant. Hamas gained seventy-six, and twenty women were elected.

In January 2005, eleven Israelis and fifty-two Palestinians were killed, most before the cease-fire went into effect.

Preliminary communications between Ariel Sharon's entourage and the advisors of Mahmoud Abbas were successful. Israel and the Palestinian Authority resumed talks, and, on February 8, under the aegis of Hosni Mubarak and King Abdullah of Jordan, the summit of hope opened at Sharm el-Sheik. It was the first time that Sharon visited Egypt since he assumed power. The Israeli prime minister and the Palestinian president proclaimed a cease-fire, and, before television cameras from throughout the world, declared the beginning of a new era of hope.

Ariel Sharon:

> We must be careful not to waste the opportunity that has been given to us. We have a chance to leave the bloody path that has been imposed upon us during the last four years. . . . For the first time in a long time, there is hope in our region for a better future for our children and grandchildren. We must proceed with caution. This opportunity is very fragile. The extremists want to destroy it, destroy this opportunity and allow our two peoples to drown in their blood. . . . I do not intend to let this opportunity pass us by. . . . That is why we have acted rapidly and with determination, understanding the needs of the Palestinian side. During the past few days, we have concluded a number of agreements that will bring tranquility and security to both peoples in the near future. Today, with President Abbas, we have decided that the Palestinians will halt all acts of violence perpetrated against the Israelis, no matter where. At the same time, Israel will halt all military activities against the Palestinians, no matter where. Today, we hope to mark the beginning of a new period of tranquility and hope. We have also agreed on a process by which to transfer responsibility for some security matters to the Palestinians. . . . Soon, we will liberate hundreds of Palestinian prisoners and establish a joint commission to arrange further liberations. . . . To our Palestinian neighbors: I assure you that we truly intend to respect your right to live in independence and dignity. I have already confirmed that Israel has no desire to continue to govern you or to control your destiny. It was necessary for us [the Israelis] to painfully renounce our dreams. . . . You must prove that you also have the strength and courage to accept compromise, to abandon unreal dreams, to master the forces opposed to peace, and to live in peace and mutual respect, side by side [with Israel].

Mahmoud Abbas:

> We decided, with Prime Minister Ariel Sharon, to put a stop
> to all acts of violence against the Israelis and the Palestinians,
> no matter where they may be. The tranquility and calm that
> shall reign over our region starting today will mark the begin-
> ning of a new era. The beginning of peace and hope proclaimed
> today represents the implementation of the first article of the
> Quartet's road map. . . . We have some disagreements about a
> certain number of questions: the settlements, the liberation of
> prisoners, the wall that encloses institutions in Jerusalem. . . .
> We will not be able to resolve all of these problems today, but
> our positions on these issues are clear and firm. The intensifi-
> cation of our efforts will lead us to another stage of the road
> map: to resume negotiations on the final status in order to end
> the Israeli occupation that began in 1967.

On February 25, a suicide bomber set off his explosives in front of
the entrance to a discotheque in Tel Aviv, killing five and wounding fifty.
Mahmoud Abbas gathered together the heads of Palestinian security
services and ordered them to arrest those responsible for the attack. And
if they failed, he warned that they would be forced to resign. Near
Tulkarm, the brothers of the terrorist were arrested the very next day.

In Lebanon, Islamic Jihad claimed responsibility for the attack and,
in a video, accused the Autonomous Authority of collaborating with the
occupier: "It shall have the same destiny as the auxiliaries of the army of
south Lebanon!" In Gaza, the leaders of the Islamic organization claimed
they were surprised by this statement and confirmed that they were observing the truce.

In February 2005, five Israelis and twelve Palestinians were killed.

SETTLEMENTS

Despite the many promises made by Ariel Sharon to the American administration, no significant outposts in the West Bank had yet been

evacuated. Indeed, new settlements and extensions of existing settlements were being built, all without official authorization. To gain time, the previous July the prime minister had invested Talia Sasson, a prominent legal expert, with the responsibility of preparing a complete report on the question. The report that she submitted on March 8 was a veritable indictment of the government:

> Some of the land confiscation and illegal construction was done with the unauthorized aid of the Ministry of Housing and the Settlement Division, while *violating the law* publicly; the State of Israel finances at least part of the establishment of unauthorized outposts; for years the Civil Administration overlooked neighborhood expansions, either nearby or far away from settlements that were completed without a lawful detailed scheme, sometimes over private Palestinian property; [the Civil Administration] does not supervise construction there; [the Civil Administration] refuses to give information regarding outposts . . . the Ministry of Defense sometimes permits caravans to enter Judea, Samaria, and Gaza even when there is no legal planning for their destination. The assistant to the Defense Minister-Settlement Affairs certifies that unauthorized outposts are settlements eligible for local authority budgets from the Ministry of Interior Affairs, while the Ministry of Defense publicly declares them as unauthorized; thousands of destruction orders remain unexecuted for years; the outposts keep increasing and getting thicker, while no delimiting orders are issued, not even regarding outposts mentioned in the March 2001 list, which Israel took upon itself an explicit political obligation to evacuate; *delimiting orders issued and approved by the High Court of Justice remain unexecuted.*[10]

Talia Sasson brought to light what was, in fact, an open secret. Anyone visiting the West Bank could easily see that the outposts possessed infrastructures that could only be authorized by the state: attachment to the national electric grid, connection to the telephone network, running water, access to roads, etc. Her report would remain a dead letter. None of the officials against whom she recommended judicial action would have reason to worry.

In March 2005, two Palestinians were killed.

On April 9 in Rafah, an Israeli tank opened fire on a group of young Palestinians, killing three, aged fifteen to seventeen. According to the Palestinians, they were playing soccer, but the IDF denied it and claimed that they were suspects who were rushing toward an Israeli unit. During the next several hours, dozens of mortar shells were launched on Israeli settlements, and Sharon accused Abbas and the Autonomous Authority of doing nothing to prevent these attacks. Soon afterward, he arrived in Crawford at George Bush's Texas ranch.

This meeting with President Bush did not go as well as those in the past. In front of the press, following the conventional niceties, George Bush asked his interlocutor to keep his promises: "I told the prime minister of my concern that Israel not undertake any activity that contravenes the road map obligations or prejudice final status negotiations. Therefore, Israel should remove unauthorized outposts and meet its road map obligations regarding settlements in the West Bank. . . ."

Ariel Sharon responded as follows: "It is the Israeli position that the major Israeli population centers will remain in Israel's hands under any future final status agreement with all related consequences."

And George Bush reiterated the promise he made on April 14, 2003: "While the United States will not prejudice the outcome of final status negotiations, those changes on the ground, including major Israeli population centers, must be taken into account in any final status negotiations."

The prime minister also criticized Mahmoud Abbas, and insisted that Israel was still suffering from terrorism. Bush responded that he "appreciate[s] the fact that they've taken some action on security.

We want to continue to work with them on consolidating the security forces."

In April 2005, five Palestinians were killed.

On May 9, the Israeli government decided to delay the beginning of the evacuation of the Gaza settlements by twenty-four hours, planned for August 14, to avoid disturbing Tisha B'Av, a symbolic day of fasting commemorating the destruction of the Temple of Jerusalem. The settlers and their supporters mobilized their troops. On May 16, protesters blocked the main roads in the region.

In May 2005, one Israeli and eleven Palestinians were killed.

ISRAELI GESTURES

On June 1, Moshe Yaalon left the army. Ariel Sharon and Shaul Mofaz chose not to extend his mandate as chief of staff of the IDF for the following year, as was customary. Yaalon had been rebelling more and more frequently. He was opposed to disengagement, which he felt was the worst mission of his entire military career. He demanded, in vain, an in-depth study of the consequences of the withdrawal on Israel's security. "The decisions," he said, "had been made without having consulted with the IDF!"[11] General Dan Halutz, his deputy and a former commander of the air force, succeeded him as head of the army.

The next day, Sharon kept his word: 398 Palestinian prisoners were freed, including militants from Fatah and Hamas, but not Islamic Jihad, which refused to respect the truce. The number should have been 400, but two decided to remain in their cells to express their solidarity with the detainees who were to remain imprisoned. On June 7, a rocket exploded in Ganei Tal, a Gaza settlement, killing three workers, one Chinese and two Palestinians. On June 20, an Israeli died in an ambush in Baka al-Sharkia in the West Bank, an attack that Shin Bet blamed on Islamic Jihad. On the morning of June 21, the IDF attempted a targeted killing for the first time since the Sharm el-Sheik summit. In Gaza, a helicopter launched a missile and destroyed a car belonging to an Islamic Jihad leader. Several hours later, Mahmoud Abbas and his advisors arrived at the government offices in Jerusalem.

Ariel Sharon announced the latest Israeli gestures: responsibility for Bethlehem and Qalqilya would be transferred to the Palestinian security services. The number of Palestinian workers authorized to work in Israel would be increased. Mahmoud Abbas promised to deploy 5,000 police officers around Gaza settlement blocs during the evacuation and asked that they be authorized to bear arms. Palestinians would remove the ruins of destroyed houses, an operation that would be financed by the international community. He also demanded the transfer to the Autonomous Authority of a sector in the West Bank containing four settlements that were to be destroyed. Sharon refused, telling Abbas that "you are taking insufficient measures against terrorism. If you do not act against Islamic Jihad, we will take it upon ourselves to do so." Abbas answered that "each bullet and each mortar shell fired at you is also fired at me." The Palestinian delegation returned to Ramallah, extremely depressed.

In June 2005, four Israelis, one Chinese worker, and five Palestinians were killed.

THE EVACUATION

IDF planning for the evacuation was moving into high gear. Units of officers and soldiers were undergoing special training involving a psychological component that aimed to prepare them to face bitter insults and moral pressure. Only around thirty religious officers and soldiers, most of whom themselves resided in West Bank settlements, refused to obey orders. Beginning in October 2004, approximately sixty rabbis had approved the appeal of the former grand rabbi of Israel, Mordechai Eliahu:

> It is clear that according to the Halakah [the religious law], any soldier who receives an order contrary to the laws of the Torah must adhere to the law of the Torah and not to secular law, . . . since it is clear that the commandment to populate the land of Israel is more important than any other commandment stipulated by the Torah. . . . Any order given by the army going against this commandment has no value. . . . It is clear that soldiers must refuse the order to evacuate the

Jewish settlements in the land of Israel; this order contradicts
the commandment of the Torah. All Jews are prohibited from
participating in any way at all in the dismantling of the Jewish settlements in the land of Israel. The land of Israel, in its
totality, is the inheritance left to us by our God.

Some rabbis insisted that, based on their faith in their interpretations
of the sacred texts, the withdrawal would not take place. Numerous religious settlers believed them. On July 4, young religious girls blocked
main roads in Jerusalem and Tel Aviv, and several dozens of them were
arrested.

On July 12th, a suicide bomber sent by Islamic Jihad set off his explosives in a commercial center in Netanya, killing five and wounding
thirty. The next day, settlements in Gaza and in the northern area of the
West Bank were declared closed military zones. Only their inhabitants
were permitted to remain. On July 14, a twenty-two-year-old Israeli
woman was killed by a Qassam rocket in an attack for which the al-Aqsa
Martyrs Brigades of Fatah, Hamas, and Islamic Jihad claimed responsibility. In retaliation, the air force bombed two apartment buildings in
Gaza. On July 18, the settlers' movement mounted a demonstration in
Netivot, the development city in the western Negev. Tens of thousands
of settlers and their sympathizers dressed in orange, the color symboliz-
ing the refusal of withdrawal. They called for Sharon's resignation.

On July 21, Sharon was invited to the municipality of Ariel, one of
the main settlements in the West Bank. He stated that "this [settlement]
bloc will be an integral part of the state of Israel forever. . . . I came in
person to see how we can develop this town and the whole bloc." Ron
Nachman, the mayor of Ariel, was standing at his side and was naturally
obliged to express his approval. A Likud deputy, he presided over the
settlement lobby in parliament. Meanwhile, settlers were organizing a
massive demonstration in Kfar Maimon, near the Gaza border. A huge
contingent of police was preventing them from reaching the settlements.

The next day, Condoleezza Rice made her first visit to the region as secretary of state. Received by Ariel Sharon at his Sycamore Ranch, she requested that he coordinate the withdrawal with the Palestinian Authority and that he not make exaggerated demands of Mahmoud Abbas who, she added, was politically very weak.

On July 23, two Israelis were assassinated by Palestinians on a road close to the Gaza Strip. On the evening of July 26, a group of extremists from the racist movement Kach prayed in the Rosh Pina cemetery, in the Upper Galilee, for Ariel Sharon's death by reciting the Pulsa de Nura, a Kabbalistic prayer.

In July 2005, eight Israelis and twenty-five Palestinians were killed.

On August 4, a large police contingent close to the city of Ofakim blocked a demonstration by opponents to the withdrawal. But the media's attention was elsewhere. Natan Zada, a young deserter from the army, had opened fire on Arab-Israeli passengers on a bus in the city of Shfaram in Galilee. He killed four people and wounded six before being lynched by an angry mob, despite attempts by the police to intervene. Officials from the settlement committee officially condemned this crime. On August 7, Sharon's government approved the withdrawal of the first section of three settlements: Kfar Darom, Netzarim, and Morag. The announcement was made in order to misdirect thousands of protesters who were planning to block the withdrawal. Five Likud ministers voted against it: Danny Naveh, Limor Livnat, Yisrael Katz, Tzachi Hanegbi, and Benjamin Netanyahu, who resigned soon thereafter. The others promptly followed his lead. On August 15, the Gaza settlers were granted a forty-eight hour extension to leave voluntarily and receive a departure subsidy. Close to 50,000 soldiers and police officers were deployed around the site in question.

That evening, Ariel Sharon addressed the nation in a speech broadcast by radio and television: "It is no secret. . . . I believed and I hoped that we would be able to keep Netzarim and Kfar Darom forever. But the reality has changed in our country, in the region, and in the world. I therefore had to change my position. . . . This operation is essential for

Israel. We cannot keep Gaza forever. More than a million Palestinians live there in overpopulated refugee camps, in poverty, without hope." Mahmoud Abbas subsequently issued a statement: ". . . The Israeli withdrawal is a very important step in our history. But it is only a beginning. Such a withdrawal must take place not only in Gaza, but also in the West Bank and in East Jerusalem. . . ."

The operation began early in the morning on August 17. The settlers made an appeal to the conscience of public opinion as well as that of any soldier participating in the expulsion. Before the cameras, families came out of their homes, hands in the air, wearing the yellow star, evoking the image of Nazi roundups. Others, seated in their dining rooms as if nothing was going on, responded with a look of surprise when soldiers came to knock at their doors: "Leave? Why? What have we done?" They were carried into the buses. All of this took place before the cameras and under the gaze of 500 journalists from throughout the world. The three main Israeli television channels and the largest satellite stations broadcast the events live. That afternoon, a settler from Shiloh, in the West Bank, shot and killed four Palestinian workers whom he was transporting. By that evening, seven Gaza settlements had been evacuated: Peat Sadeh, Bedolah, Ganei Tal, Kerem Atzmona, Morag, Rafiah Yam, and Tel Katifa. The next day, Gan Or, Kfar Yam, Netzer Hazani, and Shirat Hayam were evacuated in their turn, without the army encountering any resistance. In Kfar Darom, hundreds of young protesters barricaded themselves on the roof of the synagogue. After several hours of confrontations with the police, they were subdued and led away in handcuffs. In Neve Dekalim, 1,500 protesters who refused to leave the synagogue were expelled from it. On August 19, Gadid was evacuated, followed two days later by Slav, Katif, Dugit, Elei Sinai, Bne Atzmona, as well the final houses in Neve Dekalim. The last battle took place on August 22. Once again, a few dozen young protesters refused to leave the synagogue in Netzarim. Helmeted police officers climbed on the roof and stormed the building. The operation did not end until nightfall. In the northern West Bank, after mounting resistance for several hours, the evacuation of

Sanur and Homesh took place unobstructed. The inhabitants of Ganim and Kadim had already left at the beginning of the month. This sector would not be transferred to the Palestinian Authority.

The nationalist religious movement had just suffered its first great ideological defeat. It did not succeed in mobilizing Israeli public opinion. In the end, only around sixty soldiers responded to the call of the rabbis to refuse to participate in the operation.

In August 2005, one Israeli and eleven Palestinians were killed.

Bulldozers tore down 2,800 houses, various buildings, and twenty-six synagogues. Prior to that, teams of police officers and soldiers packed the personal belongings of the families of settlers in containers. Bodies buried in the Gush Katif cemetery were exhumed so that they could be buried in Israeli land.

Greenhouses and agricultural structures had been purchased by a group of rich philanthropists led by James Wolfensohn, the former head of the World Bank, who had become an emissary for the Quartet. They would be offered to the Palestinians who, in principle, would be able to export winter vegetables and cherry tomatoes to earn $50 million per year. These crops constituted the livelihood of hundreds of Palestinian families and were to serve as the basis for economic development in Gaza.

On September 7, in anticipation of its withdrawal from Gaza, the IDF closed the Rafah border post situated between Gaza and Egypt. Settlers and prominent religious figures attempted to prevent the destruction of the synagogues in Gaza by filing an appeal with the High Court of Justice in Jerusalem. The judges handed down their decision on September 8: the state was granted permission to destroy these houses of prayer. But, two days later, Ariel Sharon changed his mind. Saeb Erekat received a telephone call from Dov Weisglass, who told him that the synagogues were not to be torn down. Palestinians were asked to prevent any attacks upon these sacred sites. During the same call, the Israeli prime minister's advisor informed his interlocutor that the IDF would leave Gaza within twenty-four hours. Erekat was completely taken aback: he was expecting a withdrawal on September 15, three days later. Neither the Palestinian police force, nor the Egyptian force across the border, was ready. He told Weisglass that he could not guarantee the security of the synagogues.

Early in the morning on September 12, the last soldier left Gaza territory. The withdrawal was complete. Thousands of Palestinians rushed into the evacuated sectors. Before the cameras, the most enraged among them burned and destroyed four synagogues. By asking Israel to destroy them, Palestinian leaders were aiming at all costs to avoid the international dissemination of such disastrous images. Jewish organizations throughout the world condemned the Autonomous Authority. On the sites of the destroyed buildings, crowds came to scavenge anything that was usable: doors, windows, shards of metal to be sold as scrap. The Palestinian police busied itself with protecting greenhouses in order to prevent looting.

THE WORKERS IN THE TEMPLE

A page in the history of Israel's occupation of the Gaza Strip had been turned. Messianic Judaism had just endured what would perhaps remain the gravest crisis in its history. The founding father of the eschatological vision of Zionism was Avraham Yitzhak Hacohen Kook, the first head Ashkenazi rabbi in the Jewish community of Palestine in the early twentieth century. He opposed the two powerful trends of the Judaism of his era. On one hand, he opposed the ultraorthodox view that the movement created by Theodor Herzl was a heresy, since the return to Zion could only take place within the context of redemption signaled by the return of the Messiah. On the other hand, he opposed religious groups who believed that immigration to Palestine would serve to increase the strength of the Jewish community, without this necessarily having any connection to the return of the Messiah. Avraham Yitzhak Hacohen Kook proposed an alternative theological synthesis: he claimed that lay Zionists were the equivalent of the workers authorized to enter the Holy of Holies in the Temple of Jerusalem in order to repair it, or they were the donkey upon whose back "the spirit of Israel," the Messiah, would make his entrance into the land of Israel.[12] This vision of the state of

Israel assumed a political dimension after the Six-Day War, which the rabbis of Merkaz Harav (the yeshiva founded by Kook) interpreted immediately as a miracle. It was seen as an expression of the divine will to bring the Jewish people together on the historical lands of the Bible: in Nablus, which is Shechem, in Hebron, the city of the patriarchs, on the hills of Samaria, where Aaron, the brother of Moses, protected the Ark of the Covenant, in Judea, on the Temple Mount in Jerusalem. On July 4, 1967, before his Talmudic school and in the presence of a thousand invited guests, Rabbi Zvi Yehuda Hacohen Kook gave a speech to the Jewish people: "If I forget thee, O Jerusalem, let my right hand wither, let my tongue cleave to my palate if I do not remember you, if I do not set Jerusalem above my highest joy." Then, praising the president of the Jewish state and the ministers assembled for the ceremony, he continued: "May the hand that signs any agreement for the concession of the land of Israel be cut off! . . . In the Torah, there is an absolute prohibition against giving up the tiniest bit of our liberated land." Twenty-nine years later, Yigal Amir, a young religious extremist, obeyed the call of Rabbi Kook and assassinated Yitzhak Rabin, the first leader of the Israeli government to have agreed to the principle of territorial compromise. The destruction of the settlements of Gaza and the northern West Bank flew in the face of the religious vision espoused by this movement. The "workers of the Temple" rebelled. Some rabbis explained to their flocks that this trial had been inflicted upon them by God and that, before the redemption, the people of Israel in its entirety must return to the faith.

In Gaza, the leaders of the armed branch of Hamas, the Ezzedin al-Qassam, emerged from the shadows and declared victory, claiming that it was their attacks that forced the Zionists to leave. A survey conducted by the Palestinian Center for Policy and Survey Research revealed that this opinion was shared by 40 percent of the people, while 21 percent attributed the withdrawal to Fatah's armed resistance, and only 11 percent to the actions of Chairman Mahmoud Abbas.[13]

On September 12, Hamas militants used a bulldozer to open a breach in the concrete wall separating Rafah from Egypt, thereby permitting thousands of Palestinians to flood the border. They rejoined members of their families who had stayed on the other side. They took the opportunity to go shopping, for Egyptian prices were actually 30 to 60 percent lower than in Gaza. Order would only be reestablished on September 18.

On September 23, a vehicle transporting armed militants exploded during a Hamas meeting in the Jebaliya refugee camp: nineteen people were killed and 80 wounded. The Islamic organization blamed Israel, but the Palestinian Authority stated that it was an accident. Handmade rockets were again being fired regularly toward the Israeli border town of Sderot. Six Israelis were wounded, and the IDF resumed its policy of "targeted killings."

TOWARD ELECTIONS IN ISRAEL

In September 2005, one Israeli and seventeen Palestinians were killed due to attacks and military operations.

On October 16, the al-Aqsa Martyrs Brigades attacked a bus station near the Gush Etzion settlement in the West Bank, killing three Israelis. Ten days later, a suicide bomber sent by Islamic Jihad detonated his explosives at the Hadera market, north of Tel Aviv, killing six and wounding thirty, and provoking the IDF to fire missiles in response. On October 28, Eyal Arad, Sharon's chief political strategist, spoke on Israeli radio: "If the peace process with the Palestinian Authority remains in an impasse, Israel may see itself pursuing its unilateral policy of disengagement in the West Bank, annexing territories, and thereby drawing its definitive boundaries." The prime minister's office responded by issuing a statement: "There are no plans for another unilateral withdrawal!" This did not prevent politicians from viewing Arad's statement as a test engineered by Sharon to gauge the potential political response. At the core of the Likud Party, opponents to withdrawal closed ranks around Benjamin Netanyahu.

In October 2005, ten Israelis and twenty-two Palestinians were killed.

Hermetically sealed since the Israeli withdrawal, Gaza was going through a deepening humanitarian crisis. Israelis and Palestinians had not concluded any agreement that would lift travel restrictions on people or goods. The Karni checkpoint was open only to a limited transfer of food and medical supplies into Gaza. Exports of agricultural and other products rarely made it out, while the Rafah crossing with Egypt was closed most of the time. Thousands of Gazans had been waiting—sometimes for months—to go abroad for medical treatment or study, or just to return to their families.

Condoleezza Rice decided to intervene. For the first time, she extracted a concession from Ariel Sharon. After marathon negotiations in Jerusalem, she struck a deal on November 15. An international border crossing would open at Rafah, operated by the Palestinian Authority under the control of European observers. Through a video circuit, the Israelis could follow the movement of the travelers from a distance. Rice declared: "It is a major step for the Palestinian people in their own movement towards independence. This agreement is intended to give the Palestinian people the freedom to move, to trade, to live ordinary lives." But the Israelis retained the option to order the closure of the border at any time, and in the coming months and years the Gazans would often live under total closure.

The Israeli political scene was in turmoil. On November 10, Amir Peretz, the former leader of the Histadrut labor union federation, surprised everyone by carrying the primaries of the Labor Party: 42.3 percent of 62,000 members voted for him, against 39.9 percent for Shimon Peres. Once the results were made public, the new leader of the Labor Party announced that he would keep his campaign promise: the ministers from the Labor Party would resign from the government. This act was accomplished on November 20. Sharon could no longer count on the Right and the extreme Right to form a new coalition, for such a majority would oppose his disengagement policy, and so he decided to shake up the Israeli political game. The next day, the president of Likud slammed the door on the party that he had formed thirty years earlier, and created a new one. He called it Kadima, a term that in Hebrew means "forward." That same day, he tendered his resignation to the president of the Knesset, who requested that he move quickly on pending issues. On November 23, the parliamentary decree to dissolve the government was signed and legislative elections were set for March 28. Tzipi Livni, the future foreign minister, as well as fourteen Likud deputies, joined Kadima. Livni was from a family of rightist activists, her father a comrade in arms of Menachem Begin in the Irgun, the rightist Zionist militia that fought British forces before the creation of Israel. On November 30, Shimon Peres left the Labor Party that he had led for decades and, along with Haim Ramon and Dalia Itzik, joined Kadima—his old friend "Arik" promised him the position of vice-prime minister in the event that the party won the election.

In November 2005, three Israelis and fifteen Palestinians were killed.

SHARON

On December 5, an Islamic Jihad suicide attack in Netanya killed five and wounded thirty-five. On December 18, Ariel Sharon was rushed to Hadassah Hospital in Jerusalem. He had visible difficulty speaking. Doctors diagnosed him with having had a mild stroke and he recovered in a few hours. A medical examination discovered that the source of the blood clot was a dysfunction in the septum of the heart. During the next few weeks, Sharon continued to recruit candidates for the Kadima electoral roll. After having announced that he would stay with Likud, Shaul Mofaz changed his mind and joined the prime minister.

In December 2005, eight Israelis and twenty Palestinians were killed.

On January 4, 2006, the night before a heart operation and while he was returning to his farm in the Negev, Ariel Sharon fell ill. He lost consciousness in the ambulance that was transporting him once again to Hadassah Hospital. This time the cerebral hemorrhage was massive. Television teams from throughout the world set up in the courtyard of the hospital and for the next ten days followed the old general's fight against death. Sharon did not win his final battle. He would remain incapacitated. Ehud Olmert, the vice-prime minister, became the interim leader of the government.

HAMAS ASSUMES POWER IN PALESTINE

Legislative elections in Palestine were held on January 25. Prior to his illness, Ariel Sharon announced that he would prevent Hamas from presenting candidates, but Mahmoud Abbas persuaded the American administration to support an election open to all Palestinian parties, including the Islamists. After all, George Bush was promoting democracy in the Middle East. Under pressure from the White House, Sharon yielded and Ehud Olmert had no choice but to implement the decision of his predecessor.

Hamas put forth candidates on a platform for change and reform that did not adopt the charter of the Islamic organization, but rather a less virulent electoral program:

> . . . Islam is our foundation. Palestine is an Arab and Muslim land. Palestinians belong to one nation, no matter where it is located. The Palestinian people are pursuing the process of national liberation and, to realize this objective, they have the right to use all means, including armed struggle. All Palestinians have the right of return. . . . The rights of minorities will be respected. . . . Public funds will be accessible to all.

The document, in response to the Israeli policy of disengagement, proposed that "the economic and monetary system should be independent of the Zionist entity. The platform for change and reform proposes that a Palestinian currency be created. . . ."

During the electoral campaign, Hamas candidates relentlessly attacked corruption within the Autonomous Authority dominated by Fatah, and insisted that "years of negotiation with Israel have brought nothing to the Palestinian people. . . . It is time for change!" Besides its official candidate, a divided Fatah put forth one, and sometimes two, candidates in some districts. In this way they handed the victory over to an Islamic candidate, the only representative of his party. Fatah, along with the independents with whom it was affiliated, received 43.9 percent of the vote and forty-three of the 132 deputy seats. Hamas received only 38.89 percent of the votes, but obtained seventy-six seats, and thus gained an absolute majority in the Palestinian legislative council. The outcome took Israel and the international community completely by surprise. Control over the Autonomous Authority passed into the hands of a group that the American administration, Europe, and Israel designated a terrorist organization.

In January 2006, thirteen Palestinians were killed.

ELECTIONS IN ISRAEL

On February 1, 2006, in the middle of the election campaign, Ehud Olmert approved the destruction of nine houses built without authorization in the settlement of Amona, in the West Bank, as ordered by the High Court of Justice. In an operation that continued into the evening, 1,400 police and soldiers confronted several hundred young settlers. At least a hundred activists, members of law enforcement, and two extreme right members of Parliament had been lightly wounded. The new prime minister presented himself as a man who does not compromise on matters relating to the law.

In February, one Israeli and twenty-nine Palestinians were killed during attacks and military operations conducted in the West Bank and Gaza.

On March 8, Kadima presented the main points of its platform. The party founded by Sharon did not relinquish the Quartet's road map. But if the diplomatic impasse were to continue, Israel would proceed unilaterally to effect withdrawals from the West Bank. Ehud Olmert's communications specialists devised a new term to signify "disengagement." He called it "realignment." It consisted of gathering the settlers evacuated from some settlements into "settlement blocs" that Israel would maintain in the West Bank. On the morning of March 14, two weeks before the Israeli elections, agents from British and American prison monitors who were helping guard the prison in Jericho took their arms and luggage and left.[14] The IDF immediately intervened. After a siege of several hours, all of the occupants left the prison. Ahmed Saadat, the secretary general of the PFLP and the assassin of the minister Rehavam Zeevi, two of his accomplices, and Fuad Shobaki, who was responsible for chartering the *Karine A*, were captured.

Negotiations between Hamas and Fatah to form a national unity government failed. The neo-Marxist organizations PFLP and DFLP chose not to form an alliance with the Islamists, and Ismail Haniyeh formed a new government for the Autonomous Authority, composed uniquely of members of Hamas. The international community suspended all transfers of funds to the Palestinian administration.

On March 28, legislative elections took place in Israel: Kadima gained twenty-nine parliamentary seats, and the Labor Party under Amir Peretz gained nineteen. Likud, under Benjamin Netanyahu, collapsed, winning only twelve, just one more than Avigdor Lieberman's party representing Russian-speaking immigrants, which also integrated members of Shin Bet and the police.

In March 2006, five Israelis and fifteen Palestinians were killed.

The new Israeli cabinet was formed on April 17. Ehud Olmert and Amir Peretz reached an agreement for a coalition according to which the Labor Party would obtain seven ministries, including Education, which would go to Yuli Tamir, a former leader of the Peace Now movement. Peretz granted himself the position of defense minister. The next day, the al-Aqsa Martyrs Brigades and Islamic Jihad committed a suicide attack in the neighborhood of the former Tel Aviv bus station, killing eleven and wounding sixty-two. Speaking on behalf of the Autonomous Authority, Hamas claimed that the attack was legitimate, while Chairman Abbas, for his part, condemned it.

In April 2006, eleven Israelis and thirty-one Palestinians were killed. The following month, the IDF response to rockets launched toward Israeli territory and operations conducted in the West Bank resulted in thirty-six Palestinian deaths.

OLMERT IN WASHINGTON

On May 23, Ehud Olmert presented his "realignment" plan to the American administration. After six hours of discussion with the Israeli prime minister, George Bush revealed during the customary press conference that it was a question of evacuating most West Bank settlements. He also added the following:

> I would call them bold ideas. These ideas could lead to a two-state solution if a pathway to progress on the road map is not open in the period ahead. His ideas include the removal of most Israeli settlements, except for the major Israeli population centers in the West Bank. I look forward to learning more about the prime minister's ideas. While any final status agreement will be only achieved on the basis of mutually agreed changes [accepted by both parties], and no party should prejudice the outcome of negotiations on a final status agreement, the prime minister's ideas could be an important step toward the peace we both support.

Ehud Olmert:

> I intend to exhaust every possibility to promote peace with the Palestinians, according to the road map, and I extend my hand in peace to Mahmoud Abbas, the elected president of the Palestinian Authority. . . . Unfortunately, the rise of Hamas, a terrorist organization which refuses to recognize Israel's right to exist, and regards terrorism as a legitimate tool, severely undermines the possibility of promoting a genuine peace process. . . . Despite our sincere desire for negotiations, we cannot wait indefinitely for the Palestinians to change. We cannot be held hostage by a terrorist entity which refuses to change or promote dialogue. If we come to the conclusion that no progress is possible, we will be compelled to try a different route. . . .

At this time in Israel, Dan Halutz, the chief of staff, rid himself of the final vestiges of the epoch of his predecessor, Moshe Yaalon. Following an unfavorable report from the state controller, on May 30 the officials of the IDF's Operational Theory Research Institute (OTRI), Brigadier General (res.) Dov Tamari and Brigadier General (res.) Shimon Naveh, were suspended from their duties due to irregularities in the financial management of their think tank. Exit the authors of the new doctrine of low-intensity warfare. Their theories would be completely undermined two months later when the IDF confronted Hezbollah in Lebanon. Caroline Glick of the *Jerusalem Post*, herself a member of the OTRI for two years, published Yaalon's reaction in her newspaper:

> The method of operational assessment that is used today in the regional commands and in the General Staff was developed through the joint work of the OTRI with field commanders. Over the past few years, foreign militaries began noticing that something new was happening in the IDF. As Yaalon explains: 'The Americans saw there were a lot of changes in our assessment methods, and they asked us to transfer our new knowledge to them. OTRI worked with the Americans to teach them the methods we had developed.' Lieutenant Colonel David Pere, from the US Marine Corps, is now involved in authoring the Marine Corps' operational doctrine. He characterizes OTRI's contribution to the US Armed Forces thus: 'Naveh and OTRI's influence on the intellectual discourse and understanding of the operational level of war in the US has been immense. The US Marine Corps has commissioned a study of design that will result in a Marine Corps Concept of Design that is based heavily on Shimon [Naveh]'s work.'[15]

In May 2006, thirty-six Palestinians were killed.

GAZA

On June 25, eight men belonging to the Ezzedin al-Qassam commando unit and to the Popular Resistance Committees attacked an Israeli position a few dozen meters from the barrier that surrounds the Gaza Strip. They killed two soldiers and captured a third, Corporal Gilad Shalit, who was brought to Palestinian territory. The IDF responded in under twenty-four hours with a massive bombing campaign targeting strategic objectives in Gaza, including a power station and transformers providing half of the electricity. This imposed even more hardship on the Gazans, who in the heat of summer had to make do with only eight hours of electricity per day.

In the West Bank, eight ministers and thirty members of parliament from Hamas were apprehended by the army and the Israeli police. Hamas announced that it would only free its prisoner in exchange for a thousand Palestinians being held in Israeli prisons. Ehud Olmert responded immediately, saying that he refused to negotiate. Gaza was hermetically sealed, and the border post in Rafah was closed.

In June 2006, four Israelis and forty-one Palestinians were killed.

The army pursued its offensive in Gaza during the entire month of July. The offices of Prime Minister Ismail Haniyeh and of the ministers of the interior and foreign affairs were bombed, while forces on the ground effected incursions into Palestinian territory. The death rate was high: two Israelis and 177 Palestinians.

LEBANON

The region toppled on July 12. At 9 o'clock in the morning, Hezbollah fired mortars on several Israeli locations close to the Lebanese border. Several dozen meters from the town of Zarit, militants attacked two jeeps, killed three soldiers, wounded two, and captured two others, who were brought to Lebanon. The IDF sent a tank on the trail of the kidnappers, but it was destroyed by a powerful mine, killing the four members of the crew. A sniper lying in ambush opened fire on the rescuers, killing a paramedic. Sheik Hassan Nasrallah let it be known that he would demand hundreds of Palestinian prisoners in exchange for his two prisoners. Ehud Olmert and Amir Peretz, the defense minister, decided to launch a massive response to the Hezbollah attack. The security cabinet approved the proposals of General Dan Halutz, the chief of staff.

This marked the beginning of Israel's second war with Lebanon. It would end thirty-four days later. More than 1,000 Lebanese and 156 Israelis, including 117 soldiers, were killed. The Shiite neighborhoods south of Beirut and numerous Lebanese villages were almost entirely destroyed. For the first time since 1948, nearly 500,000 Israelis had to leave their homes to seek refuge in the central part of the country. For more than a month, the IDF would not succeed in preventing the bombing of northern Israel, and, in the eyes of Arab public opinion, radical Islam would leave this conflict the victor.

EPILOGUE

The war in south Lebanon marked Israel's second strategic surprise since its creation. The first occurred during the Yom Kippur War in October 1973. The second, in July 2006, primarily revealed the blindness of Israeli intelligence services obsessed with the Palestinian conflict. Not a single expert predicted that Hezbollah would have the capacity to respond to IDF bombardments for more than a month by launching barrages of hundreds of rockets. In Lebanon, paratroopers discovered, just a few hundred meters inside the border, a veritable network of fortifications. Some bunkers were found 30 meters underground, equipped with computers and video systems intended for surveillance of the area. The air force did not succeed in destroying them.

The ultramodern weaponry in the Shiite militia's possession fell as yet another surprise. They owned antitank missiles—the Sagger, of Iranian manufacture; Russian Metis and Kornets; and American Tows—capable of penetrating the armor plating of the Israeli Merkava tank, despite the fact that this model was considered to be the most modern in existence. The majority of Israeli deaths were due to these missiles.

For six years, Hezbollah had stocked armaments. They were preparing for war, unbeknownst to the ministry of defense in Tel Aviv.

How can this lack of preparation at all levels, in the army, in the government, and in the ministries, possibly be explained? Military and political leaders had systematically minimized the threats and violent anti-Jewish diatribes regularly launched by Sheik Hassan Nasrallah, the Hezbollah leader, and by his main sponsor, the Iranian regime. This miscalculation was the result of the vision Israel had forged of its neighbors. Since early 2000, Israeli governments espoused a unilateral policy based on the principle that they had no partner in the peace process, as well as on the notion that Israel's military power would allow it to impose its decisions on its weak neighbors. As the Israeli inquiry commission into the second war in Lebanon in the summer of 2006, headed by judge Eliahu Winograd, concluded:

> Some of the political and military elites in Israel have reached the conclusion that Israel is beyond the era of wars. It had enough military might and superiority to deter others from declaring war against her; these would also be sufficient to send a painful reminder to anyone who seemed to be undeterred; since Israel did not intend to initiate a war, the conclusion was that the main challenge facing the land forces would be low-intensity asymmetrical conflicts. . . . Given this analysis, there was no need to prepare for war, nor was there a need to energetically seek paths to stable and long-term agreements with our neighbors.[1]

The withdrawal from Lebanon on May 25, 2000 was the first manifestation of this Israeli policy of unilateralism. After the failure of negotiations with Hafez el-Assad two months prior, Prime Minister Ehud Barak decided to keep his campaign promise: to evacuate the security zone that Israel had maintained for eighteen years in south Lebanon. And he did this without concluding an agreement either with the government in Beirut or with its protector, Syria—the other sponsor of Hezbollah. According to General Uri Saguy, who led secret negotiations with the Syrians, it would have been possible to sign a peace treaty with the Syrians, and the withdrawal from Lebanon was a mistake.[2]

Several months after the withdrawal, following the failure of the Oslo process and the beginning of the intifada, Ehud Barak proclaimed that Arafat was no longer a viable partner with whom to negotiate peace. His successor to the seat of prime minister, Ariel Sharon, pursued this strategy by shifting all responsibility for Palestinian violence onto the shoulders of Chairman Arafat, and by confining him to his headquarters in Ramallah, effectively cutting him off from the world. This policy opened the way to the unilateral withdrawal from Gaza in 2005 and to the construction of the separation barrier in the West Bank, viewed by Palestine and the Arab world as the plan for a future border. Israel never reached out to the very moderate Mahmoud Abbas, who was calling for a resumption of negotiations on the final status of the Palestinian territories. Military officials and intelligence analysts belatedly reached the conclusion that this strategy did not produce the results they had expected.

Around 70 percent of Palestinians live below the poverty line, which is set at $2 per day. Most families survive thanks to food aid distributed by international organizations. The WFP/FAO Emergency Food Needs Assessment in May 2006 showed that 51 percent of Palestinians are food insecure in the Occupied Palestinian Territory as a whole, with 70 percent food insecurity in Gaza. Unemployment levels have increased from an average of 12 percent to 19 percent in the West Bank, and 36 percent in the Gaza Strip, compared to 30 percent in 2005. Poverty affects 46 percent of the population in the West Bank, and a "shocking 80 percent of Gazans."[3] Even worse, 22 percent of children under the age of five suffer from severe malnutrition, and 15 percent from severe anemia. These statistics appear all the more disturbing when it is taken into account that half of the Palestinian population is under the age of fifteen. This generation will no doubt be orientated toward vengeance, and its heroes will bear the names Ahmed Yassin and Abdel Aziz Rantisi, the two Hamas leaders "liquidated" by the Israeli army. After more than five years of repression during the intifada, the Palestinian nationalist movement had suffered its most devastating defeat since 1948. Today, Palestinian moderates are marginalized, and Hamas has assumed control of the Palestinian Authority.

Through and through, this policy was based upon the IDF's doctrine of low-intensity warfare developed to confront the Palestinians. The Winograd commission considers that "this new conception created problems within the army during the period preceding the conflict in Lebanon [in July-August 2006]. The idea that it is possible to win a victory by using 'indirect leverage' or '[special] effects' without launching classical operations of conquest, occupation of territory, and destroying enemy forces, arouses difficult questions when confronting a militia like Hezbollah."[4] Israel attempted to implement those same principles in Lebanon, most notably its primary principle of "burning the conscience of the population with the idea that anti-Israeli attacks do not pay," and in order to achieve that, targeting major highways, necessitating the evacuation of Shiite neighborhoods. The bombing of key infrastructures was also intended to serve as leverage against the Lebanese government. Ground operations failed because they were conducted by an army that had not trained in classical warfare for years and, too often, followed the model of military incursions into Gaza and the West Bank.

The overall result was negative. Israel was forced to accept an agreement for the cessation of hostilities that was far from the objectives it had set at the time it launched its operations. There was no immediate release of captured soldiers by Hezbollah. Despite the presence of an intensified United Nations force, the Shiite militia maintained its offensive capacity. Rocket launchers and other devices for launching missiles were left intact for the most part, and remain a threat to Israel.

The July 2006 war thus marked a failure of a doctrine, a policy, and a strategy. The only remaining possibility is to follow the proposals put forth by men like General Uri Saguy, or by the supporters of the Geneva Initiative developed with the Palestinians. First, it is important to conduct direct negotiations with the Syrian and Lebanese governments to achieve peace in due form, even at the price of a withdrawal from the Golan Heights. Second, it is necessary to conclude an agreement with Chairman Mahmoud Abbas based on the principle of "territory for peace." Unless these two objectives are achieved, radical Islam will only gain power in the region.

Charles Enderlin
Jerusalem
May 2007

POSTSCRIPT

The last nail on the coffin of the Oslo peace process was hammered in on June 15, 2007 in Gaza when Hamas defeated the underequipped, unpaid, and untrained pro-Fatah police and "preventive security." For the first time since the beginning of the Oslo peace process, Fatah and the Autonomous Authority lost control over Gaza, where one million four hundred thousand Palestinians live. Hamas—an offshoot of the Muslim Brotherhood and partly financed by Iran—now rules over part of the Palestinian territory. Radical Islam, the predominant enemy to a two-state solution of the Israeli-Palestinian conflict, has scored a major victory, whose consequences will reverberate over the entire Middle East. Could this have been possible to prevent? Certainly! If there had been a serious peace process. If there had been a halt in Israel's settlement policy. If there had been an effort by Israel and the international community to confront the problem of poverty in Gaza. If. . .

July 2007

CHRONOLOGY OF MAJOR EVENTS

2001

February 6: Ariel Sharon is elected prime minister.

May 21: Publication of the report on the Palestinian-Israeli conflict by Senator Mitchell's commission.

June 1: Hamas suicide attack at the entrance to the Dolphinarium discotheque in Tel Aviv. Casualty count: twenty-one dead, eighty-three wounded.

June 13: Cease-fire plan proposed by George Tenet, director of the CIA.

July 31: Targeted killings of Jamal Mansur and Jamal Salim, two Hamas sheiks, in Nablus.

August 9: Hamas suicide attack in a Sbarro pizzeria in Jerusalem: fifteen dead, 110 wounded.

August 27: Assassination by Israel of Abu Ali Mustafa, head of the Popular Front for the Liberation of Palestine, in Ramallah.

October 17: Assassination of Israeli minister Rehavam Zeevi by the PFLP in Jerusalem.

December 1-2: During General Anthony Zinni's arbitration mission, a series of Hamas suicide attacks causes twenty-six Israeli deaths in twenty-four hours.

December 12: The Sharon government declares Yasser Arafat "out of play."

2002

January 5: The Israeli navy captures the *Karine A,* a freighter loaded with arms and munitions, in the Red Sea.

January 14: Targeted killing of Raed Karmi, of Fatah, in Tulkarm.

January 27: First suicide attack perpetrated by a female Fatah militant. Wafa Idris detonates her explosive belt in a Jerusalem street. Casualty count: one dead, 150 wounded.

March 27: Hamas suicide attack on the evening of Passover at the Park Hotel in Netanya, killing thirty and wounding 114. Failure of the Zinni mission.

March 28: In Beirut, the Arab League approves the Saudi peace plan offering Israel complete normalization in exchange for withdrawal from all occupied territories.

March 29: Israel launches operation "Shield" and reoccupies all of the cities in the West Bank.

June 24: George W. Bush officially declares his support for the formation of an independent Palestinian state, without Arafat.

2003

January 28: Elections in Israel. Likud and the extreme right win an absolute majority.

March 19: Yasser Arafat names Mahmoud Abbas to the position of prime minister.

April 30: The road map proposed by the Quartet is delivered to Ariel Sharon and Yasser Arafat.

June 4: Bush-Sharon-Abbas summit in Aqaba.

September 6: Mahmoud Abbas resigns.

December 1: Presentation and signing of the Geneva Initiative by Yossi Beilin and Yasser Abed Rabbo.

2004

February 2: Ariel Sharon tells *Haaretz* of his intention to withdraw from settlements in Gaza and the northern West Bank.

March 22: Targeted killing of Sheik Ahmed Yassin, the founder of Hamas, in Gaza.

November 11: Death of Arafat in Paris.

2005

January 9: Mahmoud Abbas is elected chairman of the Palestinian Authority.

February 8: Bush-Sharon-Abbas summit at Sharm el-Sheik.

August 15: Beginning of the evacuation of Gaza settlements.

September 12: End of the settlement evacuation in Gaza.

November 20: Ariel Sharon leaves Likud and founds a new party, Kadima.

2006

January 4: Ariel Sharon suffers from a massive cerebral hemorrhage and falls into a deep coma.

January 25: Hamas is victorious in Palestinian legislative elections, winning seventy-six seats out of 132.

March 28: Legislative elections in Israel. Kadima wins twenty-eight seats. Ehud Olmert succeeds Ariel Sharon.

June 25: Hamas abducts an Israeli soldier, followed by a series of Israeli raids in Gaza, destroying the main power transformer.

July 12: Hezbollah abducts two Israeli soldiers. Beginning of the war in Lebanon.

August 14: Cease-fire in Lebanon. 1,300 Lebanese and 156 Israelis were killed during the war.

Between September 29, 2000 and October 1, 2006, 3,839 Palestinians and 1,070 Israelis were killed. Among those killed, B'Tselem counted 1,812 Palestinians who did not participate in combat, 767 Palestinian minors, 697 Israeli civilians, and 119 Israeli minors. Forty-eight foreign civilians were killed by Palestinians, and ten by Israelis.

APPENDIX

ROAD MAP PRESENTED TO THE ISRAELI GOVERNMENT AND TO THE PALESTINIAN AUTHORITIES BY THE QUARTET, APRIL 30, 2003[1]

A performance-based roadmap to a permanent two-state solution to the Israeli-Palestinian conflict.

The following is a performance-based and goal-driven roadmap, with clear phases, timelines, target dates, and benchmarks aiming at progress through reciprocal steps by the two parties in the political, security, economic, humanitarian, and institution-building fields, under the auspices of the Quartet (the United States, European Union, United Nations, and Russia). The destination is a final and comprehensive settlement of the Israel-Palestinian conflict by 2005, as presented in President Bush's speech of 24 June, and welcomed by the EU, Russia and the UN in the 16 July and 17 September Quartet Ministerial statements.

A two-state solution to the Israeli-Palestinian conflict will only be achieved through an end to violence and terrorism, when the Palestinian people have a leadership acting decisively against terror and willing and able to build a practicing democracy based on tolerance and liberty, and through Israel's readiness to do what is necessary for a democratic Palestinian state to be established, and a clear, unambiguous acceptance by both parties of the goal of a negotiated settlement as described below. The Quartet will assist and facilitate implementation of the plan, starting in Phase I, including direct discussions between the parties as required. The plan establishes a realistic timeline for implementation. However, as a performance-based plan, progress will require and depend upon the good faith efforts of the parties, and their compliance with each of the obligations outlined below. Should the parties perform their obligations rapidly, progress within and through the phases may come sooner than indicated in the plan. Noncompliance with obligations will impede progress.

A settlement, negotiated between the parties, will result in the emergence of an independent, democratic, and viable Palestinian state living side by side in peace and security with Israel and its other neighbors. The settlement will resolve the Israel-Palestinian conflict, and end the occupation that began in 1967, based on the foundations of the Madrid Conference, the principle of land for peace, UNSCRs 242, 338 and 1397, agreements previously reached by the parties, and the initiative of Saudi Crown Prince Abdullah—endorsed by the Beirut Arab League Summit—calling for acceptance of Israel as a neighbor living in peace and security, in the context of a comprehensive settlement. This initiative is a vital element of international efforts to promote a comprehensive peace on all tracks, including the Syrian-Israeli and Lebanese-Israeli tracks.

The Quartet will meet regularly at senior levels to evaluate the parties' performance on implementation of the plan. In each phase, the parties are expected to perform their obligations in parallel, unless otherwise indicated.

PHASE I: ENDING TERROR AND VIOLENCE, NORMALIZING PALESTINIAN LIFE, AND BUILDING PALESTINIAN INSTITUTIONS—PRESENT TO MAY 2003

In Phase I, the Palestinians immediately undertake an unconditional cessation of violence according to the steps outlined below; such action should be accompanied by supportive measures undertaken by Israel. Palestinians and Israelis resume security cooperation based on the Tenet work plan to end violence, terrorism, and incitement through restructured and effective Palestinian security services. Palestinians undertake comprehensive political reform in preparation for statehood, including drafting a Palestinian constitution, and free, fair and open elections upon the basis of those measures. Israel takes all necessary steps to help normalize Palestinian life. Israel withdraws from Palestinian areas occupied from September 28, 2000 and the two sides restore the status quo that existed at that time, as security performance and cooperation progress. Israel also freezes all settlement activity, consistent with the Mitchell report.

At the outset of Phase I:

- Palestinian leadership issues unequivocal statement reiterating Israel's right to exist in peace and security and calling for an immediate and unconditional ceasefire to end armed activity and all acts of violence against Israelis anywhere. All official Palestinian institutions end incitement against Israel.
- Israeli leadership issues unequivocal statement affirming its commitment to the two-state vision of an independent, viable, sovereign Palestinian state living in peace and security alongside Israel, as expressed by President Bush, and calling for an immediate end to violence against Palestinians everywhere. All official Israeli institutions end incitement against Palestinians.

Security

- Palestinians declare an unequivocal end to violence and terrorism and undertake visible efforts on the ground to arrest, disrupt, and restrain individuals and groups conducting and planning violent attacks on Israelis anywhere.
- Rebuilt and refocused Palestinian Authority security apparatus begins sustained, targeted, and effective operations aimed at confronting all those engaged in terror and

dismantlement of terrorist capabilities and infrastructure. This includes commencing confiscation of illegal weapons and consolidation of security authority, free of association with terror and corruption.

• GOI [Government of Israel] takes no actions undermining trust, including deportations, attacks on civilians; confiscation and/or demolition of Palestinian homes and property, as a punitive measure or to facilitate Israeli construction; destruction of Palestinian institutions and infrastructure; and other measures specified in the Tenet work plan.

• Relying on existing mechanisms and on-the-ground resources, Quartet representatives begin informal monitoring and consult with the parties on establishment of a formal monitoring mechanism and its implementation.

• Implementation, as previously agreed, of U.S. rebuilding, training and resumed security cooperation plan in collaboration with outside oversight board (U.S.–Egypt–Jordan). Quartet support for efforts to achieve a lasting, comprehensive cease-fire.

• All Palestinian security organizations are consolidated into three services reporting to an empowered Interior Minister.

• Restructured/retrained Palestinian security forces and IDF counterparts progressively resume security cooperation and other undertakings in implementation of the Tenet work plan, including regular senior-level meetings, with the participation of U.S. security officials.

• Arab states cut off public and private funding and all other forms of support for groups supporting and engaging in violence and terror.

• All donors providing budgetary support for the Palestinians channel these funds through the Palestinian Ministry of Finance's Single Treasury Account.

• As comprehensive security performance moves forward, IDF withdraws progressively from areas occupied since September 28, 2000 and the two sides restore the status quo that existed prior to September 28, 2000. Palestinian security forces redeploy to areas vacated by IDF.

Palestinian Institution-Building

• Immediate action on credible process to produce draft constitution for Palestinian statehood. As rapidly as possible, constitutional committee circulates draft Palestinian constitution, based on strong parliamentary democracy and cabinet with empowered prime minister, for public comment/debate. Constitutional committee proposes draft document for submission after elections for approval by appropriate Palestinian institutions.

• Appointment of interim prime minister or cabinet with empowered executive authority/decision-making body.

• GOI fully facilitates travel of Palestinian officials for PLC and Cabinet sessions, internationally supervised security retraining, electoral and other reform activity, and other supportive measures related to the reform efforts.

• Continued appointment of Palestinian ministers empowered to undertake fundamental reform. Completion of further steps to achieve genuine separation of powers, including any necessary Palestinian legal reforms for this purpose.

• Establishment of independent Palestinian election commission. PLC reviews and revises election law.

• Palestinian performance on judicial, administrative, and economic benchmarks, as established by the International Task Force on Palestinian Reform.

• As early as possible, and based upon the above measures and in the context of open debate and transparent candidate selection/electoral campaign based on a free, multi-party process, Palestinians hold free, open, and fair elections.

• GOI facilitates Task Force election assistance, registration of voters, movement of candidates and voting officials. Support for NGOs involved in the election process.

• GOI reopens Palestinian Chamber of Commerce and other closed Palestinian institutions in East Jerusalem based on a commitment that these institutions operate strictly in accordance with prior agreements between the parties.

Humanitarian Response

• Israel takes measures to improve the humanitarian situation. Israel and Palestinians implement in full all recommendations of the Bertini report to improve humanitarian conditions, lifting curfews and easing restrictions on movement of persons and goods, and allowing full, safe, and unfettered access of international and humanitarian personnel.

• AHLC reviews the humanitarian situation and prospects for economic development in the West Bank and Gaza and launches a major donor assistance effort, including to the reform effort.

• GOI and PA continue revenue clearance process and transfer of funds, including arrears, in accordance with agreed, transparent monitoring mechanism.

Civil Society

• Continued donor support, including increased funding through PVOs/NGOs, for people to people programs, private sector development and civil society initiatives.

Settlements

• GOI immediately dismantles settlement outposts erected since March 2001.

- Consistent with the Mitchell Report, GOI freezes all settlement activity (including natural growth of settlements).

PHASE II: TRANSITION—JUNE 2003-DECEMBER 2003

In the second phase, efforts are focused on the option of creating an independent Palestinian state with provisional borders and attributes of sovereignty, based on the new constitution, as a way station to a permanent status settlement. As has been noted, this goal can be achieved when the Palestinian people have a leadership acting decisively against terror, willing and able to build a practicing democracy based on tolerance and liberty. With such a leadership, reformed civil institutions and security structures, the Palestinians will have the active support of the Quartet and the broader international community in establishing an independent, viable, state.

Progress into Phase II will be based upon the consensus judgment of the Quartet of whether conditions are appropriate to proceed, taking into account performance of both parties. Furthering and sustaining efforts to normalize Palestinian lives and build Palestinian institutions, Phase II starts after Palestinian elections and ends with possible creation of an independent Palestinian state with provisional borders in 2003. Its primary goals are continued comprehensive security performance and effective security cooperation, continued normalization of Palestinian life and institution-building, further building on and sustaining of the goals outlined in Phase I, ratification of a democratic Palestinian constitution, formal establishment of office of prime minister, consolidation of political reform, and the creation of a Palestinian state with provisional borders.

- International Conference: Convened by the Quartet, in consultation with the parties, immediately after the successful conclusion of Palestinian elections, to support Palestinian economic recovery and launch a process, leading to establishment of an independent Palestinian state with provisional borders.

• Such a meeting would be inclusive, based on the goal of a comprehensive Middle East peace (including between Israel and Syria, and Israel and Lebanon), and based on the principles described in the preamble to this document.

• Arab states restore pre-intifada links to Israel (trade offices, etc.).

• Revival of multilateral engagement on issues including regional water resources, environment, economic development, refugees, and arms control issues.

• New constitution for democratic, independent Palestinian state is finalized and approved by appropriate Palestinian institutions. Further elections, if required, should follow approval of the new constitution.

• Empowered reform cabinet with office of prime minister formally established, consistent with draft constitution.

• Continued comprehensive security performance, including effective security cooperation on the bases laid out in Phase I.

• Creation of an independent Palestinian state with provisional borders through a process of Israeli-Palestinian engagement, launched by the international conference. As part of this process, implementation of prior agreements, to enhance maximum territorial contiguity, including further action on settlements in conjunction with establishment of a Palestinian state with provisional borders.

• Enhanced international role in monitoring transition, with the active, sustained, and operational support of the Quartet.

• Quartet members promote international recognition of Palestinian state, including possible UN membership.

PHASE III: PERMANENT STATUS AGREEMENT AND END OF THE ISRAELI-PALESTINIAN CONFLICT—2004-2005

Progress into Phase III, based on consensus judgment of Quartet, and taking into account actions of both parties and Quartet monitoring. Phase

III objectives are consolidation of reform and stabilization of Palestinian institutions, sustained, effective Palestinian security performance, and Israeli-Palestinian negotiations aimed at a permanent status agreement in 2005.

- Second International Conference: Convened by Quartet, in consultation with the parties, at beginning of 2004 to endorse agreement reached on an independent Palestinian state with provisional borders and formally to launch a process with the active, sustained, and operational support of the Quartet, leading to a final, permanent status resolution in 2005, including on borders, Jerusalem, refugees, settlements; and, to support progress toward a comprehensive Middle East settlement between Israel and Lebanon and Israel and Syria, to be achieved as soon as possible.
- Continued comprehensive, effective progress on the reform agenda laid out by the Task Force in preparation for final status agreement.
- Continued sustained and effective security performance, and sustained, effective security cooperation on the bases laid out in Phase I.
- International efforts to facilitate reform and stabilize Palestinian institutions and the Palestinian economy, in preparation for final status agreement.
- Parties reach final and comprehensive permanent status agreement that ends the Israel-Palestinian conflict in 2005, through a settlement negotiated between the parties based on UNSCR 242, 338, and 1397, that ends the occupation that began in 1967, and includes an agreed, just, fair, and realistic solution to the refugee issue, and a negotiated resolution on the status of Jerusalem that takes into account the political and religious concerns of both sides, and protects the religious interests of Jews, Christians, and Muslims worldwide, and fulfills the vision of two states, Israel and sovereign,

independent, democratic and viable Palestine, living side-by-side in peace and security.

• Arab state acceptance of full normal relations with Israel and security for all the states of the region in the context of a comprehensive Arab-Israeli peace.

THE GENEVA ACCORD:
A MODEL ISRAELI-PALESTINIAN PEACE AGREEMENT[2]

The State of Israel (hereinafter "Israel") and the Palestine Liberation Organization (hereinafter "PLO"), the representative of the Palestinian people (hereinafter the "Parties"):

Reaffirming their determination to put an end to decades of confrontation and conflict, and to live in peaceful coexistence, mutual dignity and security based on a just, lasting, and comprehensive peace and achieving historic reconciliation;

Recognizing that peace requires the transition from the logic of war and confrontation to the logic of peace and cooperation, and that acts and words characteristic of the state of war are neither appropriate nor acceptable in the era of peace;

Affirming their deep belief that the logic of peace requires compromise, and that the only viable solution is a two-state solution based on UNSC Resolution 242 and 338;

Affirming that this agreement marks the recognition of the right of the Jewish people to statehood and the recognition of the right of the Palestinian people to statehood, without prejudice to the equal rights of the Parties' respective citizens;

Recognizing that after years of living in mutual fear and insecurity, both peoples need to enter an era of peace, security and stability, entailing all necessary actions by the parties to guarantee the realization of this era;

Recognizing each other's right to peaceful and secure existence within secure and recognized boundaries free from threats or acts of force;

Determined to establish relations based on cooperation and the commitment to live side by side as good neighbors aiming both separately and jointly to contribute to the well-being of their peoples;

Reaffirming their obligation to conduct themselves in conformity with the norms of international law and the Charter of the United Nations;

Confirming that this Agreement is concluded within the framework of the Middle East peace process initiated in Madrid in October 1991, the Declaration of Principles of September 13, 1993, the subsequent agreements including the Interim Agreement of September 1995, the Wye River Memorandum of October 1998 and the Sharm El-Sheikh Memorandum of September 4, 1999, and the permanent status negotiations including the Camp David Summit of July 2000, the Clinton Ideas of December 2000, and the Taba Negotiations of January 2001;

Reiterating their commitment to United Nations Security Council Resolutions 242, 338 and 1397 and confirming their understanding that this Agreement is based on, will lead to, and—by its fulfillment—will constitute the full implementation of these resolutions and to the settlement of the Israeli-Palestinian conflict in all its aspects;

Declaring that this Agreement constitutes the realization of the permanent status peace component envisaged in President Bush's speech of June 24, 2002 and in the Quartet Roadmap process.

Declaring that this Agreement marks the historic reconciliation between the Palestinians and Israelis, and paves the way to reconciliation between the Arab World and Israel and the establishment of normal, peaceful relations between the Arab states and Israel in accordance with the relevant clauses of the Beirut Arab League Resolution of March 28, 2002; and

Resolved to pursue the goal of attaining a comprehensive regional peace, thus contributing to stability, security, development and prosperity throughout the region;

Have agreed on the following:

ARTICLE 1
PURPOSE OF THE PERMANENT STATUS AGREEMENT

1. The Permanent Status Agreement (hereinafter "this Agreement") ends the era of conflict and ushers in a new era based on peace, cooperation, and good neighborly relations between the Parties.

2. The implementation of this Agreement will settle all the claims of the Parties arising from events occurring prior to its signature. No further claims related to events prior to this Agreement may be raised by either Party.

ARTICLE 2
RELATIONS BETWEEN THE PARTIES

1. The state of Israel shall recognize the state of Palestine (hereinafter "Palestine") upon its establishment. The state of Palestine shall immediately recognize the state of Israel.

2. The state of Palestine shall be the successor to the PLO with all its rights and obligations.

3. Israel and Palestine shall immediately establish full diplomatic and consular relations with each other and will exchange resident Ambassadors, within one month of their mutual recognition.

4. The Parties recognize Palestine and Israel as the homelands of their respective peoples. The Parties are committed not to interfere in each other's internal affairs.

5. This Agreement supercedes all prior agreements between the Parties.

6. Without prejudice to the commitments undertaken by them in this Agreement, relations between Israel and Palestine shall be based upon the provisions of the Charter of the United Nations.

7. With a view to the advancement of the relations between the two States and peoples, Palestine and Israel shall cooperate in areas of common interest. These shall include, but are not limited to, dialogue between their legislatures and state institutions, cooperation between their appropriate local authorities, promotion of non-governmental civil society cooperation, and joint programs and exchange in the areas of culture, media, youth, science, education, environment, health, agriculture, tourism, and crime prevention. The Israeli-Palestinian Cooperation Committee will oversee this cooperation in accordance with Article 8.

8. The Parties shall cooperate in areas of joint economic interest, to best realize the human potential of their respective peoples. In this regard, they will work bilaterally, regionally, and with the international community to maximize the benefit of peace to the broadest cross-section of their respective populations. Relevant standing bodies shall be established by the Parties to this effect . . .

ARTICLE 3
IMPLEMENTATION AND VERIFICATION GROUP

1. Establishment and Composition
i. An Implementation and Verification Group (IVG) shall hereby be established to facilitate, assist in, guarantee, monitor, and resolve disputes relating to the implementation of this Agreement . . .

3. Coordination with the Parties
A Trilateral Committee composed of the Special Representative and the Palestinian-Israeli High Steering Committee shall be established and shall meet on at least a monthly basis to review the implementation of this Agreement. The Trilateral Committee will convene within 48 hours upon the request of any of the three parties represented . . .

ARTICLE 4
TERRITORY

1. The International Borders between the States of Palestine and Israel
i. In accordance with UNSC Resolution 242 and 338, the border between the states of Palestine and Israel shall be based on the June 4th 1967 lines with reciprocal modifications on a 1:1 basis as set forth in attached Map 1.

ii. The Parties recognize the border, as set out in attached Map 1, as the permanent, secure and recognized international boundary between them.

2. Sovereignty and Inviolability
i. The Parties recognize and respect each other's sovereignty, territorial integrity, and political independence, as well as the inviolability of each others territory, including territorial waters, and airspace. They shall respect this inviolability in accordance

with this Agreement, the UN Charter, and other rules of international law.

ii. The Parties recognize each other's rights in their exclusive economic zones in accordance with international law.

3. Israeli Withdrawal
i. Israel shall withdraw in accordance with Article 5.

ii. Palestine shall assume responsibility for the areas from which Israel withdraws.

iii. The transfer of authority from Israel to Palestine shall be in accordance with Annex X.

iv. The IVG shall monitor, verify, and facilitate the implementation of this Article.

4. Demarcation
i. A Joint Technical Border Commission (Commission) composed of the two Parties shall be established to conduct the technical demarcation of the border in accordance with this Article. The procedures governing the work of this Commission are set forth in Annex X.

ii. Any disagreement in the Commission shall be referred to the IVG in accordance with Annex X.

iii. The physical demarcation of the international borders shall be completed by the Commission not later than nine months from the date of the entry into force of this Agreement.

5. Settlements
i. The state of Israel shall be responsible for resettling the Israelis residing in Palestinian sovereign territory outside this territory.

ii. The resettlement shall be completed according to the schedule stipulated in Article 5.

iii. Existing arrangements in the West Bank and Gaza Strip regarding Israeli settlers and settlements, including security, shall remain in force in each of the settlements until the date prescribed in the timetable for the completion of the evacuation of the relevant settlement.

iv. Modalities for the assumption of authority over settlements by Palestine are set forth in Annex X. The IVG shall resolve any disputes that may arise during its implementation.

v. Israel shall keep intact the immovable property, infrastructure and facilities in Israeli settlements to be transferred to Palestinian sovereignty. An agreed inventory shall be drawn up by the Parties with the IVG in advance of the completion of the evacuation and in accordance with Annex X.

vi. The state of Palestine shall have exclusive title to all land and any buildings, facilities, infrastructure or other property remaining in any of the settlements on the date prescribed in the timetable for the completion of the evacuation of this settlement.

6. Corridor
i. The states of Palestine and Israel shall establish a corridor linking the West Bank and Gaza Strip. This corridor shall:
　　1. Be under Israeli sovereignty.
　　2. Be permanently open.
　　3. Be under Palestinian administration in accordance with Annex X of this Agreement. Palestinian law shall apply to persons using and procedures appertaining to the corridor.
　　4. Not disrupt Israeli transportation and other infrastructural networks, or endanger the environment, public safety

or public health. Where necessary, engineering solutions will be sought to avoid such disruptions.

5. Allow for the establishment of the necessary infrastructural facilities linking the West Bank and the Gaza Strip. Infrastructural facilities shall be understood to include, inter alia, pipelines, electrical and communications cables, and associated equipment as detailed in Annex X.

6. Not be used in contravention of this Agreement.

ii. Defensive barriers shall be established along the corridor and Palestinians shall not enter Israel from this corridor, nor shall Israelis enter Palestine from the corridor . . .

ARTICLE 5
SECURITY

1. General Security Provisions
i. The Parties acknowledge that mutual understanding and co-operation in security-related matters will form a significant part of their bilateral relations and will further enhance regional security. Palestine and Israel shall base their security relations on cooperation, mutual trust, good neighborly relations, and the protection of their joint interests.

ii. Palestine and Israel each shall:
1. Recognize and respect the other's right to live in peace within secure and recognized boundaries free from the threat or acts of war, terrorism and violence;
2. Refrain from the threat or use of force against the territorial integrity or political independence of the other and shall settle all disputes between them by peaceful means;
3. Refrain from joining, assisting, promoting or co-operating with any coalition, organization or alliance of a military or security character, the objectives or activities of which include launching aggression or other acts of hostility against the other;

4. Refrain from organizing, encouraging, or allowing the formation of irregular forces or armed bands, including mercenaries and militias within their respective territory and prevent their establishment. In this respect, any existing irregular forces or armed bands shall be disbanded and prevented from reforming at any future date;

5. Refrain from organizing, assisting, allowing, or participating in acts of violence in or against the other or acquiescing in activities directed toward the commission of such acts.

iii. To further security cooperation, the Parties shall establish a high level Joint Security Committee that shall meet on at least a monthly basis. The Joint Security Committee shall have a permanent joint office, and may establish such sub-committees as it deems necessary, including sub-committees to immediately resolve localized tensions.

2. Regional Security

i. Israel and Palestine shall work together with their neighbors and the international community to build a secure and stable Middle East, free from weapons of mass destruction, both conventional and non-conventional, in the context of a comprehensive, lasting, and stable peace, characterized by reconciliation, goodwill, and the renunciation of the use of force.

ii. To this end, the Parties shall work together to establish a regional security regime.

3. Defense Characteristics of the Palestinian State

i. No armed forces, other than as specified in this Agreement, will be deployed or stationed in Palestine.

ii. Palestine shall be a non-militarized state, with a strong security force. Accordingly, the limitations on the weapons that may be purchased, owned, or used by the Palestinian Security Force

(PSF) or manufactured in Palestine shall be specified in Annex X. Any proposed changes to Annex X shall be considered by a trilateral committee composed of the two Parties and the MF. If no agreement is reached in the trilateral committee, the IVG may make its own recommendations.

1. No individuals or organizations in Palestine other than the PSF and the organs of the IVG, including the MF, may purchase, possess, carry or use weapons except as provided by law.

iii. The PSF shall:
1. Maintain border control;
2. Maintain law-and-order and perform police functions;
3. Perform intelligence and security functions;
4. Prevent terrorism;
5. Conduct rescue and emergency missions; and
6. Supplement essential community services when necessary.

iv. The MF shall monitor and verify compliance with this clause.

4. Terrorism
i. The Parties reject and condemn terrorism and violence in all its forms and shall pursue public policies accordingly. In addition, the parties shall refrain from actions and policies that are liable to nurture extremism and create conditions conducive to terrorism on either side . . .

5. Incitement
i. Without prejudice to freedom of expression and other internationally recognized human rights, Israel and Palestine shall promulgate laws to prevent incitement to irredentism, racism, terrorism and violence and vigorously enforce them . . .

6. Multinational Force
i. A Multinational Force (MF) shall be established to provide security guarantees to the Parties, act as a deterrent, and oversee the implementation of the relevant provisions of this Agreement . . .

iv. The MF shall only be withdrawn or have its mandate changed by agreement of the Parties.

7. Evacuation

i. Israel shall withdraw all its military and security personnel and equipment, including landmines, and all persons employed to support them, and all military installations from the territory of the state of Palestine, except as otherwise agreed in Annex X, in stages . . .

v. Israel shall complete its withdrawal from the territory of the state of Palestine within 30 months of the entry into force of this Agreement, and in accordance with this Agreement.

vi. Israel will maintain a small military presence in the Jordan Valley under the authority of the MF and subject to the MF SOFA as detailed in Annex X for an additional 36 months. The stipulated period may be reviewed by the Parties in the event of relevant regional developments, and may be altered by the Parties' consent . . .

8. Early Warning Stations
Israel may maintain two EWS in the northern, and central West Bank at the locations set forth in Annex X . . .

ARTICLE 6
JERUSALEM

1. Religious and Cultural Significance
i. The Parties recognize the universal historic, religious, spiritual, and cultural significance of Jerusalem and its holiness enshrined in Judaism, Christianity, and Islam. In recognition of this status, the Parties reaffirm their commitment to safeguard the character, holiness, and freedom of worship in the city and to respect the existing division of administrative functions and traditional practices between different denominations.

ii. The Parties shall establish an inter-faith body consisting of representatives of the three monotheistic faiths, to act as a consultative body to the Parties on matters related to the city's religious significance and to promote inter-religious understanding and dialogue. The composition, procedures, and modalities for this body are set forth in Annex X.

2. Capital of Two States

The Parties shall have their mutually recognized capitals in the areas of Jerusalem under their respective sovereignty.

3. Sovereignty

Sovereignty in Jerusalem shall be in accordance with attached Map 2. This shall not prejudice nor be prejudiced by the arrangements set forth below.

4. Border Regime

The border regime shall be designed according to the provisions of Article 11, and taking into account the specific needs of Jerusalem (e.g., movement of tourists and intensity of border crossing use including provisions for Jerusalemites) and the provisions of this Article.

5. al-Haram al-Sharif/Temple Mount (Compound)

i. International Group

1. An International Group, composed of the IVG and other parties to be agreed upon by the Parties, including members of the Organization of the Islamic Conference (OIC), shall hereby be established to monitor, verify, and assist in the implementation of this clause.

2. For this purpose, the International Group shall establish a Multinational Presence on the Compound, the composition, structure, mandate and functions of which are set forth in Annex X . . .

ii. Regulations Regarding the Compound

1. In view of the sanctity of the Compound, and in light of the unique religious and cultural significance of the site to the Jewish people, there shall be no digging, excavation, or construction on the Compound, unless approved by the two Parties. Procedures for regular maintenance and emergency repairs on the Compound shall be established by the IG after consultation with the Parties.

2. The state of Palestine shall be responsible for maintaining the security of the Compound and for ensuring that it will not be used for any hostile acts against Israelis or Israeli areas. The only arms permitted on the Compound shall be those carried by the Palestinian security personnel and the security detachment of the Multinational Presence.

3. In light of the universal significance of the Compound, and subject to security considerations and to the need not to disrupt religious worship or decorum on the site as determined by the Waqf, visitors shall be allowed access to the site. This shall be without any discrimination and generally be in accordance with past practice.

iii. Transfer of Authority

1. At the end of the withdrawal period stipulated in Article 5/7, the state of Palestine shall assert sovereignty over the Compound.

2. The International Group and its subsidiary organs shall continue to exist and fulfill all the functions stipulated in this Article unless otherwise agreed by the two Parties.

6. The Wailing Wall

The Wailing Wall shall be under Israeli sovereignty.

7. The Old City

1. Significance of the Old City

i. The Parties view the Old City as one whole enjoying a unique character. The Parties agree that the preservation of this unique character together with safeguarding and promoting the welfare of the inhabitants should guide the administration of the Old City.

ii. The Parties shall act in accordance with the UNESCO World Cultural Heritage List regulations, in which the Old City is a registered site.

2. IVG Role in the Old City

i. Cultural Heritage

1. The IVG shall monitor and verify the preservation of cultural heritage in the Old City in accordance with the UNESCO World Cultural Heritage List rules. For this purpose, the IVG shall have free and unimpeded access to sites, documents, and information related to the performance of this function . . .

ii. Policing

The IVG shall establish an Old City Policing Unit (PU) to liaise with, coordinate between, and assist the Palestinian and Israeli police forces in the Old City, to defuse localized tensions and help resolve disputes, and to perform policing duties in locations specified in and according to operational procedures detailed in Annex X.
The PU shall periodically report to the IVG . . .

3. Free Movement within the Old City

Movement within the Old City shall be free and unimpeded subject to the provisions of this article and rules and regulations pertaining to the various holy sites.

4. Entry into and Exit from the Old City

i. Entry and exit points into and from the Old City will be staffed by the authorities of the state under whose sovereignty the point falls, with the presence of PU members, unless otherwise specified.

ii. With a view to facilitating movement into the Old City, each Party shall take such measures at the entry points in its territory as to ensure the preservation of security in the Old City. The PU shall monitor the operation of the entry points.

iii. Citizens of either Party may not exit the Old City into the territory of the other Party unless they are in possession of the relevant documentation that entitles them to. Tourists may only exit the Old City into the territory of the Party which they possess valid authorization to enter . . .

vii. Color-Coding of the Old City
A visible color-coding scheme shall be used in the Old City to denote the sovereign areas of the respective Parties.

8. Policing
i. An agreed number of Israeli police shall constitute the Israeli Old City police detachment and shall exercise responsibility for maintaining order and day-to-day policing functions in the area under Israeli sovereignty.

ii. An agreed number of Palestinian police shall constitute the Palestinian Old City police detachment and shall exercise responsibility for maintaining order and day-to-day policing functions in the area under Palestinian sovereignty . . .

9. Arms
No person shall be allowed to carry or possess arms in the Old City, with the exception of the Police Forces provided for

in this agreement. In addition, each Party may grant special written permission to carry or possess arms in areas under its sovereignty . . .

10. Mount of Olives Cemetery:
i. The area outlined in Map X (the Jewish Cemetery on the Mount of Olives) shall be under Israeli administration; Israeli law shall apply to persons using and procedures appertaining to this area in accordance with Annex X.

   1. There shall be a designated road to provide free, unlimited, and unimpeded access to the Cemetery . . .

11. Special Cemetery Arrangements
Arrangements shall be established in the two cemeteries designated in Map X (Mount Zion Cemetery and the German Colony Cemetery), to facilitate and ensure the continuation of the current burial and visitation practices, including the facilitation of access.

12. The Western Wall Tunnel
i. The Western Wall Tunnel designated in Map X shall be under Israeli administration, including:

   1. Unrestricted Israeli access and right to worship and conduct religious practices.
   2. Responsibility for the preservation and maintenance of the site in accordance with this Agreement and without damaging structures above, under IVG supervision.
   3. Israeli policing.
   4. IVG monitoring.
   5. The Northern Exit of the Tunnel shall only be used for exit and may only be closed in case of emergency as stipulated in Article 6/7.

ii. This arrangement may only be terminated by the agreement of both Parties.

13. Municipal Coordination

i. The two Jerusalem municipalities shall form a Jerusalem Co-ordination and Development Committee ("JCDC") to oversee the cooperation and coordination between the Palestinian Jerusalem municipality and the Israeli Jerusalem municipality. The JCDC and its sub-committees shall be composed of an equal number of representatives from Palestine and Israel. Each side will appoint members of the JCDC and its subcommittees in accordance with its own modalities.

ii. The JCDC shall ensure that the coordination of infrastructure and services best serves the residents of Jerusalem, and shall promote the economic development of the city to the benefit of all. The JCDC will act to encourage cross-community dialogue and reconciliation . . .

14. Israeli Residency of Palestinian Jerusalemites
Palestinian Jerusalemites who currently are permanent residents of Israel shall lose this status upon the transfer of authority to Palestine of those areas in which they reside . . .

ARTICLE 7
REFUGEES

1. Significance of the Refugee Problem
i. The Parties recognize that, in the context of two independent states, Palestine and Israel, living side by side in peace, an agreed resolution of the refugee problem is necessary for achieving a just, comprehensive and lasting peace between them.

ii. Such a resolution will also be central to stability building and development in the region.

2. UNGAR 194, UNSC Resolution 242, and the Arab Peace Initiative

i. The Parties recognize that UNGAR 194, UNSC Resolution 242, and the Arab Peace Initiative (Article 2.ii.) concerning the rights of the Palestinian refugees represent the basis for resolving the refugee issue, and agree that these rights are fulfilled according to Article 7 of this Agreement.

3. Compensation

i. Refugees shall be entitled to compensation for their refugee-hood and for loss of property. This shall not prejudice or be prejudiced by the refugee's permanent place of residence.

ii. The Parties recognize the right of states that have hosted Palestinian refugees to remuneration.

4. Choice of Permanent Place of Residence (PPR)

The solution to the PPR aspect of the refugee problem shall entail an act of informed choice on the part of the refugee to be exercised in accordance with the options and modalities set forth in this agreement. PPR options from which the refugees may choose shall be as follows:

i. The state of Palestine, in accordance with clause 1 below.

ii. Areas in Israel being transferred to Palestine in the land swap, following assumption of Palestinian sovereignty, in accordance with clause 1 below.

iii. Third Countries, in accordance with clause 2 below.

iv. The state of Israel, in accordance with clause 3 below.

v. Present Host countries, in accordance with clause 4 below.

1. PPR options i and ii shall be the right of all Palestinian refugees and shall be in accordance with the laws of the State of Palestine.

2. Option iii shall be at the sovereign discretion of third countries and shall be in accordance with numbers that each third country will submit to the International Commission. These numbers shall represent the total num-

ber of Palestinian refugees that each third country shall accept.

3. Option iv shall be at the sovereign discretion of Israel and will be in accordance with a number that Israel will submit to the International Commission. This number shall represent the total number of Palestinian refugees that Israel shall accept. As a basis, Israel will consider the average of the total numbers submitted by the different third countries to the International Commission.

4. Option v shall be in accordance with the sovereign discretion of present host countries. Where exercised this shall be in the context of prompt and extensive development and rehabilitation programs for the refugee communities.

Priority in all the above shall be accorded to the Palestinian refugee population in Lebanon.

5. Free and Informed Choice

The process by which Palestinian refugees shall express their PPR choice shall be on the basis of a free and informed decision. The Parties themselves are committed and will encourage third parties to facilitate the refugees' free choice in expressing their preferences, and to countering any attempts at interference or organized pressure on the process of choice. This will not prejudice the recognition of Palestine as the realization of Palestinian self-determination and statehood.

6. End of Refugee Status

Palestinian refugee status shall be terminated upon the realization of an individual refugee's permanent place of residence (PPR) as determined by the International Commission.

7. End of Claims

This agreement provides for the permanent and complete resolution of the Palestinian refugee problem. No claims may be raised except for those related to the implementation of this agreement.

8. International Role

The Parties call upon the international community to participate fully in the comprehensive resolution of the refugee problem in accordance with this Agreement, including, inter alia, the establishment of an International Commission and an International Fund.

9. Property Compensation

i. Refugees shall be compensated for the loss of property resulting from their displacement.

ii. The aggregate sum of property compensation shall be calculated as follows:

> 1. The Parties shall request the International Commission to appoint a Panel of Experts to estimate the value of Palestinians' property at the time of displacement.
> 2. The Panel of Experts shall base its assessment on the UNCCP records, the records of the Custodian for Absentee Property, and any other records it deems relevant. The Parties shall make these records available to the Panel.
> 3. The Parties shall appoint experts to advise and assist the Panel in its work.
> 4. Within 6 months, the Panel shall submit its estimates to the Parties.
> 5. The Parties shall agree on an economic multiplier, to be applied to the estimates, to reach a fair aggregate value of the property.

iii. The aggregate value agreed to by the Parties shall constitute the Israeli "lump sum" contribution to the International Fund. No other financial claims arising from the Palestinian refugee problem may be raised against Israel.

iv. Israel's contribution shall be made in installments in accordance with Schedule X.

v. The value of the Israeli fixed assets that shall remain intact in former settlements and transferred to the state of Palestine will be deducted from Israel's contribution to the International Fund. An estimation of this value shall be made by the International Fund, taking into account assessment of damage caused by the settlements.

10. Compensation for Refugeehood

i. A "Refugeehood Fund" shall be established in recognition of each individual's refugeehood. The Fund, to which Israel shall be a contributing party, shall be overseen by the International Commission. The structure and financing of the Fund is set forth in Annex X.

ii. Funds will be disbursed to refugee communities in the former areas of UNRWA operation, and will be at their disposal for communal development and commemoration of the refugee experience. Appropriate mechanisms will be devised by the International Commission whereby the beneficiary refugee communities are empowered to determine and administer the use of this Fund.

11. The International Commission (Commission)

i. Mandate and Composition

1. An International Commission shall be established and shall have full and exclusive responsibility for implementing all aspects of this Agreement pertaining to refugees.

2. In addition to themselves, the Parties call upon the United Nations, the United States, UNRWA, the Arab host countries, the EU, Switzerland, Canada, Norway, Japan, the World Bank, the Russian Federation, and others to be the members of the Commission.

3. The Commission shall:

a) Oversee and manage the process whereby the status and PPR of Palestinian refugees is determined and realized.

b) Oversee and manage, in close cooperation with the host states, the rehabilitation and development programs.

c) Raise and disburse funds as appropriate.

4. The Parties shall make available to the Commission all relevant documentary records and archival materials in their possession that it deems necessary for the functioning of the Commission and its organs. The Commission may request such materials from all other relevant parties and bodies, including, inter alia, UNCCP and UNRWA.

ii. Structure

1. The Commission shall be governed by an Executive Board (Board) composed of representatives of its members.

2. The Board shall be the highest authority in the Commission and shall make the relevant policy decisions in accordance with this Agreement . . .

iii. Specific Committees

1. The Commission shall establish the Technical Committees specified below.

2. Unless otherwise specified in this Agreement, the Board shall determine the structure and procedures of the Committees . . .

iv. Status-determination Committee

1. The Status-determination Committee shall be responsible for verifying refugee status.

2. UNRWA registration shall be considered as rebuttable presumption (prima facie proof) of refugee status.

v. Compensation Committee

1. The Compensation Committee shall be responsible for administering the implementation of the compensation provisions.

2. The Committee shall disburse compensation for individual property pursuant to the following modalities:

a) Either a fixed per capita award for property claims below a specified value. This will require the claimant to only prove title, and shall be processed according to a fast-track procedure, or

b) A claims-based award for property claims exceeding a specified value for immovables and other assets. This will require the claimant to prove both title and the value of the losses.

3. Annex X shall elaborate the details of the above including, but not limited to, evidentiary issues and the use of UNCCP, "Custodian for Absentees' Property," and UNRWA records, along with any other relevant records.

vi. Host State Remuneration Committee
There shall be remuneration for host states.

vii. Permanent Place of Residence Committee (PPR Committee):
The PPR Committee shall,

1. Develop with all the relevant parties detailed programs regarding the implementation of the PPR options pursuant to Article 7/4 above.

2. Assist the applicants in making an informed choice regarding PPR options.

3. Receive applications from refugees regarding PPR. The applicants must indicate a number of preferences in accordance with article 7/4 above. The applications shall be received no later than two years after the start of the International Commission's operations. Refugees who do not submit such applications within the two-year period shall lose their refugee status.

4. Determine, in accordance with sub-Article (a) above, the PPR of the applicants, taking into account individual pref-

erences and maintenance of family unity. Applicants who do not avail themselves of the Committee's PPR determination shall lose their refugee status.

5. Provide the applicants with the appropriate technical and legal assistance.

6. The PPR of Palestinian refugees shall be realized within 5 years of the start of the International Commission's operations . . .

12. The International Fund

i. An International Fund (the Fund) shall be established to receive contributions outlined in this Article and additional contributions from the international community. The Fund shall disburse monies to the Commission to enable it to carry out its functions. The Fund shall audit the Commission's work.

ii. The structure, composition and operation of the Fund are set forth in Annex X.

13. UNRWA

i. UNRWA should be phased out in each country in which it operates, based on the end of refugee status in that country.

ii. UNRWA should cease to exist five years after the start of the Commission's operations. The Commission shall draw up a plan for the phasing out of UNRWA and shall facilitate the transfer of UNRWA functions to host states . . .

NOTES

FOREWORD

1. G.W. Bush radio address, March 22, 2003, http://www. whitehouse.gov/news/releases/2003/03/20030322.html.

CHAPTER 1: *Lies and Truths*

1. Ahron Bregman, *Elusive Peace* (London: Penguin Books, 2005), 145.
2. Videotaped interview with Shimon Peres, June 25, 2004.
3. For the reproduction of the conclusions of this "simulation," see Raviv Drucker, *Harakiri* (Tel Aviv: Yedihot Aharonot, 2002), 284.
4. Videotaped interview with Amos Malka, May 10, 2005.
5. Videotaped interviews with Amos Malka, Shaul Arieli, Matti Steinberg, May 10, 2005. See also Akiva Eldar, *Haaretz*, June 11, 2004.
6. Statements made on "Democracy Now": http://democracynow. org/finklestein-benami.shtml.
7. Charles Enderlin, *Shattered Dreams* (New York: Other Press), 250. See also the extensive analysis of Camp David by Clayton Swisher, *The Truth about Camp David* (New York: The Nation Books, 2004).

8.   "Shne Kolot Shel Amman," *Haaretz*, June 11, 2004. See also the videotaped interview with Amos Malka, May 10, 2005.

9.   Interview with Ephraim Lavi, July 11, 2005. See also Yoav Stern, *Haaretz*, June 13, 2004.

10.   Enderlin, *Shattered Dreams*, 324. Videotaped interview with Shlomo Ben Ami, June 17, 2001.

11.   Videotaped interview with Shlomo Ben Ami, June 17, 2001.

12.   Gilead Sher, *Be Merhak Neguiah* (Tel Aviv: Yedihot Aharonot, 2001).

13.   During exchanges of fire on May 15, 2000 in the West Bank and Gaza, four Palestinians had been killed and 300 wounded.

14.   Dennis Ross, *The Missing Peace* (New York: Farrar, Straus and Giroux, 2004), 730–31.

15.   Videotaped interview with Zvi Fogel, May 4, 2005.

16.   Sher, *Be Merhak Neguiah*, 366.

17.   Amos Harel, "Mediniot Hazigzag Nimshechet," *Haaretz*, December 29, 2000.

18.   Ofer Shelakh, *Yedihot Aharonot*, December 22, 2000.

19.   Sher, *Be Merhak Neguiah*, 368.

20.   Shlomo Ben Ami, *Khazit le lo Oref. Massa el ha gvoulot taalikh ha shalom* (Tel Aviv: Yedihot Aharonot, 2004), 319.

21.   General (res.) Amnon Lipkin-Shahak never publicly spoke of the efforts he himself made to arrive at a cease-fire.

22.   Ami Ayalon, head of Shin Bet until May 2000, and his deputy, Israel Hasson, were opposed to "Field of Thorns" when it was presented to them by Shaul Mofaz.

23.   Videotaped interview with Amos Malka, May 10, 2005.

24.   Alex Fischman, *Yedihot Aharonot*, January 19, 2001. See also Amir Rappoport, "Bemetzh Lo Yodim Et Havoda," *Maariv*, January 1, 2005.

25.   B'Tselem, *Use of Firearms*, http://www.btselem.org/English/Firearms.

26.   Videotaped interview with Zvi Fogel, May 4, 2005.

27.   Interview with Colonel Shaul Arieli, April 5, 2004.

28.   Interviews with Israeli officers, personal communications.

29. Videotaped interview with General Dov Sedaka, May 14, 2006.

30. About the influence of this think tank on Israeli military thinking, see chapter 15 of Ofer Shelakh and Yoav Limor, *Shvuim be Levanon* (Tel Aviv, Yedihot Aharonot, 2007).

31. In Hebrew, the expression *Tsriva Todaatit* was a success, becoming the theme of numerous debates.

32. Cited by Aluf Benn, "Larsen Takaf Et Mediniot Haseger Haisraelit," *Haaretz*, February 15, 2001.

33. Merkaz le Bitakhon Leoumi, *Iounim Be Bitakhon Leoumi*, University of Haifa, July 2001, vol. 2, 79.

34. Videotaped interview with Moshe Yaalon, Washington, June 7, 2006.

35. In February 1983, Judge Yitzhak Kahan's investigative commission concluded that Ariel Sharon had to step down as defense minister for having ignored the risk of massacres when authorizing the Lebanese Phalange militia to pass through Israeli lines and enter two refugee camps in September 1982. According to various estimates, from 700 to 3,500 Palestinians, men, women, and children, had been murdered on this occasion: ". . . [W]e hold that it would be right for the Defense Minister to undergo the appropriate personal consequences for the lapse committed in exercising his duties. If necessary, the Prime Minister should consider the exercise of his authority according to section 21-A(a) of the fundamental Law: the Prime Minister can, after having informed the government, remove a minister." Translations of the Kahan report exist on several Web sites. See also *The Beirut Massacre: The Complete Kahan Commission Report* (Princeton, NJ: Karz-Kohl, 1983).

36. Vered and Amnon Barzilai, "Ahavat Arik," *Haaretz*, November 29, 2002.

37. The quotation marks appear in the original text.

38. Nahum Barnea, *Yedihot Aharonot*, September 13, 2002. Elements of this plan already appeared in an article by Alex Fischman in *Yedihot Aharonot*, December 14, 2001.

39. Videotaped interview with Avi Dichter, May 4, 2006.

40. Videotaped interview with Ami Ayalon, July 6, 2004.

41. *A Clean Break: A New Strategy for Securing the Realm* (Washington, DC: The Institute for Advanced Strategic and Political Studies, 1996).

42. David Frum and Richard Perle, *An End to No Evil: How to Win the War on Terror* (New York: Random House, 2003), 182.

43. Marc Zell, *A Settler's History of Settlements*, http://www .internationalwallofprayer.org/A-143-A-Settlers-History-of-Settlements.html.

44. Several quotes from Douglas Feith against the creation of a Palestinian state can be found on the Web site of the Center for Security Policy, http://www.centerforsecuritypolicy.org/index .jsp?section=papers&code=96-D_130.

45. Elliott Abrams, *Faith or Fear: How Jews Can Survive in a Christian America* (New York: The Free Press, 1997), 181.

46. Palestinian source, personal communication.

47. Eyewitness account of a Palestinian leader, personal communication.

48. Reuters, February 21, 2001.

49. Zeev Schiff, "Bidei Mi vuhue Tik Habitahon," February 23, 2001.

50. In Hebrew, the word signifies both "colonization" and "settling on the land."

CHAPTER 2: *Let's Act Like We Didn't Know*

1. Cited by Nahum Barnea, *Yedihot Aharonot*, March 20, 2001.

2. American sources, personal communications.

3. American and Israeli sources, personal communications.

4. *Yedihot Aharonot*, March 30, 2001. The poll was conducted on a sample of 504 people, with a margin of error of 4.5 percent.

5. *Peace Index*, March 2001. Tami Steimetz Research Institute for Peace, University of Tel Aviv, http://www./tau.ac.il.peace.

6. *JMCC Public Opinion Poll*, no. 40, http://www.jmcc.org.

7. Israeli source, personal communication.

8. Palestinian sources, personal communications.

9. Interview with Mohammed Dahlan, April 10, 2001.

10. Military sources. Videotaped interview with General Dov Sedaka, May 14, 2006. This scene was also described by Raviv Drucker and Ofer Shelakh in *Boomerang* (Tel Aviv: Keter, 2005), and also Amos Harel and Avi Issacharoff, *Hamilhama Ha Shviit* (Tel Aviv: Yedihot Aharonot, 2004).

11. Interviews with Israeli officers, personal communications.

12. Gal Hirsch in Hagaï Golan and Shaul Shaï (dir.), "Mi Oferet Yetzuka le Derekh Akheret Hitpatkhut Ha maarakha be Pikud Ha Merkaz, 2000–2003," *Ha Imout Ha Mougbal* (Tel Aviv: Minister of the Defense, 2004), 239.

13. "The Combatants' Letter," http://www.seruv.org.il.

14. This territory, occupied by Israel in June 1967, belongs to Syria according to the UN, but Lebanon claims it.

15. Israeli sources, personal communications.

16. Videotaped interviews with Generals Dov Sedaka and Ilan Paz, May 14, 2006. See also Amir Oren, "Lo Hargno Amar Hamagad Hargno lefi Horaat Mofaz," *Haaretz*, June 13, 2001.

17. Videotaped interview with Ilan Paz, May 14, 2006.

18. Videotaped interview with Saeb Erekat, December 16, 2005.

19. On August 26, 2000, a special Israeli unit had already made an attempt to kill Abu Hamoud.

20. Videotaped interview with Ilan Paz, May 14, 2006.

21. The author's source, personal communication.

22. On this episode, see Enderlin, *Shattered Dreams*, 288–291. The Mitchell report can be found at http://www.state.gov/p/nea/rls/rpt/3060.htm.

23. These were the seventh and eighth meetings between Israeli and Palestinian security officials since April.

24. Hamad would be killed on the roof of his house in Qalqilya by an Israeli sharpshooter on October 13, 2001.

25. Videotaped interview with Yasser Abed Rabbo, November 18, 2005.

26. Videotaped interview with Ilan Paz, May 14, 2006.

27. Videotaped interview with Moshe Yaalon, Washington, June 7, 2006.

28. Interviews with Yasser Abed Rabbo and Saeb Erekat, October 20, 2005.

29. Source requesting anonymity.

30. Videotaped interview with Saeb Erekat, Jericho, October 20, 2005.

31. "Muqata": the "district" in Arab.

32. The author's sources, personal communications.

33. This secret coordination of security had been established by Alistair Crooke, the security advisor to the European emissary, Miguel Moratinos, who had himself negotiated with the Israelis and the Palestinians.

34. Interview with General Dov Sedaka and General Ilan Paz, May 14, 2006.

35. Ariel Sharon had in fact spoken of 42 percent.

36. Jamal Mansur, *Al-Tahwwul Al-Dimuqrati Al-Filastini, Markaz Al-Buhuth w-Al-dirasat Al-Filastiniyya* (Nablus, March 1999).

37. Interview with Matti Steinberg, September 12, 2005.

CHAPTER 3: *9/11*

1. http://www.btselem.org/English/.

2. Videotaped interview with Salah Taamri, April 14, 2006.

3. This neighborhood was constructed on land occupied in 1967, and subsequently annexed.

4. *Haaretz,* August 20, 2001.

5. *Yedihot Aharonot,* August 24, 2001.

6. The Israeli police announced, on September 4, the arrest in East Jerusalem of six members of the PFLP who, they claimed, were preparing attacks, notably against a kindergarten.

7. *Ynet,* August 30, 2001.

8. *Ynet,* September 5, 2001. *Haaretz,* September 7, 2001. *Maariv,* September 7, 2001.

9. Karmi admitted that he had assassinated the two Israelis to avenge his uncle, Thabet Thabet, the head of Fatah in Tulkarm, killed by the IDF on December 31, 2000.

10. "Hamilhama Ha Shviit," ed. *Yedihot Aharonot,* Tel Aviv, 2004, 165–166.

11. *Haaretz,* September 13, 2001.

12. Interview with Yasser Abed Rabbo, Ramallah, November 18, 2005.

13. Interviews with Saeb Erekat, October 20, 2005; Yasser Abed Rabbo, November 18, 2005; and Miguel Moratinos, January 17, 2006. Information on the scene at Shifa Hospital was provided by the author's sources.

14. Interview with Binyamin Ben-Eliezer, with *Yedihot Aharonot,* September 14, 2001.

15. *Jerusalem Post,* September 17, 2001.

16. *Yedihot Aharonot,* Rosh Hashanah supplement, September 17, 2001.

17. AFP, September 17, 2001.

18. Interview with Avi Gil, May 4, 2004.

19. Israeli military source, personal communication.

20. For nearly a year, Palestinian security officials had been demanding the option of transferring forces and maintaining order between Gaza and the West Bank.

21. Videotaped interview with Dan Kurtzer, Princeton, June 9, 2006.

22. Ibid.

CHAPTER 4: *Hamas*

1. Author's sources, personal communication.

2. Interview with Jibril Rajoub, Ramallah, February 15, 2006.

3. American diplomatic source, personal communication.

4. October 26, 2001. Conversation confirmed by an American source, personal communication.

5. An official in one of these services would confirm later: Arafat was, for us, "totally transparent." The author's source, personal communication.

6. *Maariv,* November 18, 2001.

7. *Years of Blood,* televised documentary, Discovery Channel, January 2007.

8. Videotaped interview with Dan Kurtzer, June 9, 2006.

9. Tom Clancy, with General Zinni, *Battle Ready* (London: Sidwick and Jackson, 2004), 383.

10. Interview with Saeb Erekat, October 20, 2005.

11. Tom Clancy, *Battle Ready*, 386.

12. Videotaped interview with Avi Dichter, April 4, 2006.

13. Videotaped interview with Anthony Zinni, December 12, 2005.

14. Videotaped interviews with Anthony Zinni and Aaron Miller, December 12, 2005.

15. Videotaped interview with Saeb Erekat, October 20, 2005.

16. Those security sources deny claims published in the Israeli press that a conversation was recorded between Arafat and Fuad Shubaki, the Palestinian official in charge of the military purchase, in which the PLO chairman authorized the purchase of the *Karine A*. Until his capture by the IDF in 2006, Shubaki denied any link to the *Karine A*. In Israeli custody, he was quoted as having told his Shin Bet interrogators that Arafat approved the arms deal with Iran. It has not been possible to interview Shubaki independently since his arrest.

17. Videotaped interview with Anthony Zinni, December 12, 2005.

18. Videotaped interview with Moshe Yaalon, June 7, 2006.

19. Interview with Matti Steinberg, May 19, 2005.

20. Cheney's statement had been published widely in the Israeli press. American sources would subsequently deny it. See *Haaretz*, February 11, 2002.

21. Ron Leshem, "Va Binataym Begvul Hatsafoun," *Yedihot Aharonot*, February 2, 2002.

22. Thomas Friedman, "An Intriguing Signal from the Saudi Crown Prince," *New York Times*, February 17, 2002.

23. Daniel Sobalman, "Saudi Plan Wins Egyptian Backing," *Haaretz*, February 28, 2002.

24. http://telaviv.usembassy.gov/publish/peace/archives/2002/february/022701.html.

25. *Haaretz*, February 26, 2002.

26. *Haaretz*, March 4, 2001. Israel only accepted the English-language version of resolution 242, which called for the evacuation of territories and not the evacuation of *all* territories.

27. Videotaped interview with Anthony Zinni, December 12, 2005.

28. Videotaped interview with Avi Dichter, May 4, 2005.

29. The author's sources, personal communications.

30. Videotaped interview with Mohammed Dahlan, April 8, 2005.

31. Videotaped interview with Saeb Erekat, December 16, 2005.

32. Interview with Mohammed Dahlan, April 8, 2005.

33. http://www.al-bab.com/arab/docs/league/peace02.htm.

34. http://www.mfa.gov.il.

35. Videotaped interview with Saeb Erekat, December 16, 2005.

CHAPTER 5: *A Strong Hand and an Outstretched Arm*

1. Soldiers had given the intifada the name "High Tide, Low Tide."

2. Interview with Dov Sedaka, May 14, 2006.

3. Raviv Drucker and Ofer Shelakh, *Boomerang*, 243–246.

4. Military sources, personal communications.

5. Interview with Jibril Rajoub, February 15, 2006, and videotaped interview with Zakariah Mousleh, commander of preventative security, February 27, 2006.

6. Interview with Jibril Rajoub.

7. All visitors who entered Rajoub's office could clearly see this plaque.

8. Tom Clancy, *Battle Ready*, 404.

9. Videotaped interview with Miguel Moratinos, January 17, 2006.

10. Israeli sources, personal communications.

11. *Maariv*, April 13, 2002.

12. Interview with Saeb Erekat, December 16, 2005.

13. Videotaped interview with Uzi Dayan, April 14, 2006.

14. Raviv Drucker and Ofer Shelakh, *Boomerang*, 221.

15. Representative Council of French Jewish Institutions (Conseil représentatif des institutions juives de France).

16. A movement in France that promotes social integration and secularization.

17. Interviews with Saeb Erekat, October 20, 2005, and Yasser Abed Rabbo, November 18, 2005. American diplomatic sources.

18. Videotaped interview with Saeb Erekat, October 20, 2005.

19. American sources. Raviv Drucker and Ofer Shelakh also recount the anecdote in *Boomerang*.

20. Bob Woodward, *Bush at War* (New York: Simon & Schuster, 2002), 325.

21. Videotaped interview with Larry Wilkerson, June 6, 2006.

22. http://www.btselem.org/English/index.asp.

23. Tel Aviv, *Yedihot Aharonot*, 2004, p. 338.

24. Interview with Ilan Paz, December 19, 2005.

25. Report by Talia Sasson, March 8, 2005. http://www.pmo.gov.il/ NR/rdonlyres/0A0FBE3C-C741-46A6-8CB5-F6CDC042465D/0/ sasson.2.pdf-.

26. B'Tselem report: http://www.btselem.org/english/Settlements/ Land_Takeover.asp.

27. Ahmed Saadat was captured by the IDF on March 24, 2006, during an attack launched against the Jericho prison. Meni Mazuz, the Israeli attorney general, would state that sufficient proof to accuse him of Rehavam Zeevi's murder did not exist. See Chapter 8.

28. Israeli source, personal communication.

29. René Backmann, *Un mur en Palestine* (Paris: Fayard, 2006), 70.

30. *San Jose Mercury News*, June 4, 2002.

31. Videotaped interview with Mohammed Dahlan, November 7, 2001.

32. *Haaretz*, June 24, 2002.

33. See Chapter 1.

34. Article by Gal Hirsch in Hagaï Golan and Shaul Shaï (dir.), *Ha Imout Ha Mougbal*, 399–400.

CHAPTER 6: *The Failure of Abbas*

1. *Yedihot Aharonot*, September 26, 2006; *Haaretz*, August, 29, 2002; *Yedihot Aharonot*, August 30, 2003.

2. Translated by Vivian Eden.

3. *Washington Post*, November 28, 2000. On May 14, 2006, a Tel Aviv judge deemed Yom Tov Samia's reconstruction as "non-scientific and non-professional" (File A .043040/04, Case of Yossef Doriel against Aharon Hauptman).

4. *Jerusalem Post*, April 15, 2003.

5. Videotaped interview with Miguel Moratinos, January 17, 2006.

6.   Videotaped interview with Terje Larsen, December 17, 2004.

7.   Interview with Dan Kurtzer, June 9, 2006. See the appendix for the text of the road map in its entirety.

8.   *Maariv*, May 1, 2003.

9.   Amendments that the Palestinian Authority rejected.

10.   Author's sources, personal communications.

11.   Charles Enderlin, *Les années de sang* (France 2, 2006).

12.   That is to say, including the amendments presented by the Israeli government.

13.   The previous day, Israel had released approximately one hundred Palestinians, "administrative" detainees, jailed without a trial. Mahmoud Abbas viewed this measure as insufficient.

14.   Interview with Yasser Abed Rabbo, November 18, 2005.

15.   http://www.mifkad.org.il/en/principles.asp.

16.   € 400 million. The defense budget reached 12 percent of the gross national product in Israel, as opposed to 3.5 percent in the United States.

17.   Ben Kaspit, *Maariv*, September 15, 2006.

18.   http://www.state.gov/secretary/former/powell/remarks/2003/23111.htm.

19.   Enderlin, *Les années de sang*.

20.   Interview with Yasser Abed Rabbo, November 18, 2005.

CHAPTER 7: *Withdrawal from Gaza*

1.   In 2006, the projected length of the "wall" was to exceed 600 kilometers, some segments still being disputed in the Israeli high court.

2.   Michael Cherney is a Russian oligarch established in Israel.

3.   *Yedihot Aharonot; Maariv*, October 29, 2003.

4.   Ariel Sharon, *Entretien intimes avec Uri Dan* (Paris: Michel Lafon, 2006), 392.

5.   Interview with Giora Eiland, June 31, 2006.

6.   The West Bank.

7.   Ariel Sharon, *Warrior: An Autobiography* (New York: Simon & Schuster 1989), 364.

8. According to B'Tselem and the Israeli minister of foreign affairs.

9. Videotaped interview with Avi Dichter, May 4, 2006.

10. Videotaped interview with Mike Scheuer, June 9, 2006.

11. Interview with Saeb Erekat, April 4, 2004.

CHAPTER 8: *Olmert*

1. http://www.globalsecurity.org/military/library/news/2004/04/
    mil-040418-usia01.htm.

2. See B'Tselem: http://www.btselem.org, OCHA: http://www
    .humanitarianinfo.org; UNISPAL: http://domino.un.org/
    unispal.NSF.

3. Mohammed Dahlan is apparently alluding to the total sum
    received by the Autonomous Authority since its creation.

4. *Al-Wattanin*, August 1, 2004.

5. These figures were presented by Avi Dichter during a press
    conference.

6. In September 2004, eleven Israelis and 113 Palestinians had been
    killed.

7. Videotaped interview with Yasser Abed Rabbo, November 18,
    2005; interview with Saeb Erekat, December 16, 2005.

8. Steve Erlanger, *New York Times*, September 8, 2005.

9. Ariel Sharon, *Entretiens intimes*, 401–403.

10. Italicized phrases appear that way in the report, available at http:
    //www.fmep.org/documents/sassonreport.html.

11. Interview with Moshe Yaalon, June 7, 2006.

12. According to Seffi Rachlevski, in his book, *Hamoro Shel Ha
    Mashiakh* (Tel Aviv: Yediot Aharonot, 1998), which received a
    very critical reception from religious Zionists.

13. Associated Press, September 12, 2005.

14. These American and British agents stated that security in the
    Jericho prison did not allow them to perform their duties.

15. *Jerusalem Post*, June 8, 2006. In 2007, U.S. military sources
    denied this assertion that the army's new doctrinal publication
    on Operations (Field Manual 3.0) was "heavily based on Naveh's
    work."

EPILOGUE

1.   The Winograd interim report (April 30, 2007). Havvada le Bdikat Iroe Hamaarakh Belevanon 2006, 31. http://www.vaadatwino.co. il/press.html#null.

2.   Interview with Uri Saguy, July 20, 2006. See also Enderlin, *Shattered Dreams*, 125–142.

3.   www.wfp.org.

4.   The Winograd interim report, 74

APPENDIX

1.   See http://www.mideastweb.org/quartetrm3.htm.

2.   Extracts from the text of the Geneva Initiative of December 1, 2003. See http://www.geneva-accord.org/Accord.aspx?FolderID= 33&lang=en.

INDEX